Puritans in Conflict

Puritans in Conflict

THE PURITAN GENTRY
DURING AND AFTER THE CIVIL WARS

J. T. Cliffe

ROUTLEDGE

London and New York

First published in 1988 by
Routledge
11 New Fetter Lane, London EC4P 4EE

Published in the USA by
Routledge
in association with Routledge, Chapman and Hall, Inc.
29 West 35th Street, New York NY 10001

Set in 10/12 pt Trump Medieval
by Pentacor Ltd.,
and printed in Great Britain by
T.J. Press (Padstow) Ltd.,
Padstow, Cornwall.

British Library Cataloguing in Publication Data

Cliffe, J. T. (John Trevor), 1931–
    Puritans in Conflict:
    The Puritan gentry during and after the Civil Wars.
    1. England. Puritanism, 1640–1660
    I. Title
    285'.9'0942

Library of Congress Cataloging in Publication Data

Cliffe, J. T. (John Trevor), 1931–
    Puritans in Conflict: The Puritan gentry during and after the civil
    wars/J. T. Cliffe.
    p.   cm.
    Bibliography: p.
    Includes index.
    1.Puritans—England—History—17th century. 2. England—
    Gentry. 3. England—Church history—17th century. 4. England—
    Social conditions—17th century. I. Title.
    BX9333.C59 1988
    941.06'3'08825–dc19   88–2952

ISBN 0–415–00879–4

Contents

Acknowledgments

I should like to record my grateful thanks to the following for allowing me to make use of material in manuscript collections: Mr J. T. L. Jervoise (Jervoise of Herriard Collection in the Hampshire Record Office); the Director of Libraries and Information Services, Sheffield Central Libraries, and Olive Countess Fitzwilliam's Wentworth Settlement Trustees (Wentworth Woodhouse Muniments, Bright Papers); Trustees of the late Mrs C. Dryden (Dryden MSS in the Northamptonshire Record Office); Dr Williams's Library (Baxter and Morrice MSS); the City of Bristol Record Office (Ashton Court MSS); and the Devon Record Office (Drake of Buckland Abbey MSS).

Acknowledgments are also due to the British Library Board and all libraries and record offices listed in the Bibliography.

Abbreviations
Used in References

A. & O.	Sir Charles Firth and R. S. Rait (ed.), *The Acts and Ordinances of the Interregnum, 1642–1660*, 3 vols, 1911
Baillie	Robert Baillie, *Letters and Journals of Robert Baillie*, ed. David Laing, 3 vols, 1841–2
BL	British Library
C. J.	*Commons Journals*
C. S. P. Dom	Calendar of State Papers Domestic, Public Record Office
Clarendon	*The History of the Rebellion and Civil Wars in England . . . . by Edward, Earl of Clarenddon*, ed. W. D. Macray, 6 vols, 1888
DNB	*Dictionary of National Biography*
Fast Sermons	*The English Revolution, I. Fast Sermons to Parliament*, 34 vols, 1970–1
HMC	*Historical Manuscripts Commission Reports*
Hutchinson Memoirs	Lucy Hutchinson, *Memoirs of the Life of Colonel Hutchinson*, ed. James Sutherland, 1973
L. J.	*Lords Journals*
Lyon Turner	G. Lyon Turner (ed.), *Original Records of Early Nonconformity under Persecution and Indulgence*, 3 vols, 1911–14
Oxford Royalist	*The English Revolution. III, Newsbooks I. Oxford Royalist*, 4 vols. 1971

Abbreviations

Parliamentary History	*The Parliamentary or Constitutional History of England*, 24 vols, 1762–3
PRO	Public Record Office
Puritan Gentry	J. T. Cliffe, *The Puritan Gentry*, 1984
Rushworth	John Rushworth, *Historical Collections of Private Passages of State, Weighty Matters in Law, Remarkable Proceedings in Five Parliaments*, 8 vols, 1721
Shaw	W. A. Shaw, *A History of the English Church, 1640–1660*, 2 vols, 1900
VCH	*Victoria County History*

Introduction

In *The Puritan Gentry*, which was published in 1984, I showed that in the early seventeenth century there were a considerable number of prominent county families which were strongly attached to the cause of godliness; that this was primarily a reflection of genuine religious conviction rather than political dissent; and that concern about the future of 'true religion' was a key factor in the growing alienation of families of this type during the 1630s. Such families ensured that their children received a godly education; presented Puritan ministers to livings in their gift and employed Puritan chaplains; and diligently engaged in religious exercises in the privacy of their country houses. The present volume takes up the story where *The Puritan Gentry* left off, that is to say at the end of 1641, and carries it on through the period of the Civil Wars and the Commonwealth into the reign of Charles II.

As before it is the leading Puritan gentry, most of them with landed estates worth £1,000 a year or more, who occupy the centre of the stage, though their clerical associates also figure prominently. A comprehensive list of families at this income level can be found in the Appendix together with a list of other Puritan gentry who are mentioned in the text.

In the introduction to *The Puritan Gentry* I described a true Puritan of the early seventeenth century as 'a zealous Calvinist who placed a very high value on piety and holiness (to the extent that he might be considered "precise") and who preferred a plain form of religious worship with the emphasis on godly preaching'. In the present work I have continued to be guided by this definition which embraces both Presbyterians and Independents in the religious sense of those terms.

ONE

Reformation Deferred

In a fast sermon preached before members of the Commons in December 1641 Edmund Calamy made it clear that there was much still to be done. Drunkenness, he thundered, had 'growne to that Gyant-like bignesse as that there is no hope of redresse but in the Parliament.' Blasphemous swearing was so prevalent that it appeared that men took a pride in offending God, while adultery and fornication were spreading through the kingdom like an epidemic. The Sabbath continued to be profaned and in the churches idolatry and superstition were flourishing. The time had come, he stressed, 'to bury all superstitious Ceremonies in the grave of oblivion and perfect a Reformation according to the Word of God.'[1] The Puritan squires who sat in the Long Parliament would have wholeheartedly agreed with his account of the evils of the day and with his proposal that there should be a national synod of divines which would provide advice on the settlement of religion. Some of these men had ministers under their patronage whose views were at least as radical as those of Calamy. The same month Stanley Gower, the minister of Brampton Bryan in Herefordshire, wrote in a letter to his patron, Sir Robert Harley, who was the senior knight of the shire that he was now expecting a major alteration in religion: 'The Atheists, papists and prelats, our common enemys, are now to be scoured and swept away . . . our Land hath bene long sick and yow are the physicians.'[2] In April 1641 Samuel Fairclough, the pastor of Kedington in Suffolk, had exhorted Parliament in another fast sermon to extirpate the Achans, a name which he applied to papists, 'idle, scandalous, negligent ministers', blasphemers, Sabbath-breakers and others whom the Puritans regarded with disfavour. When the sermon was published he dedicated it to his patron, Sir Nathaniel Barnardiston, who was one of the knights of the shire and in his estimation a man who had proved to be a true Joshua by 'countenancing and incouraging the vertuous and opposing the profane and vitious.'[3]

Shortly after Calamy delivered his sermon the Commons considered a report from a committee which had been charged with the task of preparing an order for the speedy execution of the laws against swearing, drunkenness and profanation of the Sabbath and decided that a bill should be drafted for this purpose. During the debate Sir Simonds D'Ewes argued that justices of the peace who were guilty of the sins of swearing and drunkenness should be removed from office.[4] In the ecclesiastical field there was little to suggest that the dreams of a new Jerusalem were about to be realized. With Laud and most of his bishops in confinement the system of episcopal government was no longer functioning but at the parish level there were many clergymen whom the Puritans condemned as unworthy of their calling; and in most counties there were relatively few churches which had godly preaching ministers. In February 1642 it was claimed in a petition from Oxfordshire that the county had 'many corrupt and scandalous Ministers' and that there were 'not above thirty Ministers that were constant preachers' in a diocese with nearly 280 parishes. Similarly, Sir Robert Harley was informed that a survey of the parishes in his own county of Herefordshire had revealed that there were 225 churches and chapels but only twenty ministers who regularly preached two sermons each Sunday. In a Herefordshire petition which was presented to the Commons in May 1642 it was stressed that the county was in great need of more preaching ministers,

> it now abounding with insufficient, Idle and Scandalous Ministers, whereby the people generally are continued in Ignorance, Superstition and prophanenesse and are ready to

become a prey to popish seducers, which Idolatrous profession hath of late yeares with much boldnesse appeared in this County.[5]

Sir Simonds D'Ewes had spoken in favour of legislation for the abolition of all idolatry and had served on the committee which had been assigned the task of preparing a bill. In the event the bill had failed to make headway and on 8 September 1641 the Commons had decided instead to issue a parliamentary order for sweeping away the Laudian innovations in the parish churches. In some areas Puritan magistrates like Sir Robert Harley and John Hutchinson had sought to ensure that the order was complied with but on the whole it appears to have had only a limited impact.[6]

With the Church in a state of considerable disarray Puritan divines were now able to preach with much greater freedom than had normally been possible in recent years and many Puritan books and pamphlets were published which would previously have fallen foul of the Laudian censorship regime. At the same time the breakdown of ecclesiastical discipline had opened up the way for the gathering of Independent congregations which had no parochial affiliations and the emergence of sectaries who boldly claimed that they owed no allegiance to the established Church. According to a Kentish gentleman the sectaries were maintaining that 'there is noe nationall church, and so seperat from us and the puritans as being no true church.'[7] These separatist tendencies were viewed with growing concern by most Puritan squires because of their attachment to the concept of a national Church; what they wanted was a Church which had been thoroughly cleansed and purified and which offered a fruitful abundance of godly preaching. Of all the ecclesiastical issues which had still to be resolved the most pressing was the question of how the Church was to be governed in the future. During the course of 1641 the attempts of the Root and Branch party to secure the abolition of episcopacy had sharply divided both the Commons and the country at large. In the House there were many wealthy Puritans who were in favour of putting an end to the

3

institution of bishops, among them Sir Robert Harley, Sir Arthur Hesilrige, Sir Nathaniel Barnardiston, Sir John Wray, Sir Henry Vane the younger, Sir Thomas Barrington, Sir Simonds D'Ewes, Sir Walter Erle, Sir William Brereton, John Pyne and John Hampden. This upper-class radicalism, which often went hand in hand with an innate conservatism in other respects, was the product of a number of factors: in particular, the conviction that there was no scriptural justification for a hierarchical system of church government; an antipathy towards bishops which had been generated by their activities during the Laudian era; and a belief, which sometimes reflected apocalyptic influences, that it would never be possible to achieve a true reformation of religion so long as the Church remained under episcopal control.[8] John Pyne, who in the words of Bulstrode Whitelocke was 'of the more rigid party' in the Commons, had been incensed by the thoroughgoing way in which William Peirs, the Bishop of Bath and Wells, had implemented Laud's ecclesiastical policy in Somerset. In December 1640 Pyne had written to a friend that he was confident that the county would soon be delivered 'from soe oppressive a Person, the excommunications for not Bowinge att the Name of Jesus, not turneinge the Communion Table Alterwise &c doubtlesse will be held sufficient charges.'[9] No doubt many Puritan MPs would have agreed with the view expressed by Sir Thomas Widdrington, when advocating the impeachment of Bishop Wren, that an arbitrary government in the Church was 'more dangerous, more grievous then that in the state; this is exercised upon men's consciences, the most tender parts, and is the very penacle of tyranny, and of all other most intollerable.'[10]

Some Puritan MPs did not consider it necessary or expedient to abolish episcopacy altogether. Harbottle Grimston had made a scathing attack on Laud and his 'popish' bishops and had pointed out that 'we meete not with the name of Arch Bishopps or a deane or Archdeacon in all the new Testament'; but he had subsequently argued in favour of doing no more than depriving the bishops of their temporal powers on the grounds that abolition could have far-reaching political consequences.[11] Another Puritan opponent of the Root and Branch approach was John Crewe who was described as 'a man of a very exact strict life' and 'a person of great parts, piety, and a great countenancer of Religion'. As a member of the Commons he displayed no little zeal in the cause of ecclesiastical reform but he caused some surprise by suggesting that it would be sufficient to reduce the powers of the bishops.[12] In spite of this disagreement such men as Grimston and Crewe would remain loyal to Parliament. More politically significant was the opposition to the Root and Branch party among wealthy Protestants whose religious sympathies lay somewhere between Puritanism and Laudianism. This opposition was motivated not only by genuine anxieties about the future of the Church but by fears that the abolition of episcopacy might encourage the common people to question the legitimacy of other institutions and eventually lead to a major social upheaval.[13] In some counties Root and Branch petitions were followed by counter-petitions which favoured the *status quo*. In December 1641 Robert Sutton, one of the knights of the shire for Nottinghamshire, sought to present a petition for the continuance of bishops which was in effect a belated response to a petition calling for their abolition which his colleague Sir Thomas Hutchinson had sponsored in April. Sir Samuel Luke claimed that the authors of this new petition had resorted to unscrupulous practices in collecting signatures, pretending that it was for the removal of altar rails; and Sutton was refused leave to introduce the petition.[14]

In the Grand Remonstrance it had been alleged that the bishops had been guilty of introducing popery into the Church.[15] Many Puritans were convinced of the truth of this accusation and believed that Laudianism was intimately linked with such features of Charles I's reign as the prevalence of Catholic influences at Court, the indulgence shown towards Catholics and the growth of recusancy which this policy had helped to encourage. Apocalyptic prophecies about a final conflict between the contending forces of Protestantism and Catholicism which would end in the downfall of the Roman Antichrist acquired increased significance in the light of the war which was raging in Germany and the rebellion of the Irish Catholics which broke out in October 1641. The Irish rebellion made a particularly profound impression on Puritan minds. Lucy Hutchinson comments, with some exaggeration, that in this 'cursed rebellion . . . about 200,000 were massacred. . . . and many of them most inhumanely butcher'd and tormented.' While Parliament wanted to see it suppressed with all speed, the king's response was dilatory and half-hearted; and his ambivalent attitude offended 'all the good protestants in England, and confirm'd that this rebellion in Ireland receiv'd countenance from the King and Queene of England.'[16] Another consequence of the rebellion was that English Catholics now became the object of intense suspicion and hostility. In this overcharged atmosphere rumours were circulating that the papists were conspiring together and might even be planning to stage an armed insurrection. Considered objectively, the idea that the Catholics might rise up in rebellion was highly implausible, if only because they were a relatively small minority; indeed a papal emissary who had visited England in the 1630s had estimated that the number of Catholics, both recusants and conformists, was only of the order of 150,000.[17] However, the marked decline in their total strength which had occurred since the reign of Elizabeth had been obscured by the fact that convictions for recusancy had been increasing; and in some counties the Old Religion still commanded the allegiance of a significant number of gentry families. Moreover, the revelation that in 1639 wealthy Catholics had been collecting money for the support of the king's expedition against the Scottish Covenanters seemed to suggest that they were capable of taking concerted action when the need arose.[18]

In November 1641 Sir Walter Erle informed the Commons that he had received a report that in the neighbourhood of Portsmouth 'the Papists and ioviall clergimen were merrier than ever' and that this had aroused concern that 'ther was some new designe in hande'. Sir Walter was reluctant to name the source of his information but it was generally believed that this was his son-in-law Richard Norton, another Puritan squire, whose estates were situated near Portsmouth.[19] In

January 1642 John Browne composed a parliamentary speech in which he declared that Dorset, the county which he represented, was under threat from the Catholics (though it was not in fact a particularly Catholic county). Lord Digby's tenants, he claimed, were mainly recusants. 'The root of all the evils already come upon us' was 'Papisticall heresie . . . And is it not high time then to grub up that root that produces such fruit?' In the event the speech was never delivered but Browne considered it important enough to have it published.[20] The following month the knights of the shire for Yorkshire heard from Sir Edward Rodes that the inhabitants of the county were anxious that steps should immediately be taken for the disarming of recusants; and in a Yorkshire petition which was drawn up about the same time there was the further request that guards should be posted at the houses of papists and popishly affected persons.[21]

If the Puritans were convinced that the English Catholics presented a genuine threat to the peace of the kingdom there were others who had very different perceptions. Writing from London in January 1642, an Essex gentleman commented that the Puritan faction, with the sectaries and schismatics, was so prevalent in the capital and the country at large that no one could tell which party would be the stronger in the event of a rupture between king and Parliament.[22] Before long the term 'Roundhead' was being freely applied to those who were regarded as hostile to the Crown; and this carried with it the implication that there was now a distinctive opposition party which was essentially Puritan in character.

During the early months of 1642 the Puritan gentry in the counties were heavily involved in a major petitioning campaign which had a number of common themes.[23] The recusants (it was pleaded) should be disarmed and the whole kingdom put into a military posture. The bishops and popish lords should be deprived of their seats in the Upper House. Scandalous clergymen should be ejected from their livings; godly preachers should be planted in every parish and provided with adequate maintenance; and the Church should be reformed on lines to be determined by Parliament in accordance with the Word of God. Not infrequently a petition was brought up with great pomp and circumstance by a troop of gentlemen and their followers: Thomas May writes that 'It was then grown a custom, which proved accidentally very unhappie to the Kingdom ... to come in great numbers to Westminster when they presented Petitions to the Parliament.'[24] On 21 January there was a meeting at the Swan tavern in Northampton which had been called for the purpose of framing a petition in the name of the county. At this meeting the assembled company included such leading Puritans as Sir Francis Nichols, formerly the patron of Robert Bolton and a man who had suffered at the hands of the High Commission, and Richard Knightley whose minister at Fawsley was the celebrated John Dod. The petition which was drawn up was delivered to the Commons by Sir Rowland St John who was said to have been accompanied on his journey by a greater number of gentlemen of quality than had so far appeared in support of any other county petition. In the course of a long recital of measures which they considered necessary the petitioners prayed that the House would continue its endeavours 'towards the perfecting such a Reformation in Church and Commonwealth as in your Wisdome shall be thought fit' and that they would be 'assured of the freedome of their persons as well as of the propretie in their estates.'[25]

Writing to her son Edward on 11 February Lady Brilliana Harley expressed her delight at the news that the Bishops' Exclusion Bill had passed both Houses and added 'I hope the Lord will perfect His owne glorious worke.' Three days later Sir William Eliott commented in a letter to his brother-in-law Sir Simonds D'Ewes that he did 'much desyre to know whether the king hath passed the Bill for the taking away the Bishopp votes and Baronyes'; in fact it had received the royal assent the day before he put pen to paper. 'This week', wrote Sir John Wray on 17 February to Lord Montagu of Boughton, 'hath produced so happy effects as gives us hopes of better times. Valentine Day was the welcome commission read for disvoting of Bishops.'[26]

On 12 February a meeting took place at York which resulted

in the submission of three petitions, one to the king, another to the Lords and a third to the Commons. In the passages relating to ecclesiastical matters the petitioners sought the removal of ceremonial burdens and the settlement of religion in such a way that godly ministers would no longer have to endure persecution. The signatories included Sir Thomas Gower, the sheriff of Yorkshire, and Sir Marmaduke Langdale, neither of whom had Puritan sympathies (and indeed the latter would eventually be converted to Catholicism). In the main, however, it was a show of strength by the Puritan gentry, men such as Sir Matthew Boynton, Sir Richard Darley, Sir John Bourchier and Sir Edward Rodes, who had never previously acted in concert on such a major scale.[27]

A Somerset petition which was presented to the Commons on 25 February still contained a plea for the removal of the bishops from the House of Lords. Sir Thomas Wroth, who though he was not yet an MP was allowed to deliver a speech, explained that while the petition had been 'ambulatory in our Country for Hands' the renowned act concerning bishops and others in holy orders[28] had been passed 'to the unspeakable content of all the well-affected Christians of the Kingdome.' This, he hoped, would be followed by further legislation aimed at promoting true religion:

> when the Bill of Pluralities (the next great worke towards the blessed Reformation) is perfected I will then say Lord, now let thy servant depart this World in peace, for mine eye hath seen the great Salvation thou art beginning to worke for England.
>
> God blesse England.[29]

Sir Simonds D'Ewes noted in his journal that the petition was on the same general lines as the earlier petitions which had been directed against the bishops. He was more enthusiastic about the Derbyshire petition presented by Sir John Curzon, one of the knights of the shire, on 14 March: while there was nothing particularly new about the substance, it 'expressed moore zeale and earnestnes for the Reformation of Religion then any other petitions had done.' The petition had been drawn up, or first offered for consideration, at a meeting attended by a considerable number of the country gentry. Among the signatories at this meeting were representatives of some of the leading Puritan families in the county: Sir John Gell, Sir Thomas Burdett and his son Francis, Sir Samuel Sleigh and two of the sons of Sir John Curzon. Subsequently copies of the petition were dispatched to the towns and villages where ministers and other persons of standing who sympathized with its objectives helped to organize the collection of signatures. In the parish of Foremark, where Sir Thomas Burdett was seated, both he and his son subscribed for a second time and the Puritan incumbent, Nathaniel Barton, also put his hand to the petition.[30]

In the preamble to the Derbyshire petition the signatories expressed their gratitude to God for the work of reformation which had already been started and their desire that it might be brought to 'a sweet perfection'. They went on to declare that the malignant party had endeavoured to infringe the lawful power and liberties of Parliament, to continue popish innovations, to oppress their consciences with unnecessary ceremonies and to destroy the legitimate rights of the subject. They ended with a rhetorical flourish and an allusion to the Book of Revelation which may be regarded as evidence of clerical influence:

> that the Doctrine and Discipline of Christ may be vindicated from all corruptions. . . . That England may still continue one of Christ's golden Candlesticks. . . . the whole Kingdome and people in Covenant with God, and in the blessed peace of the Gospell we may sit every man under his own Vine and Fig tree and enjoy a happy peace to us and our posterity to the world's end.[31]

Two days after the Derbyshire petition was presented, the Commons received a similar petition from Bedfordshire, a county whose MPs, Sir Oliver Luke and his son Samuel, Sir Roger Burgoyne and Sir Beauchamp St John, were all men of Puritan outlook. Among those associated with the petition were two other Puritan gentlemen, Sir Thomas Alston who was sheriff of the county and Sir John Burgoyne, the father of Sir Roger, who brought it to Westminster accompanied by a cavalcade of 2000 horsemen. In the matter of ecclesiastical reform the petitioners were insistent that further changes were necessary but they were prepared to leave much of the detail to the discretion of Parliament. Having assured the Commons that they were 'truely sensible of your pious care in the reformation of Religion' they prayed that 'all burdensome and scandalous Ceremonies be taken away, and such an Ecclesiasticall Discipline and Governement as is agreeable to God's word may be settled by such wayes and meanes as to your wisedomes shall seeme expedient.'[32]

While the Puritans were organizing petitions calling for a further reformation of religion, the more moderate or conservative elements among the gentry and clergy were gathering support for petitions in favour of maintaining the *status quo*. The framing of a Surrey petition for the retention of bishops appears to have been prompted by a Puritan-inspired petition which Sir Ambrose Browne, one of the knights of the shire, had presented in the name of the county on 17 December 1641. Much to his amazement, Sir William Eliott was invited to sign a copy of the petition by Nicholas Andrews, the vicar of Godalming, whom he was seeking to oust from his living.[33] On 17 January Sir William wrote to his brother-in-law, Sir Simonds D'Ewes:

These popish and proud Cleargye were never at a greater heighte. What hopes they may conceave I know not. Our Popishe and Treacherous vicar was not ashamed this last weeke to come unto me to have my hand to a peticyon in the behalf of the bishops and pressed me so farr for my Reasons of Refusing until some course language passed between us.[34]

In February Sir Robert Harley was informed that Wallop Brabazon and Fitzwilliam Coningsby, two of the most prominent squires in Herefordshire, had no liking for his friend John Tombes, the Puritan vicar of Leominster, nor for any who welcomed the leaving off of the ceremonies; and that they had subscribed to a petition in favour of bishops, ceremony and liturgy. On 5 March these men, along with other Herefordshire landowners, wrote to Sir Robert and his fellow knight of the shire, Humphrey Coningsby, expressing their concern about the Puritan pressures for further reform and declaring their desire for 'the defence and maintenance of our Religion, his Majesty's Royall Person, Honor and estate, our owne rights and liberties, and the power and Priviledge of Parliamente' so far as they had statutory authority or were consistent with 'those other Relations we stand to maintain by former oathes, the Lawes of God, nature and the Land'. In a further letter which was dispatched on 28 April they commented, in response to a reply which they had received from the knights of the shire, that 'you tell us truely that the constitution of this Kingdome is composed of three states, King, Lords and Commons: it is a triple cord and it would be dangerous to untwist it.'[35]

Divisions which reflected a conflict of views over the future of the Church of England were also in evidence in other counties. In Somerset, which had been described in 1639 as a county 'full of Facion', there were two petitions circulating in January, one calling for a Root and Branch settlement and the other 'tending much to the Confirmation of Episcopall power'. After hearing the speech delivered by Sir Thomas Wroth on 25 February, the Commons proceeded to discuss the latter petition, which had been presented by Sir John Poulett, one of the knights of the shire, and decided to lay it aside.[36] On 8 March Sir Robert Harley drew the attention of the Commons to a letter sent from Oxfordshire by John Fiennes, a son of Lord Saye and Sele, and his fellow Puritan Sir William Cobb. In this letter it was reported that great efforts were being made to raise a faction within the county and to gather support for a petition arguing for the continuance of bishops and the Book of Common Prayer and laying a false aspersion on those responsible for the submission of an earlier petition which had been hostile to episcopacy. After considering this intelligence the House resolved to send for Sir William Waller who, it was alleged, had been striving for some time to organize a party or faction among the Oxfordshire gentry.[37]

While the king was gaining support from those who were

implacably opposed to any major alteration in religion, the Puritans in the House of Commons were anxious to make it clear that they had not abandoned the goal of ecclesiastical reform. On 7 April John Crewe presented the draft of a declaration indicating that it was the intention of both Houses to carry out 'a due and necessary reformation of the Government and Liturgy of the Church' and to seek the advice of godly and learned divines on the nature of the changes to be introduced. In the political situation which was then prevailing at Westminster the declaration met with no serious opposition and on 12 April the Commons accepted a suggestion made by Sir Robert Cooke, the Puritan MP who sat for Tewkesbury, that MPs should be asked to put forward names for membership of the synod. The list as finally agreed contained two names for each county of England and Wales. A number of those selected held livings in the gift of Puritan patrons: Henry Wilkinson, for example, had been nominated by Arthur Goodwin for Buckinghamshire; William Mew by Nathaniel Stephens for Gloucestershire; John Langley by Richard Whitehead for Hampshire; Thomas Coleman by Sir John Wray for Lincolnshire; and Thomas Hill by Sir Gilbert Pickering for Northamptonshire. Predictably, Sir Robert Harley recommended Stanley Gower, his minister at Brampton Bryan, as one of the Herefordshire representatives: in a letter written on 7 May Lady Harley told her son Edward that Mr Gower was very pleased to have been chosen and added 'I pray God derect them all, that theare may be a full reformation.' The Commons committee which was made responsible for working out the procedures for consultation with the synod mainly consisted of Puritan MPs, men such as John Hampden, Sir Robert Harley, Bulstrode Whitelocke, Sir Thomas Barrington, Sir Arthur Hesilrige, Sir Gilbert Gerard and Sir Samuel Rolle.[38]

The declaration, together with the list of nominated divines, was issued towards the end of April. Clarendon comments that the object was to encourage the factious and schismatical party which thought that the pace towards reformation was not brisk and furious enough.[39] As Parliament gave order that the declaration was to be published by the sheriffs of the various counties it must soon have become a matter of common knowledge; and although the bill for the calling of an assembly was refused the royal assent[40] it was stressed in the Nineteen Propositions which were approved by Parliament on 1 June that ecclesiastical reform was still high on the agenda. Such messages may indeed have helped to reassure the godly but they also exacerbated the fears of those who rejected the view that the Church was in urgent need of renovation.

TWO

Drifting into War

On 5 March 1642 the Long Parliament took a fateful step which significantly increased the likelihood of a civil war. The Militia Ordinance appointed new lords lieutenant for the various counties and made them responsible, on behalf of Parliament, for controlling the trained bands.[1] The deputy lieutenants for each county were initially selected by the lord lieutenant who then submitted their names for the consideration of both Houses. As a general rule the lord lieutenant's nominations were endorsed, though on occasion some additional names might be recommended to him. By the beginning of August well over 200 deputy lieutenants had been appointed.[2] Most of them would remain loyal to Parliament following the outbreak of hostilities; and indeed they would be a key element in the county committees which were established by parliamentary ordinances from December onwards. Many were Puritan squires who were clearly regarded as men who could be trusted. For Devon the list of deputy lieutenants includes Sir John Northcote, Sir George Chudleigh, John Bampfield and his son Sir John and Sir Nicholas Martyn; for Essex Sir Thomas Barrington, Sir William Masham, Sir Thomas Cheke, Sir Martin Lumley, Sir Henry Mildmay and Harbottle Grimston; and for Northamptonshire Sir Christopher Yelverton, Sir Gilbert Pickering, John Crewe, Richard Knightley and Zouch Tate.[3] Among the papers of Sir Thomas Pelham, who was one of the most substantial landowners in

15

Sussex, there is a letter of appointment which Algernon Earl of Northumberland issued to him on 23 April; and in his accounts there are entries of about the same date which refer to the cleaning of his armour and the making of a key for the armoury door. Sir Thomas Jervoise's letter of appointment has also survived; dated 28 April, it bears the signature of Philip Earl of Pembroke in his capacity as lord lieutenant of Hampshire.[4]

Since Pelham and Jervoise had previously held the office of deputy lieutenant under the Crown[5] there was an appearance of continuity which possibly helped to mitigate any doubts which they may have had about the legality of the Militia Ordinance. This, however, was not true of the great majority of those who were nominated. In many cases a gentleman who was invited to serve as a deputy lieutenant must have hesitated before coming to a decision for if he accepted the offer he would be acting in defiance of the king and manifesting his loyalty to Parliament in a way which could put both him and his family at risk. Some men made it clear that they had no wish to be nominated. On 23 May the Commons heard that Sir Edward Gresham, one of the deputy lieutenants for Surrey, had refused to carry out the duties of the office and agreed that he should be replaced.[6] Bulstrode Whitelocke, who was asked to assume this responsibility in two counties, Buckinghamshire and Oxfordshire, writes that 'I was not without some perplexity in my thoughts, whether I should accept of these Deputations . . . the King not consenting to the Ordinance.' Some of his friends considered that the Ordinance was illegal, others that it was not. In the end he decided to accept, mainly because of the solemn protestations of the most powerful and active members of the Commons that they had not the slightest intention of waging a war against the king but simply wanted to arm themselves for their necessary defence 'without which the king would so grow uppon them and his evill Counsellers so prevayle that they would undoubtedly bring their designs to pass, of a speedy introducing of Popery and Tyranny.' If, it was argued, Parliament put itself into a good posture of defence and it was evident that the people generally would support it, the king would be forced to come to terms without a blow being struck. Although he was fervently hoping that a conflict could be avoided, Whitelocke did not neglect to make military preparations. At his house (he tells us) he was well furnished with pikes, muskets, pistols and gunpowder and had good horses which were regularly trained.[7]

Early in March the king arrived at York and before long a distinctive royalist party began to emerge with the Court as its focal point. From time to time there were reports that recusants and others who were disaffected in religion were flocking to the Court; and it was even alleged that the Catholics 'give all lost if a Civill Warre ensue not or this Parliament be not subdued'.[8] The suspicions about the king's intentions were fully reciprocated. On 16 May Sir John Bankes was writing from York that the king and his advisers were afraid that there was a revolution in prospect:

> Heere be impressions and ffeares that there bee endeavours to alter the forme of the Government . . . .That there be such intrusions upon his prerogative as cannot stand with monarchy. Justice is not done for the King against those who scandalise the King's person and government by speaches, sermons, and pamphlets . . . .That the peace of the Church hath been, and is, daylie disquieted, and the liturgie and discipline thereof scandalised, and endeavours to bring in a Presbyteria[n] government as an introduction to a Commonwealth.

There had so far been no suggestion that Parliament wanted to adopt a Presbyterian system but it appears to have been assumed that any new form of church government was likely to be based on the Scottish model. In Sir John's view the differences between the king and his Parliament were not so great as to prevent a reconciliation if both parties were willing.[9] That same month the king decided to provide himself with a guard for his personal security and issued a proclamation forbidding the trained bands to act in accordance with the Militia Ordinance. Most of the Yorkshire gentry were either sympathetically inclined towards the king or at least acquiescent, but there was a dissident group which opposed his military proceedings and urged him to put his trust in Parliament. Significantly, this group included such leading Puritans as Sir Matthew Boynton, Sir John Bourchier and Sir Thomas Fairfax.[10]

In his parliamentary journal Sir Simonds D'Ewes records that on 16 May a number of MPs moved that the House should consider how an accommodation might be reached with the king while others stressed the need for Parliament to make necessary preparations for its defence.[11] There were many in the Commons who favoured the latter course, not because they were convinced that a war was either necessary or inevitable but because they felt that this would help to prevent a war and enable Parliament to negotiate from a position of strength. From the end of May onwards Parliament gave orders for the execution of the Militia Ordinance, in the sense of mustering and exercising the trained bands, in counties where the situation did not appear wholly unpropitious.[12] On 4 June Harbottle Grimston, who was no militant, introduced an order which stipulated that Parliament should be informed of any deputy lieutenants who refused or failed to attend the musters which were to be held.[13] Subsequently, on 10 June, Parliament issued a declaration or propositions for the bringing in of money, plate, arms and horses. Along with the Militia Ordinance these propositions represented a test of loyalty to Parliament, though it was emphasized that the purposes for which such assistance was sought were basically defensive in character: namely to maintain the Protestant religion, the king's authority and his person in his royal dignity, the free course of justice, the laws of the land, the peace of the kingdom and the privileges of Parliament against any force which should oppose them.[14] A week later it was agreed that the parliamentary deputy lieutenants should have authority to tender the propositions in their several counties and to appoint receivers to handle the contributions.[15] The king, for his part, resorted to the issue of commissions of array with the object of placing control of the county militia in the hands of 'estated and sober men'. Among those named were some Puritan squires who remained faithful to Parliament: Sir William Eliott, for example, was included in the Surrey list and Sir Edmund Bacon and Sir William Soame in the Suffolk list.[16]

Looking back on the Civil War, Clarendon argues that the spirit of rebellion had been fomented in no small degree by the seditious sermons of Puritan divines who had not only been busily engaged in vilifying the existing system of ecclesiastical government but had endeavoured to stir up the people against the king. Such men, he maintains, were 'trumpets of war and incendiaries towards rebellion'. John Milton was no less critical of these preachers, describing them as 'Pulpit-firebrands' and 'Ministers of sedition, not of the Gospel, who while they saw it manifestly tend to civil Warr and blood shed, never ceasd exasperating the people' against the king.[17] Clarendon and Milton were primarily referring to the monthly fast sermons which from February 1642 onwards were regularly preached at St Margaret's Westminster in the presence of members of the House of Commons and were usually ordered to be printed for the benefit of others outside Parliament.[18] Some of the militant preachers had close connections with members of the Puritan gentry. Stephen Marshall had actively supported the candidature of Sir Thomas Barrington and Sir Harbottle Grimston during the election which led to their return as knights of the shire for Essex in the Short Parliament. Simeon Ashe had been given shelter by the Burgoyne family after he had been deprived of his benefice for nonconformity. He and Cornelius Burgess preached at the second of the monthly fasts and must presumably have impressed Sir Arthur Hesilrige who moved in the Commons that they should be thanked for their sermons. Thomas Goodwin had been one of the pastors of the English church at Arnhem in the Dutch Netherlands where the congregation had included Sir Matthew Boynton and Sir William Constable. On 12 April 1642 Arthur Goodwin proposed that he should be invited to preach at the next parliamentary fast and this was duly arranged.[19] Sermons of a kind which the king's supporters regarded as treasonable were also being preached within the city of London and in some of the more Puritan parishes in other parts of the country. In addition, Puritan divines might seek to exert influence by more informal means. When Sir John Hotham was garrisoning Hull on behalf of Parliament William Chantrell, a neighbouring minister, revealed where his sympathies lay in a letter to his patron, Sir Thomas Barrington. Clearly delighted over Hotham's determination to prevent the king from gaining control of the town, which he described as a place of singular importance in the northern parts, he told him that his purpose in writing was 'to stirre up those flames of pietie and holy zeale to god's cause which (I heare) hath not only warmed your frendes in the south but your well willers in this cold north.'[20]

Preaching which appeared to be aimed at promoting a holy war must have alarmed many of the peers and MPs who joined the king at York during the course of 1642. In the main, however, the Puritan squires who had openly associated themselves with the cause of Parliament, whether as MPs or deputy lieutenants, showed no signs of changing their allegiance. After years of exposure to godly preaching, of private discourse with their spiritual counsellors and of religious exercises and reading of the scriptures they would generally have been more receptive to the exhortations of pulpit firebrands than most of their fellow gentry. Certainly the Puritan MPs in the congregation at St Margaret's Westminster would not only have been quick to appreciate the import of the biblical references in the sermons which they heard but would have no difficulty in accepting the contention that godliness was in peril; that its enemies were ranged on the side of the king; and that it was the duty of Parliament to safeguard and secure the advancement of true religion. Such arguments provided an ideological justification for adhering to Parliament which weighed heavily with upper class Puritans who apart from their religious zeal had much in common with the country gentry who would take up arms for the king. On the other hand, the conviction that Parliament was in the right did not necessarily generate any enthusiasm for the idea of resolving the quarrel on the battlefield. It is perhaps ironic that although Sir Robert Kemp, who was Stephen Marshall's patron at Finchingfield in Essex, appears to have had a high regard for his preaching he was a relatively inactive parliamentarian who did not even become a member of the county committee until 1645.[21]

In his parliamentary journal Sir Simonds D'Ewes refers with scorn to the fiery or violent spirits, as he termed them, who constituted the war party in the House of Commons. These included John Hampden, who according to D'Ewes was the 'chiefe captain and ringleader' of this group, Sir Henry Vane the younger, Sir Peter Wentworth, Sir Henry Mildmay, Sir Philip Stapleton, Sir John Evelyn of Wiltshire, Henry Marten, Nathaniel Fiennes, Miles Corbet, Cornelius Holland, Denis Bond, John Gurdon and William Strode. Most of them were Puritans but D'Ewes stressed that Marten was 'generallie knowen to be an Atheisticall liver and notorious whoremaster' and that Strode was 'a notable prophaner of the scriptures and a man doubtless void of all truth of pietie'.[22] There were, however, many Puritan gentry both inside and outside the Commons who though their sympathies lay with Parliament were reluctant to take up arms against a lawful sovereign and, above all, feared that such a conflict could have the most damaging consequences both for the nation in general and the propertied classes in particular. Even before the outbreak of the Civil War some landlords were having difficulties with their tenants. Writing to his steward in Yorkshire on 30 May, Godfrey Bosvile, one of the Puritan MPs who sat for Warwick, told him to 'acquaint my tenants that I now expect them (as they value my respect) to pay in the rent without delay' and added 'The Lord direct us in our loyalty to the King and care for the safety of the Kingdome.'[23] Over a decade earlier Sir Simonds D'Ewes had thought it likely that before the downfall of the Roman Antichrist (which according to the apocalyptic prophecies of Thomas Brightman was now imminent) some of the godly would 'witnes the truth of the gospell by a cheereful laying downe of our lives in the power of Faith for that truth.' In the summer of 1642, however, he was desperately hoping that England would remain at peace. During the course of a Commons debate on 8 June about the propositions for the

21

bringing in of money, plate, arms and horses he argued that such a measure was dangerous because it would fill men's hearts with the fear and expectation of a civil war

> soe as the verie underwriting to finde horses may disable men to doe it for most men's estates who are of ranke and qualitie doe arise out of the labors and sweat of other men's browes; and if they shall once perceive that all is like to come to confusion will perhapps forbeare paying in of those rents which must finde and maintaine these horses.

He therefore felt that the surest way to be prepared was not to talk of preparation. In any case the king's party was not militarily strong and he could see no reason for stirring up fears of a civil war 'till ther be an absolute necessitie'. Subsequently, on 21 June, he was writing to his brother that

> I could be willing to redeeme the re-union of his Majestie and the two Howses with my dearest bloud, that soe Religion might be established in that power and puritie amongst us and preaching soe setled in those places wheare Atheisme, profanenes and ignorance now raigne as that all men might know their dutie to God and the King, soe as his Majestie might raigne many and many yeares over us with much honour and praise. For doubtles by a civil warre he will be the greater looser whosoever gaines.

A week later he was arguing in the Commons that the wicked prelates had been seeking to ruin all godliness and conscientious preaching and advocating an alteration in the government of the Church according to the example of other Protestant churches in Europe. For D'Ewes ecclesiastical reform was the most urgent requirement and a primary means of defusing the political crisis.[24]

According to his daughter-in-law Sir Thomas Hutchinson, whom D'Ewes describes as 'my very entire friend', never wavered in his loyalty to Parliament, largely no doubt because of his religious commitment. Yet he was also very anxious that 'the difference might rather have bene compos'd by accommodation than ended by conquest' and therefore made no attempt to involve his native county of Nottinghamshire in the quarrel 'which, if he could have prevented, he would not have had it come to a warre'. Sir Thomas was a moderate by temperament but he may also have been influenced by the fact that there was very strong support for the king among the Nottinghamshire gentry. Significantly, he had informed the Earl of Clare, who was the parliamentary lord lieutenant of the county, that he had no wish to be nominated as a deputy lieutenant.[25]

When the question of raising an army was debated in the Commons on 9 July Sir Benjamin Rudyerd declared that the present differences between the king and Parliament made the entire kingdom stand amazed in a fearful expectation of dismal calamities to fall upon it. Every member of the House, he maintained, was obliged as a matter of conscience to do everything in his power to prevent the outbreak of a civil war: 'let us save our liberties and our Estates, as we may save our Souls too.'[26] In the same debate Bulstrode Whitelocke suggested that the sins of the nation might have provoked God to punish it by a civil war 'to make us executioners of divine vengeance uppon our selves'. It was strange, he went on, to see how the country was sliding, by one accident after another, towards a civil war. Although no one could know what the outcome of such a conflict would be he was disposed to fear the worst, perhaps because of what was happening in Germany:

> We must surrender up our lawes, liberties, properties and lives into the hands of insolent mercenaries whose rage and violence will commaund us and all we have and reason, honour and justice will leave our land, the ignoble will rule the noble and basenes will be preferred before virtue, prophaneness before piety.

Whitelocke did not object to preparations being put in hand for the just and necessary defence of 'our religion, lives and liberties' but considered that the main essential was to seek an agreement with the king.[27] Sir Simonds D'Ewes, for his part, feared that if Parliament provided itself with an army the king would be obliged to respond in kind and before long 'a fire of civill warre' would be kindled which might not easily be quenched.[28] On 12 July, however, the Commons agreed that an army should be raised for the safety of the king's person, the defence of both Houses of Parliament and the laws, liberty and peace of the kingdom and that it should be placed under the command of the Earl of Essex.[29]

In the meantime steps were being taken in a number of counties to execute the Militia Ordinance, in some cases on the initiative of one or two of the Puritan deputy lieutenants who were also MPs, men such as John Hampden and Arthur Goodwin of Buckinghamshire and Sir William Brereton of Cheshire. The declared objective of these military measures was the preservation of the peace in the county concerned; at the beginning of 'these sad distractions', wrote Brereton in 1645, 'it was thought necessary that every particular County should be put in a posture of Defence that soe the whole kingdome might not be ruined.'[30]

When the arrangements for mustering the Northampton-shire militia were discussed in the Commons on 8 June it was decided that only four MPs who were deputy lieutenants should take part on the grounds that the House would otherwise be 'too thin' and that these should be Sir Christopher Yelverton, Sir Gilbert Pickering, John Crewe and Richard Knightley. The following day one of the sons of Lord Montagu of Boughton wrote in a letter to his father that Lord Spencer, the lord lieutenant, and Zouch Tate, another of the Northamptonshire MPs, would be travelling down in a coach and that Crewe and Pickering would be joining them. On 20 June Sir Gilbert, who appears to have been a key figure in this undertaking, informed the Commons that the county had readily yielded obedience to the Militia Ordinance and at least 900 volunteers had come forward. Writing to his friend Sir Rowland St John on 13 July he told him that Parliament was sending an order or commission into Northamptonshire with the view to securing contributions of horses, money or plate for the necessary defence of the kingdom and that it contained the names of 'most of the gentry of our county if not all'. He hoped that all men would be prepared to acknowledge that if the kingdom was attacked it must defend itself. This meant that it must have a stock of money, though this would have to be provided voluntarily since there could be no compulsion without legal authority. He went on:

Wee may save our owne stakes by complyance but posterety will rue it. There are now some overtures of accomodation come from his Majesty and most men thinke they smell the ayre of peace yet provide for warr.[31]

Pickering was described by a hostile contemporary as 'a most furious fiery, implacable Man'[32] and he clearly believed that Parliament must be ready to fight if necessary. No doubt he was present (as was Sir Simonds D'Ewes) on 27 July when Thomas Hill, who as pastor of Titchmarsh enjoyed his patronage, delivered a parliamentary fast sermon in St Margaret's Westminster. 'It is true', declared Hill, that 'we are now full of sad distractions; blacke and bloody clouds beginne to gather; yet, may not Faith (through them) spy out the Sunne of righteousnesse shining graciously upon unworthy England?' At one point he resorted to metaphorical language drawn from the prevailing military situation:

let us be sure of this Militia, which is the Word of God ....Guard that Magazine, wherein are laid up the weapons of our warfare, that are mighty through God, to the pulling downe of strong holds ....So shall we be put into a good posture for Reformation.

The primary need in his view was for a synod of divines which would consider the precise nature of the ecclesiastical reformation. In dedicating the printed version of his sermon to the House of Commons he offered the comment that 'to effect an happy correspondence betwixt our Soveraigne and his people, a blessed compliance betwixt England and Religion, here's work for the strongest shoulders.'[33]

Although the execution of the Militia Ordinance went relatively smoothly in some of the more Puritan counties such as Buckinghamshire, Essex and Northamptonshire, there were other counties where it proved more difficult to assert the authority of Parliament. In Cheshire, Leicestershire and Dorset the parliamentary deputy lieutenants met with opposition from the royalist commissioners of array.[34] Among the gentry of Dorset there were only a few major Puritan families: in particular, the Trenchards, Erles and Brownes of Frampton who had a number of godly ministers under their patronage.[35] Relations between the Erles and the Trenchards were strained as the result of a long-runnning property dispute which had given rise to a new round of litigation in 1640 and would do so again in 1653. Moreover, Sir Thomas Trenchard had been responsible, as sheriff of Dorset, for levying ship money and in 1636 had reported Sir Walter Erle and John Browne, among others, for refusing to pay their assessments. During the political crisis of 1642, however, the common bond of religion enabled them to sink their differences and all three of them accepted appointment as deputy lieutenants under the provisions of the Militia Ordinance. When the king issued a commission of array for Dorset on 29 June it included the names of a considerable number of leading gentry, among them Sir John Strangways who, in the words of a fellow squire, was no friend of the Puritans and Richard Rogers who as sheriff had shown great diligence in collecting ship money. Sir Thomas Trenchard was also nominated but was not prepared to change sides. Although Parliament agreed on 1 July that the Militia Ordinance should presently be put into execution in Dorset it was not until 28 July that an order was approved for this purpose. According to the preamble to this order the Lords and Commons had been informed of warlike preparations and many threatening speeches in Dorset and the parts adjoining. In view of these developments Trenchard, Erle and Browne, together with Denzil Holles, were authorized to arm, train and put in readiness all the male inhabitants of the county. It was an assignment which would have stirred the blood of Sir Walter Erle who had once fought in the Low Countries and, it was said, 'valued himself upon the sieges and service he had been in'. At the same time he was under no illusion about the strength of the forces which the royalists under the leadership of Strangways and Rogers were gathering together. On 6

August he obtained authority from the Commons to transport into Dorset five hampers with saddles and pistols, three chests, a small bundle of carbines and firelocks with horsemen's arms for the service of the Commonwealth and two 'murthering Pieces' for the defence of his house.[36] The deputy lieutenants who were entrusted with the execution of the Militia Ordinance in Bedfordshire included Sir Beauchamp St John, Sir Oliver Luke and his son Sir Samuel. On 28 July it was reported that Sir Lewis Dyve, the most active royalist in the county, had placed an order for the manufacture of 500 bullets at Bedford and had said 'Now, you Roundheads, I have provided for you'. When Sir Samuel Luke and the sheriff, Sir Thomas Alston, had sought to arrest him Sir Lewis had declared that he was commanded by the king and would kill anyone who attempted to secure his person. He had then fired a pistol at Luke and wounded him in arm and thigh with his sword. Sir Samuel, however, soon recovered, and in October was involved in the battle of Edgehill.[37]

In some counties the parliamentarian gentry considered that the implementation of the Militia Ordinance would be likely to precipitate rather than prevent a conflict of arms. Sir John Potts and Sir John Holland, who were both MPs and deputy lieutenants for Norfolk, took the view that there was a reasonable prospect that the county might be spared the tribulations of a civil war if the Militia Ordinance and the commission of array were allowed to sleep. On 1 August a parliamentary order was approved which required Sir Thomas Wodehouse, Sir John Holland, Sir John Potts, Sir Edmund Moundeford and other MPs to go down into Norfolk for the purpose of suppressing the commission of array, securing the county magazine and executing the Militia Ordinance. Three days later, however, we find Holland informing Potts that he had moved in the Commons that for the present no orders should be dispatched to Norfolk for the setting in hand of military preparations; and that he had written to many of his friends emphasizing the importance of suspending all action on the commission of array. On 11 August Potts was writing to his nephew Sir Simonds D'Ewes that the county was still 'free from blowes but not without divisions . . . .I laboure to preserve peace.' In a further letter to D'Ewes which is dated 19 August he assured him that he fully shared his concern about the potential consequences if the common people were drawn into a civil war:

I concur with you in your feares of ungovernable numbers, from whence my thoughts alwaies apprehended the most remediless dangers, which God avert. My own endeavours heer have been for peace and hitherto wee are quiet; whensoever necessity shall enforce us to make use of the multitude I doe not promise my self safety.[38]

THREE

An Unnatural War

DURING the months of uneasy peace which preceded the king's formal declaration of war the parish clergy were often drawn into the propaganda battle which was raging. On 14 July Sir Edward Harrington, one of the parliamentary deputy lieutenants for Rutland, informed the Commons that the innovating clergy were very forward in publicizing the king's declarations but ignored those which were issued by Parliament.[1] Not infrequently such ministers were summoned to Westminster to be questioned about their conduct. On 20 July the Commons decided to send for John Gwyn, the vicar of Cople in Bedfordshire, after hearing allegations that he had read a royal declaration but had categorically refused to read a declaration emanating from Parliament; and the following day Sir Nathaniel Barnardiston presented similar accusations about Frederick Gibb, the minister of Boxted in Suffolk. During the 1630s Gwyn had been at loggerheads with his Puritan parishioners of whom the most prominent was Sir Samuel Luke, who had obtained permission from the ecclesiastical authorities to worship at other churches in the neighbourhood. On 26 July the churchwardens testified that Gwyn had received copies of two declarations from Parliament and one from the king; and that he had contemptuously thrown aside the declarations from Parliament with the comment 'But judge whether I am to obey God or Man. By God's Word I am commanded to obey the King; I find no such Command for the Parliament.' They also

29

claimed that he was a man of a debauched, lewd and contentious disposition and that he had spoken of the Commons in opprobrious and scandalous terms. In the light of this evidence Gwyn was committed to prison and fined £100.[2]

On the other hand, the Commons had nothing but sympathy for godly ministers who, it was reported, had been forced by the sheriffs of their counties to read the king's declarations in their churches.[3] In some areas, however, Puritan clergymen were subjected to more severe forms of harassment. On 27 July Sir William Brereton wrote indignantly in a letter to Oliver Cromwell that in Cheshire the commissioners of array were proceeding with great violence against those who opposed them and, among other things, had called before them some of 'our best ministers'. These included John Ley, the Puritan vicar of Great Bedworth, who was the author of *A Pattern of Pietie* which had been dedicated to Lady Brilliana Harley and Lady Alice Lucy. To Sir William it was important that steps should be taken for the security and protection of such ministers.[4]

In areas where the royalist party was dominant the Puritan laity also had reason to feel isolated and exposed. Richard Baxter writes that in Worcestershire, Herefordshire and Shropshire 'they were wholly for the King and none, to any purpose, moved for the Parliament.'[5] Among the Herefordshire gentry Sir Robert Harley was the only squire of the first rank who was wholeheartedly committed to the cause of Parliament, but since he chose to remain at Westminster there was little he could do to influence the course of events in the county which he represented. As early as 4 June his wife, Lady Brilliana, was writing to him from Brampton Castle, the family's principal seat, that 'the Cuntry growes very insolent and if theare should be any rising I thinke I am in a very unsafe Place.' She went on to suggest that it would be advisable for her to remove to London, adding that 'theare is no body in the Cuntry that loves you or me, but I hope the Lord will be mercyfull to us.' Sir Robert, however, assured her (somewhat implausibly) that Herefordshire was as safe as any other county and to add to her troubles complained about the way in which his estate was being managed in his absence. Writing to her son Edward (who was also in London) on 5 July, Lady Harley told him that the king had issued a commission of array for Herefordshire and expressed the hope that Parliament would send down men to take charge of the militia; there was, however, no possibility of the Militia Ordinance being executed in the summer of 1642. 'Your father' she went on 'they are growne to hate. I pray God forgive them. My deare Ned, I am not afraide, but sure I am, we are a dispised company.' Further letters to her husband and son revealed her growing fears about the situation which was developing. Many in Herefordshire, she related, were saying that within six weeks the county would be rid of Puritans. If Sir Robert considered that Brampton Bryan was the safest place for her she hoped he would send down an acquaintance who was religious to stay with her until the storms were over and to advise her on how the house might be defended. 'Nowe', she told her son, 'the intention is to route out all that feare God, and surely the Lord will arise to healpe us: and in your God let your confidence be, and I am assured it is so.' Despite her forebodings Lady Harley and her younger children remained at Brampton Castle where they continued to have the spiritual counsel of Stanley Gower, who had recently commented in a letter to his patron that the wonders of God as manifested in the Long Parliament would never be forgotten.[6]

Nottinghamshire, writes Lucy Hutchinson, was one of those counties which were 'so wholly for the king that the godly . . . were forc'd to forsake their habitations, and seeke other shelters'. Her husband, John Hutchinson, was marked down as a man well affected to Parliament. On hearing that a troop of Cavaliers was approaching his house, Owthorpe Hall, he retired for a time into Leicestershire where he was joined by his wife.[7] In Yorkshire, where the king's military power was mainly concentrated during this period of tension, men who were known supporters of Parliament were also coming under pressure. In July marauding bands of royalist troops began to carry out raids on the houses of Roundhead squires. The first victim of this lawlessness was Christopher Legard, a Puritan gentleman who was seated at Anlaby in the neighbourhood of Hull and was serving as an officer in the parliamentary garrison there. When the royalist soldiers appeared at Anlaby they plundered his house and drove away all his horses, sheep and cattle. At Nun Monkton some royalists broke into the house of George Marwood, who had recently been struck off the commission of the peace, during his absence and insulted his wife, calling her 'Puritan whore'.[8] Lady Fiennes Jackson, who was sister to Sir William Waller, thought it prudent to send all the estate deeds of her late husband, Sir John Jackson of Hickleton, to Hull for safe keeping; and other wealthy Puritans such as Sir Richard Hawksworth and Sir Edward Rodes entrusted money or plate to the care and protection of the garrison.[9]

In the early summer Bulstrode Whitelocke went down to his house, Fawley Court, in Buckinghamshire with a view to spending some time with his family. There he found that his wife, 'being very neer her time of childbirth, was much frighted by the newes and preparations of warre'. Since, however, she was 'of a gallant spirit and exceedingly affected to the Parlament she bore it out with the more Courage and contentment.' As the political situation continued to deteriorate he decided that it would be best if she and their two eldest daughters moved to London. His other five children were left at Fawley with one of his tenants, William Cooke, who was asked to ensure their safety and do what he could to safeguard his house and goods in the event of a royalist incursion.[10]

In August a number of Puritan squires, among them Sir Robert Cooke and Sir John Hobart, secured parliamentary authority for carrying down arms to their country houses. Cooke was one of the few major landowners in Gloucestershire who were firm supporters of Parliament. On 13 August the Commons decided that he and a fellow MP should go down to Gloucestershire with the object of preserving the peace there; and on 19 August he was given leave to take two cases of pistols with him. Shortly after this the House noted that Sir John Hobart was intending to transport five cases of pistols, three carabines and two small firing pieces from London to his home, Blickling Hall, in Norfolk and gave order that he should be allowed to pass quietly and freely.[11]

Well before the king raised his standard at Nottingham on 22 August many of the principal gentry of the kingdom had in effect already declared which side they would take in the event of a war. A considerable number of MPs had left Westminster for York but a solid majority in the Commons had held firm. In the main the commissioners of array continued to support the king while virtually all the deputy lieutenants who had been appointed under the provisions of the Militia Ordinance remained loyal to Parliament. For many Puritan squires the key question in the late summer of 1642 was not whether they should come out in favour of Parliament or the king but how far they should commit themselves in the cause of Parliament, taking into consideration both the general situation which obtained and the particular circumstances with which they were faced in their own localities. Some like John Hampden, Arthur Goodwin and Sir Arthur Hesilrige were heavily engaged in military operations at a very early stage. Sir William Waller recounts that on the outbreak of the Civil War 'my passion to the Parliament imbolden'd me to offer my service, as farr as to the raising of first a troop (when there were but six appointed in all, and it was something to find gentlemen that would engage) and after of a regiment of horse.' He also tells us, however, that he abhorred the war, 'though I acted in it as upon the defensive (which I thought justifiable).'[12] Within the ranks of the parliamentarians there was a belief which was encouraged by Pym, Hampden and other leading figures in the Commons that if Parliament acted decisively the king would quickly capitulate since he had little popular support. Either a war could be avoided altogether or it would be relatively short. In a letter addressed to the parliamentarian gentry of Suffolk Arthur Goodwin and two other Buckinghamshire deputy lieutenants told them that their whole county was rising; that Hertfordshire had promised to help them; and that they presumed Northamptonshire would join them. If, they went on, Suffolk 'will appear zealous a short time' it would soon put an end to the present troubles.[13] Edmund Ludlow writes that he considered it his duty as an Englishman to serve in the army of the Earl of Essex and thought that the justice of the cause in which he had engaged to be so self-evident that 'I could not imagine it to be attended with much difficulty.' He assumed that a majority of the clergy who had been 'the principal authors of our miseries' together with some of the king's courtiers and dependants would give him their support but regarded it as inconceivable that many of the people, who had long been oppressed with heavy burdens, would be unwilling to side with Parliament.[14] When it became clear that hopes of a speedy conclusion to the war had proved to be ill-founded, Bulstrode Whitelocke complained in the Commons that 'it was an unhappy mistake of those who told us in the beginning of our warfare that it would be only to show our selves in the field with a few forces and then all would be presently ended.'[15]

In contrast, there were many wealthy parliamentarians who believed that it might be possible to ensure that their counties remained insulated from the Civil War if they followed a policy of masterly inactivity. When they eventually bestirred themselves this was generally occasioned by such factors as pressure from Parliament, royalist threats or civil disorder. In June the parliamentary commissioners at York had reported that the county was 'so inclinable to peace' that there was little for them to do. Clarendon observes that in Yorkshire 'they who were most inclined to Parliament (whereof the Lord Fairfax and his son were the chief) . . . were rather desirous to look on than engage themselves in the war, presuming that one battle would determine all disputes.' On 29 August the Fairfaxes, Sir Richard Hawksworth and other parliamentarians who were gathered together at Otley in the West Riding put their signatures to a protestation in which they complained that the activities of the royalists at York were likely to promote 'the worst of all evills', namely 'to beget a warre in the bowels of this County'. After making it clear that they could not consent to the raising of forces on behalf of the king they declared their willingness to meet the rest of the gentry and other considerable inhabitants of Yorkshire in order to consider how such a war could be prevented.[16] Henry Clifford, Earl of Cumberland, who was at that time the senior royalist commander in Yorkshire, was no less anxious to maintain peace in the county. On 16 September he wrote to his daughter Elizabeth that 'my caryage hathe beene soe equal as all my actions have tended to keepe this County in peace, and have set it in such a waye as (if the divell be not in it) I shall perfecte that quiate peace which few other Cuntryes enioys.' Following negotiations between the two parties a treaty of neutrality was concluded at Rothwell, near Leeds, on 29 September. The parliamentarians who subscribed to the treaty consisted of Lord Fairfax and his son, Sir William Lister (who was related to the principal royalist signatory, Henry Bellasis) and several other Puritan landowners. There was, however, another Puritan squire who took exception to these proceedings. Sir Edward Rodes had already suffered at the hands of the royalists: on 20 September there had been a report that a band of Cavaliers had plundered his house at Great Houghton, burnt down all the outhouses and taken away goods to the value of £600. Clearly incensed by this incident, he was determined to make sure that the treaty was stillborn. On 1 October he and John Hotham, who had been undertaking forays in the East Riding, sent a copy of the agreement to the House of Commons, describing it as most disadvantageous to the service of the kingdom and the safety of the county, and asked for instructions to be issued for the supply of horses, money and plate. On receiving this letter the Commons roundly condemned the treaty and before long the two sides were engaged in heavy fighting.[17]

In the neighbouring county of Derbyshire many substantial landowners were sympathetically inclined towards the royalist cause and for a time it looked as though they could safely discount the possibility that the handful of parliamentarian squires might attempt to use military force. After setting up his standard at Nottingham the king made his way to Derbyshire, where he was welcomed by a considerable number of country gentlemen together with the trained bands. On 13 September it was reported from Derby that royalist troops had pillaged the houses of three of the parliamentary deputy lieutenants, Sir John Gell, Sir Thomas Burdett and Sir Samuel Sleigh. At Hopton, where Sir John had his seat, they 'rifled his house, spoyled his goods, carried away his cattle and made a lamentable devastation of all he had.' He himself would later write that 'I had my House plundered and nothing left but the bare walls, and the malice of the Enemy extended so farre as to ruine and deface the Tombs and Monuments of my deceased Ancestors.'[18] At the end of September he went with his brother Thomas to Hull, where he was hoping to be given the command of some troops. During their absence Sir Francis Wortley, one of the most active royalists in Yorkshire, entered the county with a band of about a hundred soldiers. On hearing of this incursion Sir John hastened back to Derbyshire, taking with him a company of foot troops. While he was engaged in raising further troops at Chesterfield a number of Derbyshire noblemen and gentry met together at Tutbury which was just across the border in Staffordshire and sent him a threatening letter in which they condemned him for his temerity in appearing in arms. In reply Sir John protested that 'it seemed strange they should growe so quickly jealous of hym, theyre own countrieman, and known to them, and that had no other end then the cleareing of his county from theeves and robbers, to mayntaine the lawes of the land and liberties of the subject.' He then put Wortley to flight and at the end of October took possession of Derby, which he fortified and garrisoned on behalf of Parliament. Even at this stage, however, there was a general reluctance on the part of his fellow deputy lieutenants to become involved in military operations: referring to his seizure of Derby Sir John writes that Sir George Gresley 'was now joyned with us, the only Gentleman of quactly in this county that cordyally appeared to be on our side.'[19]

In East Anglia the deputy lieutenants of Norfolk and Suffolk feared that the execution of the Militia Ordinance would precipitate a full-scale conflict in their counties. Not surprisingly, the equivocation of men like Sir John Potts and Sir John Holland in Norfolk occasioned some suspicion at Westminster. On 2 September Potts was emphasizing in a letter to his nephew Sir Simonds D'Ewes that there was no truth in the scandalous rumours that he had changed sides: 'Sir, I assure you my conscience leads me to uphold the Commonwealth to which I will prove no changling.'[20] Shortly afterwards the Norfolk deputy lieutenants began to set some military preparations in hand, but essentially for the purpose of maintaining peace within the county. Contributions of arms, horses, plate and money were sought in accordance with the propositions of 10 June and the commanders of the militia formally declared at a meeting held at Norwich that they accepted the authority of the Earl of Warwick as lord lieutenant. When D'Ewes heard that troops were being mustered and exercised he was filled with dismay, partly no doubt because he was afraid that his own county of Suffolk might be put in danger, and on 28 November he wrote to his uncle that he was sorry to hear that 'you beginne alreadie in Norfolke to send for commanders, and that the face of things beginne to looke after an hostile manner amongst you.' At a meeting held on 7 December a number of Norfolk gentlemen joined with the deputy lieutenants in an agreement for the defence of the county and the protection of its inhabitants from all kinds of plunderers. On the following day Sir John Hobart, Sir John Holland and some of the other deputy lieutenants signed a letter addressed to Sir John Potts as colonel of a regiment of foot in which he was requested to send them the names of those who refused to appear at his musters 'as persons disaffected to the peace and safetie of this County'.[21]

In Suffolk, where Puritan influences were stronger, there appeared to be little danger of a royalist uprising at the beginning of the Civil War. During a Commons debate on 22 September one MP commented that Suffolk was in as good a condition, in the political sense, as any county in England and Sir Simonds D'Ewes conceded that 'it is indeed verie true that wee doe yet enioy quiet ther', though he felt it necessary to add that 'my tenants doe learne warines from other places and pay little rent.'[22] In the main the parliamentary deputy lieutenants were Puritans, men such as Sir Nathaniel Barnardiston and his son Sir Thomas, Sir William Spring, Sir John Wentworth, Sir Robert Brooke, Sir William Soame, Brampton Gurdon and his son John. On 5 July John Gurdon, whom D'Ewes characterizes as one of the fiery spirits in the Commons, had moved that the Militia Ordinance should be put into execution in Suffolk and the House had approved the proposal on the basis that the lord lieutenant and his deputies should have three weeks' notice; but in the event nothing happened.[23] Most of the leading parliamentarians were apparently convinced that it would be the height of folly to go ahead with military preparations when there was at least a possibility that the Civil War would never be more than a distant prospect. Although there were a considerable number of gentry with royalist sympathies[24] they showed no inclination to execute the commission of array; and the king's army presented no immediate threat. Very soon, however, there was an unexpected development which introduced a major new factor into the situation. On 25 August the House was informed that a report had been received from Sir Robert Crane, one of the deputy lieutenants, about some rioting which had broken out in the neighbourhood of Sudbury. The rioters, who were said to be 2,000 strong, plundered a number of houses, including those belonging to Lady Savage at Long Melford and Sir Francis Mannock at Stoke by Nayland. The disturbances led Sir William Castleton, the sheriff of the county, to order the trained bands to assemble but this action was clearly not to the liking of Sir Nathaniel Barnardiston. Writing from Westminster on 1 September he told the sheriff that he had heard from Ipswich that warrants had been issued for the raising of troops; such measures, he went on, 'wee conceave dangerous in these Turbulent times.'[25]

On 10 September Sir Simonds D'Ewes recorded in his parliamentary journal that the Speaker had been informed that 'a great number of rude and disorderly people' had lately gathered together and 'had pillaged the houses as well of the Protestants as Papists'. Faced with this situation the magistrates, with the assistance of the sheriff, had raised 'the power of the county' and apprehended the principal offenders. In the ensuing debate the House heard that there was to be a meeting of the gentry at Stowmarket and that Sir Nathaniel Barnardiston was going down with a Commons order prohibiting all riotous assemblies. Following this meeting the deputy lieutenants finally proceeded with the execution of the Militia Ordinance.[26]

In December Parliament approved an ordinance for associating the counties of Norfolk, Suffolk, Essex, Cambridgeshire and Hertfordshire for the purpose of promoting military co-operation, and on 9 February 1643 representatives of these five counties agreed that the Eastern Association should be established as soon as possible. This effectively put an end to attempts to keep Norfolk and Suffolk out of the war but in general the Puritan squires on whom Parliament was primarily dependent for support never gave the impression that they were able or willing to view the struggle in national as well as local terms.[27]

The first parliamentary lord lieutenant of Surrey was Charles Howard Earl of Nottingham, a man of doubtful loyalty who in the course of the summer thought it best to procrastinate when ordered by Parliament to execute the Militia Ordinance.[28] Among his deputy lieutenants the dominant figure was Sir Richard Onslow, the senior knight of the shire, who was one of the wealthiest Puritans in the county. According to an eighteenth-century account of the Onslow family, he was 'a man of high spirit, of a large fortune and of great parts, knowledge and courage, with the gravity and sobriety of the times' and was highly esteemed in his own county 'where he bore the principal sway in all business and interests.'[29] Probably it was at Sir Richard's instigation that on 6 August the Commons agreed on the speedy execution of the Militia Ordinance in Surrey. Six days later Nottingham summoned his deputy lieutenants to a conference at his house in Leatherhead in order to 'settle the country in a posture of arms'. Within a matter of weeks he was dead and on 5 October the Commons consented to the appointment of the Earl of Northumberland as his successor. The same day it was also agreed that the deputy lieutenants should be required to tender the propositions for bringing in of money, plate and horses and, significantly, it was Sir Richard Onslow who was entrusted with the responsibility of seeking the approval of the House of Lords.[30]

Later in the year the king's advance on London aroused growing alarm among Surrey landowners whose sympathies lay with Parliament. Sir William Eliott, a Puritan squire who was seated to the south of Guildford, found the situation thoroughly disturbing. Writing to her brother Sir Simonds D'Ewes, on 1 December, Lady Eliott asked him whether he would like to spend Christmas with them at Busbridge Hall, adding that she feared that it might be as sad a Christmas as had ever been kept in England, 'the god of heaven and earth helpe us'. Her husband, she went on, was

> so sad and overtrobled with the danger and misiry of these distracted times that he hath worne himselfe leane and denied his health. I have done what I am abell by perswading him and comforting him. Let me entreat you to joine with me in your next letter to him that he may cast of these worldly feares and cares and confidently rest on god who is alsufficient.

On 11 December Sir William told D'Ewes that in these dangerous times he considered it unwise to absent himself from his home: soldiers of both sides were continually traversing the county and his house had been visited by them, though so far there had been little damage. When the king had briefly stopped at Oatlands (his country residence near Wey-bridge) while travelling with his army towards Reading he had felt it prudent to hasten there and pay his respects; and he had also met Richard D'Ewes, the brother of Sir Simonds, who was now an officer in the king's service. Sir William continued:

> I Beseech god sett an end to these miseryes under which most of the Southerne and Northerne Countryes of this kingdome doe much suffer, and must doe much more to the ruine of the whole if a blessed peace or a present fight give not a determination thereunto.[31]

The following year he became a member of the parliamentary committee for Surrey but he was certainly no activist. In sharp contrast, Sir Richard Onslow displayed his zeal for the cause by joining the army of Sir William Waller.[32]

Even when the Militia Ordinance had been executed at an early stage there was often a tendency to think only in terms of ensuring the peace and safety of the county and to rest content so long as this requirement was satisfied. On 1 July the trained bands of Devon had been brought firmly under the control of the Earl of Bedford, as lord lieutenant, and his deputies, though it was generally agreed that they should be used solely for the defence of the county. In October the deputy lieutenants issued letters calling on the principal gentry to appear at Exeter with a view to pledging material support. In one of these letters the signatories, among them Sir Samuel Rolle, Sir Nicholas Martyn and Sir John Bamfield, emphasized the defensive nature of the military preparations which they considered necessary in view of the possibility of a royalist incursion from Cornwall:

> you know in what a sadd posture the body of the kingdome now stands. You remember that lately 500 horse passed through ours into our neighbor county, whoe now hang over us as a terrible cloude, threatning rayne, if wee provide not to withstand them. To be prepared for the worst brings noe disadvantage to any but strength and confidence to all.[33]

On 11 November Alexander Carew, Francis Buller and other Cornish parliamentarians who had been obliged to seek shelter at Plymouth wrote in a letter to the Committee for the Safety of the Kingdom that they were very surprised that their county should have been so neglected by Parliament and asked for money and arms to be dispatched to them with all possible speed. Devon, they added, 'pretends but little, and will act less'.[34] In March 1643 two of the Lincolnshire deputy lieutenants, Sir Edward Ayscough and Thomas Grantham, made it clear in a letter to the Speaker of the Commons that for them the paramount objective was to preserve their county from ruin and expressed the hope that they would receive some encouragement from Parliament in this respect.[35] Although Essex made a regiment available for service outside the county its joint commanders, Sir Thomas Barrington and Sir Thomas Honywood, did not consider it their duty to accompany it. Writing to Barrington in May 1643 Lord Grey of Warke complained that the regiment was in a mutinous state and left him in no doubt that his presence was necessary if discipline was to be restored.[36]

FOUR

A Nation Divided

LOOKING back on the Civil War Richard Baxter observes that 'all over the kingdom, save here and there a sober Gentleman and a formal Clergyman, the Religious Party and all that loved them were generally for the Parliament. . . . And the Profane Party in all Countries (Debaucht Gentlemen, Malignant Haters of Piety, the Rabble of Drunkards, Blasphemers) were generally against the Parliament'.[1] This view of the Civil War as essentially a conflict between the godly and the unregenerate enjoyed a wide currency within the ranks of the parliamentarians. In a parliamentary speech delivered in 1659 John Lambert declared that

> For the King, it is plain that Papists, prelates and delinquents, all such as had places or tithes, pluralists of honour or profit, and generally all debauched people ran with that stream. For the Parliament's party, an honest, sober, grave people, that groaned under oppression, thirsted after grace, the reformed party of the nation . . . that had no by-ends, and expected no advantage from the King or from the court.[2]

In an account of the war in Derbyshire which was written or commissioned by Sir John Gell the point was made that some of the royalists there were popish in religion while others were of lewd life and little fortune; and there was also a reference to the king's northern popish army.[3]

Similarly, Lucy Hutchinson writes that all over England the

king was able to count on the support of the papists, the debauched nobility and gentry and their dependants, and 'the lewder rout of people'.[4]

Not surprisingly, the royalists had rather different perceptions. The allegations that the king was heavily dependent on the support of his Catholic subjects were dismissed as scurrilous propaganda. In August 1643 it was reported in a royalist newspaper that letters which had been received from Dorchester had shown 'how miserably the people thereabouts have been cousened' by the Puritan ministers of the town, John White, Hugh Thomson and William Benn. From their pulpits they had claimed that the mass was celebrated openly in Oxford and that 'none but Papists were about His Majesty'.[5] Clarendon's observations on the parliamentarians suggest that he had no interest in systematic analysis. In his view some of the MPs who took up military commands in the service of Parliament did so because they were in financial difficulties or because they were anxious to be considered reformers in the belief that this would be a means of acquiring places of honour or offices of profit.[6] It was generally acknowledged, however, that there were many Puritans to be found on the side of Parliament. In November 1642 Sir Marmaduke Langdale, who was to gain some fame as a royalist commander, told Sir William Savile that in the northern counties those who were engaged in hostilities against the king were much infected with the hot zeal of Puritanism;[7] and indeed the parliamentarians were sometimes described as 'the Puritan party'.[8]

Some Puritan gentry threw in their lot with the king. Sir Henry Slingsby, the Yorkshire royalist who was executed in 1658, had received his formal education at the hands of Puritan divines: Phatuel Otby, the vicar of Foston near York, and the celebrated John Preston who was his tutor at Cambridge. His views on ecclesiastical matters were generally austere: he considered, for example, that it came too near idolatry to adorn a church 'with rich cloaths and other furniture and to command to use towards it bodily worship'. But although he was in favour of depriving the bishops of their secular powers he was strongly opposed to the abolition of episcopacy because he

43

feared it would encourage the common people to question the legitimacy of other institutions; and it was probably this factor above all which led him to support the royalist cause.[9] Another Yorkshire Puritan, Sir Gervase Cutler, was named as a member of the West Riding parliamentary committee after the king had appointed him a commissioner of array but he remained firm in his loyalty to the Crown.[10] In September 1642 Sir Simonds D'Ewes admitted in the Commons that his brother (who had been educated under a Puritan tutor at Cambridge) was serving as an officer in the royal army. Six months later Richard D'Ewes was killed in a skirmish at Reading and in one of his journals Sir Simonds paid testimony to his piety and recalled that he had often reproved the swearing of his fellow officers and punished 'that sinne in the Souldiers under his command'.[11]

Sir Robert Cooke, a leading Gloucestershire Puritan, died in battle while commanding a regiment of parliamentarian troops but in November 1643 the Commons heard that his eldest son, William, had gone over to the enemy and as a result the estate was under sequestration.[12] The Wilbrahams, who were one of the principal Puritan families in Cheshire, at first sided with Parliament. Sir Richard Wilbraham was taken into custody by royalist troops in the autumn of 1642 and died the following year. His son Sir Thomas, on the other hand, was adjudged a delinquent by Parliament for having forsaken his house and resided in the enemy's quarters. Writing from Cheshire in November 1645 Sir William Brereton asked the Speaker of the Commons for a pass which would enable the young man to travel up to London for the purpose of compounding for his estate. Sir Thomas, he stressed, had never been active or in arms. His wife was 'a very Godly and gracious woman, and one who from the begining hath manifested her zeale and Good affections to this Cause, the prosperitie and success whereof I believe shee preferrs before any outward Interests or Respects whatsoever'. At present Sir Thomas was little better than a prisoner but he intended to make his escape as soon as a favourable opportunity presented itself.[13]

A number of major Puritan families cannot readily be identified as either royalist or parliamentarian. In the main these were families which had sustained a minority; families such as Cope of Oxfordshire, Elmes of Northamptonshire, Townshend of Norfolk and Wise of Devon. Edward Wise's grandfather, Sir Thomas Wise, had declared in his will that he craved the assistance of Christ's holy spirit during the rest of his earthly pilgrimage so that he might be led 'the directest waie to the mount Syon, that heavenlie Jerusalem, which thorough his meare mercie I undoubtedly hope to enioy'. His father had been elected to the Long Parliament as one of the knights of the shire for Devon but had died in 1641 after contracting smallpox. In defiance of the king the guardianship was assumed by Francis Buller, a Cornish parliamentarian squire, and it was apparently for this reason that the estate was seized and plundered by the royalists.[14]

On the outbreak of the Civil War there were over 700 gentry in England with estates worth £1,000 a year or more.[15] Within this group 197 heads of families were ranged on the side of Parliament at the beginning of 1643 while two years later the figure had fallen to 172, mainly because of defections during the months when the royalist forces were achieving some success. A substantial number of these wealthy parliamentarians can be identified as Puritans: 128 out of 197 and 126 out of 172. In fact most Puritan squires of good estate chose to link their fortunes with Parliament, though with varying degrees of commitment.

Among the rest of the parliamentarian gentry with landed incomes of £1,000 a year or more were Sir Hugh Cholmley and Sir John Hotham who both went over to the king during the course of 1643. We are told that neither Sir Hugh nor his brother Sir Henry (a parliamentarian colonel) was a professor of religion, though they were 'kind and friendly' to the Puritans; and it is significant that in November 1641 Sir Hugh had taken exception to a clause inserted in the Grand Remonstrance which alleged that the bishops had introduced idolatry and popery into the Church.[16] Sir Henry Slingsby writes that Hotham was 'manly for the defence of the liberty of the subject and priviledge of Parliament, but was not at all for their new opinions in Church government'; and Sir Hugh

45

Cholmley offers us a similar assessment.[17] Sir Henry Foulis was the son of a Scottish courtier who had settled in Yorkshire and subsequently come into conflict with Strafford. The father, Sir David, was 'never accounted inclined to the Puritans as such, but a lover of them as Englishmen'. This attitude was shared by Sir Henry himself and it seems likely that the main reason why he took up arms for Parliament was the fact that his father had been heavily fined and imprisoned for opposing the levying of knighthood compositions.[18] There was also a considerable number of men whose private conduct offended Puritan susceptibilities. Sir Edward Baynton was a libertine who fathered at least two illegitimate children. Sir Robert Crane was 'very prone' to lechery and 'declin'd few that came his way, fitt for that sport'.[19] Henry Marten was an atheist who was noted for his hard drinking and sexual promiscuity; in the words of John Aubrey he was 'as far from a Puritane as light from darknesse'.[20] Edmund Waller the poet was described by Sir Simonds D'Ewes as a man who had led a 'prophane and luxurious life' and had been 'extreamely addicted and given up to the use of strange women'.[21] According to John Aubrey's testimony, Sir William Playters 'was a merry man in the raigne of the Saints'; in particular, he was 'a great admirer and lover of handsome woemen, and kept severall'. In March 1643 the House of Commons was informed that he did very ill offices and was given to riding about at night in Suffolk; and that his heir had joined the royalists.[22] To some Puritans at least the presence of such men on the side of Parliament was acutely embarrassing.[23]

Although Puritan divines were generally depicted as 'seditious levites' in royalist literature, they were far from unanimous in the way in which they viewed the Civil War. Some of them were certainly no firebrands. According to his biographer, Samuel Fairclough chose to remain passive during both Civil Wars and was deeply grieved by the spectacle of Protestants killing one another. The celebrated John Dod, who was now very aged, remained at Fawsley, the Northamptonshire parish where Richard Knightley was both squire and patron of the living. In a letter written to Lady Vere in

December 1642 he expressed his dismay about the present tribulations which had fallen on the kingdom and quoted a passage in the Book of Revelation which proclaimed that God 'shall come upon all the world, to try them that dwell upon the earth', adding that the hour 'sure cannot now be farr off'. Subsequently his house was plundered by royalist troops but in the midst of this turmoil he remembered his old maxim 'sanctified afflictions are good promotions'.[24] Many Puritan ministers who were beneficed in areas which were under parliamentary control from the outset went on quietly performing their pastoral duties. In the main, however, their sympathies lay with Parliament. At Somerleyton in Suffolk Sir John Wentworth lent £300 on the propositions for the support of the parliamentary forces while his minister, John Brinsley, contributed £10. Some time later Brinsley preached a sermon at Beccles when the National Covenant was taken there and dedicated the published version, which was entitled *The Saints' Solemne Covenant with Their God*, to Sir John and his colleagues on the Suffolk committee.[25] Ralph Josselin, the vicar of Earl's Colne in Essex, recorded in his diary that when he was at the house of Lady Hester Honywood, the wife of the parliamentarian Sir Thomas Honywood, on 14 June 1645, it was agreed that there should be a special day of humiliation 'to seeke God for our armyes'; but that in the meantime the parliamentary forces were overcoming the royalists at the battle of Naseby.[26]

When the Earl of Essex's army entered the field in September 1642 it was accompanied by a number of Puritan divines, among them Stephen Marshall, Cornelius Burgess, Simeon Ashe and Obadiah Sedgwick. On 30 September it was reported that Sedgwick had preached a fast sermon which had made a profound impression on many of the soldiers and prepared them for death. As Richard Baxter points out, however, most of the ministers who initially took on the role of regimental chaplains went home after the battle of Edgehill in October and the way was then clear for the sectaries to exert their influence.[27] As governor of Newport Pagnell in Buckinghamshire Sir Samuel Luke had the services of seven 'able divines' at his disposal and arranged a programme of public worship which involved two sermons every Sabbath, a Thursday sermon, and prayers and a Bible reading every morning before the sentries were posted. In November 1644 he told his father that he had appointed one of these ministers, his cousin Thomas Ford, as chaplain to his regiment.[28]

Among the Puritan ministers who were particularly singled out by the royalists as political incendiaries were John White of Dorchester, 'a man of such excellent rare sedition', who was a close friend of the Dorset MPs Sir Walter Erle and John Browne; John Strickland who had once been an associate of White and more recently had enjoyed the patronage of Sir John Horner; and John Tooker who was chaplain to Richard Whitehead, a knight of the shire for Hampshire, at Portsmouth. In June 1643 a royalist newspaper carried a report that the parliamentarians had organized a solemn fast at Southampton, Portsmouth and Hursley (near Winchester) for the speeding of Sir William Waller's great design against the king in the West Country and that Strickland had been pleased to say in his prayers 'O Lord thy honour is now at stake, for now (O Lord) Antichrist hath drawn his sword against thy Christ, and if our Enemies prevaile thou wilt loose thine honour.'[29]

Godly divines who served as regimental chaplains or were otherwise closely associated with the parliamentary troops sought to encourage them and fire them with zeal for the cause by assuring them that the taking up of arms was both lawful and necesssary, that God was on their side and that with his help Parliament would finally emerge triumphant. According to an account of the royalist siege of Cirencester in January 1643 the dying men in the ranks of the parliamentarians cried out that the gentry, among them Sir Robert Cooke, and their preachers had undone them.[30] Some Puritan ministers saw it as their duty to expose any backsliding on the part of those who had been appointed to the parliamentary committees in the various counties. In October 1644 a group of Sussex ministers and freeholders alleged in a petition to the Commons that Sir Thomas Pelham and Sir Thomas Parker had been backward in the service of Parliament while the following year

Sir Samuel Luke was informed by his father that a minister had complained to the House that half the members of the Bedfordshire committee were 'malignants'.[31]

At Westminster the fast preachers exhorted and counselled, gave thanks to God for the victories achieved on the field of battle and continued to insist that Parliament was above all engaged in the cause of God. When one of Thomas Case's sermons was published in 1643 he dedicated it to his friend Sir William Brereton, who had just defeated the royalists at Nantwich in Cheshire, and told him that among all the worthies who had participated in the battles of the Lord of Hosts 'in these latter dayes' (and he presumably included King Gustavus Adolphus of Sweden in this number) none had

> seen more of God then your self have done; and without flatterie I speake it, I verily beleeve none have observed God more in the passages of his providence than your selfe . . . . for one without the verge of danger to interest and hazzard himself in a publike rescue of Religion and Countrey is a character of true Fortitude.

And he went on, in language which was redolent of the Old Testament, to call for an all-out war against the enemy:

> And let the sword of the Lord and of Brereton be as dreadfull as once the sword of the Lord and of Gideon that you may smite your enemies as one man.[32]

On 9 April 1644 Case delivered a thanksgiving sermon following a victory by Sir William Waller over Sir Ralph Hopton. Subsequently he dedicated the printed version to Waller who had recently been described in a royalist newspaper as 'a Puritanicall Idoll' and declared that through the working of free grace he stood in the first division of those worthies 'to whose fidelity God hath given ample testimony, what exploits a people can do that know their God.'[33]

When Edmund Calamy preached a thanksgiving sermon before members of the House of Lords in June 1643 he took the opportunity to offer some forthright comments on the wealthier adherents of Parliament. There were many, he alleged, who were reluctant to show too much zeal. The time-server was prepared 'to dive no farther into the deepes of Religion, to appeare no farther in this great cause of Religion then he can be sure to save his estate, and to save his carcasse'. Not many of the great had been called. Outward prosperity and happiness ought to ensure obedience to God but for the most part they proved to be the Devil's most dangerous snare for the entrapping of souls; and for this reason few of the nobility and gentlemen of the kingdom were to be found on the side of Parliament. It was a principal aim of the ministry to convert great men since 'if they were once converted, hundreds would follow their example'. There was a widely held belief that it was fitting only for poor men who had nothing to lose to appear openly in a good cause; and that for those who were substantial landowners 'it becomes them to be wary and circumspect, and to seeke rather to save their Estates then to hazard all.' However, a true Christian was glad that he had riches and honours to lose for God. God, he told his aristocratic listeners, expected some extraordinary service from them in this time of necessity. 'You have incouraging company', he assured them, 'you have the Lord of Hosts to accompany you . . . you have the major part of God's people on your side.'[34]

Cornelius Burgess and Edmund Calamy were leading figures among the Presbyterian majority in the Westminster Assembly which wanted a national Church without bishops and strongly opposed the concept of religious toleration. Ministers of this persuasion, who were for the most part beneficed clergy with a university background, had close ties with many of the well-to-do Puritan gentry for whom they were the principal source of spiritual guidance. Calamy's circle of friends included Sir Simonds D'Ewes, Sir Robert Harley and Zouch Tate. Harley had a number of other clerical associates with the same kind of Presbyterian outlook, among them Thomas Gataker, Jeremy Whitaker and Stanley Gower. When Gower preached an apocalyptic fast sermon before members of the Commons in July 1644 he was no longer Harley's minister at Brampton Bryan but it is a measure of the high regard in which he held his former patron that he quoted an observation of his to the effect that Germany's tribulations were likely to continue because of the prevalence of Sabbath-breaking.[35] Although such ministers might argue for a vigorous prosecution of the war they were by no means in favour of any fundamental political or social changes. In the sermon which he delivered in June 1643 Calamy assured the noblemen who were listening to him that it was not the intention of the well affected party 'to take away Temporall Lordships, or the distinction between Lords and Commons, and to bring all to a popular equality'. That, he stressed, was 'an Anabaptisticall fury'.[36] On the other hand, there was growing evidence that some of the more radical sectaries, who were generally of lower-class origin, were openly questioning the justification for a hierarchical society in which there were such great disparities of wealth. Shortly before Calamy addressed the Lords a royalist newspaper was reporting that Chelmsford in Essex was full of sectaries, particularly Brownists and Anabaptists, who were preaching

> That Kings are the burdens and Plagues of those People or Nations over which they governe. . . .
> That the Honours and Titles of Dukes, Marquesses, Earles, Viscounts, Lords, Knights, and Gentlemen are but Ethnicall and Heathenish distractions not to be retained amongst Christians. . . .
> That one man should have a Thousand pounds a yeare, and another not one pound . . . . but must live by the sweat of his browes, and must labour before he eate, hath no ground neither in Nature or in Scripture.

It was now fitting, they were saying, that the nobility and gentry should serve their servants or at least work for their living; and if they were not prepared to work they ought not to eat.[37] Reports of this kind, together with the breaking down of enclosures and other manifestations of popular discontent, seemed to bear out the fears of Puritan landowners like Sir Simonds D'Ewes and Sir John Potts who had an uncomfortable feeling that the war might lead to anarchy or revolution.[38] For the propertied classes the great danger was that such levelling ideas might gain ground among the rank and file of the parliamentarian army.

Although Parliament was by no means wholly dependent on the godly it is difficult to believe that there could have been any effective resistance against the king without their support. It is no coincidence that there were relatively few Puritans in predominantly royalist counties such as Cornwall, Herefordshire, Worcestershire, Shropshire, Oxfordshire, Nottinghamshire, Durham and Northumberland; or that the more Puritan counties such as Devon, Buckinghamshire, Bedfordshire, Northamptonshire, Cambridgeshire, Suffolk and Essex remained under parliamentary control throughout the first Civil War. Henry Jessey, who had served for some years as chaplain to Brampton Gurdon in Suffolk, had been impressed by the number of 'precious Christians' both there and in the adjoining county of Essex; and in June 1643 John Hampden wrote in a letter to his kinsman Sir Thomas Barrington that Essex was 'a place of most life of religion in the land'.[39] Since, however, the godly party embraced great extremes of wealth there was always a possibility that it might eventually split asunder. It was symptomatic of the strains which existed from the outset that when John Hutchinson became governor of Nottingham he had problems with the Puritan rank and file 'who thought it scarce possible for any one to continue a gentleman and firme to a godly interest'.[40]

FIVE

For Liberty
and Religion

DURING the first Civil War a Derbyshire squire wrote in his
commonplace book that it was the king who had begun the
war 'for it apeares he had it first in designe, both by his warre
upon Scotland, his declining the former parliament', by which
he meant the Short Parliament, 'and his vanitie of design
against this.' On the question of whether Parliament was
justified in taking up arms he acknowledged that men were
forbidden to resist authority in the Bible but did not accept that
this was a valid objection: 'we resist not authority but
Tyrannie and Tyranny is no power or ordynance from God.'[1]
Wealthy parliamentarians did not consider themselves to be
involved in either a revolution or a rebellion; in their view it
was essentially a defensive war which Parliament had been
obliged to wage in response to royalist threats. At the outset
Parliament had no intention either of overthrowing the king or
of abolishing the institution of monarchy. Referring to the
outbreak of the Civil War, Sir Arthur Hesilrige was emphatic
that 'There was at this time no thought to alter Government.'[2]
If the king had accepted the Nineteen Propositions which were
put to him in June 1642 there would have been a considerable
shift of power from the Crown to Parliament but, as Hesilrige
was suggesting, there was a complete absence of any republican sentiment at Westminster when hostilities began. Signi-

ficantly, the formal objectives of Parliament included the defence and maintenance of the king's person, honour and estate.[3]

In 1642 the harshest critic of the king in the House of Commons was Sir Henry Ludlow, the father of Edmund Ludlow the regicide, who also had pronounced views on the constitutional status of the monarchy. On 7 May he declared that Charles was not worthy to be king of England and was admonished by the Speaker for his presumption. Subsequently, on 9 November, Walter Yonge recorded in his parliamentary journal that Sir Henry had said that 'the parliament was inferiour to the whole body of the kingdome, the king inferior to the parliament, to the lawe and to God. But in himselfe was superior to any man in the kingdome.' The House, however, 'would not heare him out'.[4] Far more typical was the attitude of Harbottle Grimston who in April 1643 wrote in a letter to his friend Sir Thomas Barrington that 'my trust is nowe. . . . in you, who I am assured is faithfull to God, The Kinge and Country.'[5] Sir William Waller considered that by virtue of the laws of the land, the oath of allegiance and the Solemn League and Covenant which received parliamentary approval in September 1643 he was formally committed to the preservation of the monarchy with its just rights and prerogatives. This, however, was not all: he was also personally convinced that monarchical government must be maintained 'both as it is in itself a form of politic the most ancient and natural, and as it is unto this nation, of all others, the most congenial.'[6]

Richard Baxter observes that the motives of the wealthier parliamentarians tended to be more complex than those of the rank and file: although, he writes, 'the public safety and liberty wrought much with the nobility and gentry who adhered to the parliament, yet was it principally the differences about religious matter that filled up the parliament's armies and put the resolution and valour into their soldiers.'[7] Among the Puritan gentry who were actively engaged on the side of Parliament it was generally agreed that the main issues were religion and liberty. Parliament's declared aims included the defence of the true Protestant religion, the just rights and liberties of the subject and the privileges of Parliament.[8] Bulstrode Whitelocke writes that many persons of quality and fortune took up arms for Parliament because of the great affection that they had for their religion and the rights and liberties of their country.[9] Edmund Ludlow tells us that following his capture by the royalists he was pressed to expound on 'the justice of our cause. . . . and thought myself obliged to maintain the necessity of our taking up arms in defence of our religion and liberties'.[10] Writing to the Earl of Essex in November 1644 Sir Samuel Luke expressed the hope that he would finish the work for liberty and religion for which he had spared neither his person nor his estate. In the course of some acrimonious correspondence with his kinsman Colonel Charles Fleetwood in June 1645 Luke expostulated:

> you have knowne mee a long tyme, and I hope in all that tyme I have not varyed from my first principles. The sole cause that drew mee into these warrs was the maintenance of Religion and Libertyes of Parliament.

So convinced was he that these were the basic reasons why Parliament was at war with the king that he had the words Liberty and Religion emblazoned on the ensign which he bore as the colonel of a regiment.[11] When John Pyne, one of the leading parliamentarians in Somerset, found himself in trouble with the authorities after the Restoration he informed them that in accordance with his judgment, duty and conscience he had acted 'for the Parliament upon their declarations whereby they promised the preservation of the privileges and freedom of the people both in civills and spiritualls which end he only persued.'[12]

In his work *A Healing Question*, which he wrote in the 1650s, Sir Henry Vane the younger advanced the view that the grounds of the quarrel between the king and Parliament were twofold: the people's true liberty and freedom in matters of religion. In this latter respect he meant not simply freedom from 'episcopal tyranny' but a general toleration. According to his contemporary biographer he was opposed to sacrilegious and tyrannical domination in Church or State and was 'well skilled in setting the right bounds to civil and spiritual Power in the outward government of Worldly States'. For him civil and religious liberty were intimately linked. In the final testament which he prepared before his execution in 1662 he observed that the cause to which he had committed himself had been set forth in the Grand Remonstrance and the Solemn League and Covenant; in the final analysis, however, it was clear that 'from all put together . . . this Cause which was owned by the Parliament was the CAUSE of GOD, and for the promoting of the kingdom of his dear Son, JESUS CHRIST, wherein are comprehended our Liberties and Duties, both as Men and as Christians.'[13]

For most wealthy landowners civil liberty meant in particular an assured constitutional role for Parliament and freedom from arbitrary taxation and imprisonment. Many of the leading Puritan gentry had been imprisoned for their opposition to the forced loan of 1626; and many had also had their goods distrained for refusing to pay ship money.[14] For such men, and indeed for other Puritan squires who had been more compliant, civil liberty was an issue of no small importance. Among those who had been deprived of their liberty for resisting the forced loan of 1626 were two of the richest Puritans in England, Sir William Armyne and Sir Nathaniel Barnardiston. According to one of his ministers Sir William was 'alwaies of too brave a spirit to endure vassalage, or to see his Countries liberty bound to the chaine for a Gally-slave.' At Sir Nathaniel's funeral Samuel Fairclough testified that

> for his countrey, and the defence of the just liberties therof, he did not refuse voluntarily to expose himself to a gulph of hazard and sufferings: witnesse his suffering under the imposition of ship-money, coat and conduct-money and the loan, for refusing whereof he was long time imprisoned in the gate-house.[15]

John Hampden had already acquired a national reputation as a result of his attempt to challenge the legality of ship money. In November 1637 Strafford had described him as 'a great Brother' and claimed that the guiding spirit of such men led them

'always to oppose civilly as well as ecclesiastically' all that
authority ordained for them. Some years later Bulstrode
Whitelocke wrote in his autobiography that Hampden's 'affection to publique liberty, and applause in his countrey', by
which he meant Buckinghamshire, 'exposed him to many
difficulties and troubles'.[16] Sir Arthur Hesilrige, who had also
refused to pay ship money, won praise as 'one that was a true
patriot of his country's liberties'. In a parliamentary speech
delivered in 1659 he declared that 'I was bred a Puritan, and am
for public liberty', though he felt obliged to add that he was no
leveller.[17]

Sir Edward Peyton, who had been a persistent opponent of
the Crown in the House of Commons, expressed the view , in a
work published in 1652, that 'it was just the Parliament should
defend themselves by a war, yea subdue the king's power,
which would destroy the Representative, which maintained
the liberty of the subject and property of their personall and
reall estates.'[18] There were indeed some Puritan gentlemen
who considered that the basic justification for taking up arms
against the Crown was the need to preserve the constitutional
rights of the subject. Edward Harley, the eldest son of Sir
Robert Harley, often used to say that he had fought for
Parliament for no other reason than a sincere regard for the
laws and liberties of the kingdom.[19] After studying all the
available literature about the matters in dispute John Hutchinson 'became abundantly inform'd in his understanding and
convinced in conscience of the righteousnesse of Parliament's
cause in poynt of civill right.' Although he was satisfied that
attempts had been made to bring back popery and subvert the
true Protestant religion, 'he did not thinke that so cleare a
ground of the warre as the defence of the just English
liberties.'[20]

While there was a good deal of emphasis on the preservation
of the liberty of the subject many of the Puritan gentry were
also convinced that the cause of Parliament was the cause of
God. This was true even of John Hutchinson: according to his
wife he was in no doubt that he had been called by God 'to the
carrying on of the interest of truth, righteousnesse and

57

holinesse, and to the defence of his country.'[21] For Sir Robert Harley and his wife there was no question that the conflict was primarily religious in character. In July 1642 Lady Harley wrote in a letter to her son Edward that

> I hope you and myself will remember for whose cause your father and we are hated. It is for the cause of our God, and I hope we shall be so fare from being ashamed of it or trubelled that we beare the reproche of it, that we shall binde it as a crowne upon us.

Sir Robert subsequently related that when he first became engaged in the cause of Parliament it was his understanding, after careful consideration, that it was the cause of God. When Timothy Woodroffe, one of many Puritan ministers who had enjoyed his patronage, published a spiritual treatise in 1659 he commented in the epistle dedicatory, which was addressed to Edward Harley, that his father 'was eminently known to be a Worthy indeed, one of the Gospel's great worthies, heaven's favorite, Christ's friend and Christ his friend, for whose sake he cheerfully forsook all and exposed himself and all that he had on earth to the fury of his and Christ's enemies.'[22]

If John Hampden was widely regarded as a champion of public liberty he was also a committed Puritan who had once been in trouble with the church authorities for travelling to other parishes to hear godly preaching.[23] Following his death in 1643, the author of some elegiac verse which the event inspired was emphatic that it was religion which had led him to take up arms for Parliament:

> That he was pious, his firme zeale of heav'n
> Hath to the world cleare testimony giv'n,
> For if Religion had not been the ground
> Of this great quarrell, his sheath'd sword had found
> No way to opposition; but since that
> Armed Popery hath proudly levell'd at
> The Churches ruine, then bold Hambden, none
> More bravely active or more forward knowne

In its resolv'd defence: he only can
Prove the stout Souldier that's a righteous man.

Arthur Goodwin, who was one of his closest friends, made the
same kind of point (and in so doing revealed his own
interpretation of the Civil War) in a letter addressed to his
daughter, Lady Wharton: 'All his thoughts and endeavours of
his life was zalously in for this cause of god's which he
continued in all his sickness even to his death'.[24]

Bulstrode Whitelocke tells us that his friend Rowland
Wilson, who was soon in arms for Parliament, was persuaded
that the honour and service of God and the flourishing of the
Gospel of Christ and the true Protestant religion might in
some degree be promoted by this means. At Wilson's funeral in
1650 the preacher, Obadiah Sedgwick, testified that he was
'often exposing his very life . . . in the High places of the Field,
Not counting it too dear for Christ and His Cause.'[25]

Lucy Hutchinson writes that no man knew why Sir John
Gell, who was the leading parliamentarian in Derbyshire, had
taken the side of Parliament since 'he had not understanding
enough to judge the equity of the cause, nor noe pietie or
holinesse, being a fowle adulterer all that time he serv'd the
Parliament.' In contrast, the author of *A Survey of England's
Champions*, which appeared in 1647, described him as the
'religious Sir John Gell, whose worth is such as speaks him to
bee a man beloved of his Countrey and feared by his enemies,
valiant in his actions and faithfull in his ends to promote truth
and peace.' Whatever his personal traits (and Lucy Hutchinson's assessment does not appear to have been entirely
objective), the fact remains that Sir John was a friend and
patron of godly ministers and for a time at least had a Puritan
chaplain in his household. In November 1642, not long after he
had taken possession of Derby on behalf of Parliament, he
received a letter from one of his servants which emphasized
the importance of his role in the cause of religion. Sir John, he
wrote, was engaged in 'manifold and urgent imployments for
the maintenance of god's true religion and the protection of our
Country [i.e. Derbyshire]. . . . by this shewing your selfe a good

magistrat but by the other a singular christian'. He went on to express the hope that God,

> who hath begun so pious an act in yow, may confirme itt, strengthen, stablish yow that by it god may be glorified, religion advanced, popery suppressed, our country protected and yow (with my mistris your vertuouse good Lady) for all your losses and crosses in this life everlastingly rewarded.[26]

The conviction that God was on the side of Parliament was often reflected in the inscriptions which appeared on the flags of the Roundhead officers. Sir William Brereton adopted the motto *Deus Nobiscum*; Sir Edward Hungerford's flag bore the words *Et Dieu Mon Appuy*; while Sir Arthur Hesilrige's motto was *Only in Heaven*, which was a contraction of *Hope Only in Heaven*. Sir William Waller, for his part, contented himself with the words *Fructus Virtutis* or *Fruit of Virtue*.[27]

Many Puritans who supported Parliament believed that the whole future of true religion was now in the balance. Only Parliament could bring about a thorough reformation of the Church in fulfilment of God's will; but if the king emerged victorious it seemed likely that godliness would be under even greater threat than in the years of his personal rule. Writing from Scotland in February 1643 Sir William Armyne declared that the Protestant religion was in imminent danger of ruin at the hands of the popish and prelatical faction.[28] During the latter part of 1642 there were reports that the king was seeking to enlist the aid of his Catholic subjects and that many of them were being given commissions. The papists in Lancashire, relates Bulstrode Whitelocke, were allowed to bear arms and this led many Protestants to criticize the king for 'too much favouring and entertaining them in his Army'.[29] In January 1643 Ferdinando Lord Fairfax told the Speaker of the House of Commons that 'the Strength of the Enemies will be found to consist much of Papists and popishly affected, the Earl of Newcastle granting his Commissions for raising of Men to Papists for the most Part.' He had heard that in York, where many recusants had settled, 'Mass is ordinarily said in every Street, and such Affronts offered to the Protestants and their

Ministry as few dare resort to Church.'[30] While Catholic support for the king was particularly strong in northern England it also attracted comment elsewhere in the kingdom. In January 1643 Sir John Potts was writing that there was a need for wiser men than himself in Norfolk 'to keep all quiet for the Parliament's frends are jealous and apprehensive and the Papists' side are indiscreet and bold'; and later that year Lady Brilliana Harley claimed that all the papists from many parts had been gathered against her when the family's Herefordshire mansion had come under siege.[31] If Parliament was guilty of polemical excess in employing such terms as 'the king's popish army' there was certainly some substance in the genuinely held conviction that the Catholics were making an important contribution to the royalist cause. Although some of the Catholic gentry remained neutral many of them threw in their lot with the king and very few were to be found in the ranks of the parliamentarians.[32] Moreover, it has been shown that of 815 royalist officers in the northern counties whose religious loyalties can be identified no fewer than 282 had Catholic sympathies.[33]

For Puritans who were heavily influenced by the apocalyptic prophecies which were prevalent in the early seventeenth century[34] the Civil War represented a further stage in the conflict between the forces of light and darkness which would culminate (and perhaps very soon) in the establishment of God's kingdom on earth. This kind of perception coloured the thinking of such men as Sir James Harrington, who foresaw the imminent ruin of the spiritual Babylon, and Sir Edward Peyton, who considered it likely that God had decided to destroy all monarchy throughout Christendom.[35] Edmund Ludlow observes that although the king 'was not the Anti-Christ spoken of by the Apostle, yet he was one of the kinges that gave the power to the Beast.' So far as he was able he sought to obstruct the propagation of the Gospel, 'no other doctrine being willingly permitted to be taught within his dominions but such as suited with and supported his corrupt interest of tyranny and domination.'[36] The Harleys were convinced that a new age was dawning in which the righteous would come into

61

their inheritance and true godliness would reign, though they seemed disinclined to draw the conclusion that this could have far-reaching political consequences.[37]

Sir Henry Vane the younger, whose views on the causes and nature of the Civil War were firmly set in a millenarian framework, writes that the war had been undertaken 'upon mutual Appeals of both Parties to God, desiring him to judge between them, to give the Decision and Issue by the Law of War'.[38] When the parliamentary forces secured a victory over the enemy or escaped from a difficult situation this was attributed to the providence of God[39] and regarded as a sign of his favour towards those who were engaged in his cause. In March 1643, following his defeat of the royalists at Middlewich in Cheshire, Sir William Brereton told a fellow MP that he believed that

> since the begininge of this unnaturall warre god hath not given manie more Compleat victories. . . . I desire the whole Praise and glorie may be ascribed to God who hath infused Courage into those who stood for his cause and struck the enemy with terror and amazement.

This was in spite of the fact that they had been unable to preserve the Sabbath because of the need to make preparations for their defence. Subsequently, in February 1645, Sir William informed Parliament that Shrewsbury had fallen to him and added that this was due to the many supplications which had been put up to

> that God which heareth prayers and giveth successe to those that seeke him and make theire whole dependance upon him, soe hath hee now dispenced (blessed be his great name) to his humble and unworthy servants who have been long plotting and contriving that which the Lord hath now brought to passe.[40]

Referring to the first battle of Newbury which was fought in September 1643, Bulstrode Whitelocke writes that God was pleased to strengthen the courage of the parliamentary forces and to give them the victory, 'and indeed all successe in War as well as in other matters is the free guift of the Lord of Hosts.'[41] Sir William Waller relates that at Farnham in Surrey his troops were heavily outnumbered by the royalist forces under Lord Hopton and Sir Jacob Astley but the Lord intervened and

> sent so thick a mist all the morning that by reason of the darkness the ennemy durst not give on, and when the mist brake upp I had such an advantage of the ground that my weakness remained undiscovered, and he drew off from me. I was that day delivered from an imminent destruction.[42]

When, conversely, the parliamentary forces suffered a reverse the godly were inclined to interpret this as God's punishment for sin. In January 1643, following a military setback in the West Country, Sir Thomas Wroth commented in a letter to John Pym that 'I doubt we have not been thankful enough for the late and former deliverances, and therefore God did in this action withdraw himself from our assistance.'[43] During the course of a parliamentary fast sermon preached in July 1644 Stanley Gower emphasized that a major reason why God's deliverance was still awaited was that the godly wise men were not 'so purified, made white and tried' as they should be. It was essential, he told the assembled MPs, that they should aspire to a more than ordinary purity (though it was said that a little holiness was accounted a great deal among the nobility and gentry). At the same time they should not be discouraged by the present tribulations. The wickedness of the enemy was a sufficient assurance that they would not prevail; they lay under the vials of God's wrath.[44] Edward Harley, who had lived for some years under Gower's ministry, was fully seized of the need to maintain his trust in God's providence even if it appeared that Parliament had incurred his displeasure. When informing his father in July 1643 of a royalist victory near Devizes he expressed his conviction that God intended by this means to 'make us looke more to him, who I am confident when we are weakest will shew himself a glorious God over the enemyes of his Truth.'[45]

Among the Puritan gentry who fought on the side of Parliament it was readily assumed that God had a particular care for their own personal safety. This was partly because they were in no doubt that it was his cause in which they were engaged and partly because they considered themselves to be members of the elect. According to his wife, John Hutchinson believed that he had been called by God to take up arms on behalf of Parliament and 'found the Lord's protection and glorious presence not only in all he did but in all he suffer'd for him and from him.'[46] Sir William Waller tells us that at the battle of Edgehill his horse was killed but through God's providence he emerged unscathed; and that at Lansdown in Somerset, when his troops were retreating, he escaped a shower of shot.[47] In 1650 Edward Harley recalled that during the Civil War God had given him courage and esteem among men and preserved his life on many occasions. Although he had once been shot in the shoulder he was anxious to acknowledge the mercy which God had shown him in ensuring that it 'tooke not away my life, nor the use of my Arme'.[48]

During the course of 1643 two of the most prominent upper-class Puritans who sided with Parliament died while engaged in military operations. Robert Lord Brooke was killed at Lichfield, shot in the forehead by a royalist sniper, and not long afterwards John Hampden sustained a fatal injury when his pistol backfired (though it was generally assumed at the time that a royalist bullet had been responsible). Sir Simonds D'Ewes found it impossible to believe that their deaths were merely random strokes of fate: there was no doubt in his mind that the bullets which had struck home were the instruments of God's will, however inexplicable that might be. Referring to these events in a sermon preached before members of the House of Lords, Edmund Calamy told them that 'God permits the enemy to exercise great cruelty upon his own people, and to take away his choicest servants.' They should, however, take comfort from the fact that Parliament's enemies 'can doe nothing but what our wise and most loving God permits and fore-decrees for the good of his children.' And he went on to say that 'He that dies fighting the Lord's battels dies a Martyr.'[49]

SIX

Degrees of Loyalty

SOME of the wealthy Puritan squires who sided with Parliament took a very active part in military affairs. Among the most notable of these men were Sir William Waller and Sir William Brereton, both of them generals, Sir Arthur Hesilrige, Sir John Gell, Sir Robert Cooke, Sir Richard Onslow, Sir Thomas Honywood, John Hampden, Richard Norton and John Hutchinson. Sir William Brereton played a key role in advancing the cause of Parliament in Cheshire when it apparently had little support there. In December 1642 a treaty of neutrality was concluded with the aim of insulating the county from the Civil War but the following month he arrived with some troops, proceeded to inflict defeats on the royalists at Northwich and Middlewich and gradually won over the gentry 'who had conjoyn'd in the late accommodation with the Commissioners of Array'.[1] Such men, however, were relatively few in number. Of 128 Puritan gentry with estates worth £1,000 a year or more who were to be found in the ranks of the parliamentarians at the beginning of 1643, approximately two-thirds were never directly involved in military operations though in some cases their sons appeared in arms. Even among the remainder there were instances where the period of active service was extremely limited. When the deputy lieutenants had been appointed under the provisions of the Militia Ordinance the main consideration in their selection had been the need to enlist the support of persons of wealth

65

who exercised real power and influence within their counties. During the war some of them commanded troops in the field but there were many who remained at home. In Derbyshire several members of the parliamentary committee felt it pertinent to ask whether it was fitting that those deputy lieutenants or committeemen who were not soldiers should be on the local council of war.[2]

A few major Puritan landowners spent some time on the Continent during the first Civil War. In February 1643 the Commons agreed that Sir William Drake, a Buckinghamshire MP and deputy lieutenant, should be permitted to go to the Low Countries for 'recovery of his health' and that notwithstanding this he should continue as a member of the House without any prejudice. In the event he did not return to Westminster until October 1644, by which time the fortunes of Parliament had significantly improved.[3] In April 1643 two other Puritan squires, Sir John Holland and Sir John Cutts, were allowed to travel abroad. Holland was soon back in England but his wife, who was a Catholic, took up residence at Utrecht. In September 1643 the Commons granted him leave to visit his wife who was said to be very ill, and stay with her for six weeks; in January 1644 it was noted that he was still absent; and in October 1644 it was decided that he could remain abroad until the end of March 1645.[4] Some well-to-do parliamentarians, among them Sir Samuel Luke, Sir John Bourchier, Sir Christopher Yelverton and Sir Thomas Pelham, thought it prudent to send their sons to the Continent during the Civil War. In December 1642 Sir Samuel Luke obtained a licence to travel for his son Oliver, a young kinsman Ralph Freeman and their tutor Ralph Mowat. As time went on he began to receive disturbing reports about his son's general conduct and his neglect of God. In February 1645 he dispatched an anguished letter in which he instructed him to be diligent in performing all such duties and services as God should require of him and in particular to hear and read his Word at every opportunity. That same month Mowat was writing to Lady Luke that because of the 'differences at home' they had met with some hostility and partly for this reason had concluded that it would be advisable not to travel into Italy but to sojourn at Geneva instead.[5] Sir Richard Hawksworth claimed in the course of litigation that he had been completely surprised on hearing that his son Walter was in France since he had given no indication that he was planning such a journey.[6] Sir Gilbert Gerard's heir, Francis Gerard, who like him was an MP, went abroad without a warrant from the Speaker and in February 1644 was recorded as absent. Although there was some suspicion that he had turned royalist it was agreed in April 1645 that he could take his seat again in the Commons.[7]

Some MPs such as Sir William Brereton and Sir William Waller were absent for long periods on military duty; others went down to their counties from time to time for the purpose of discharging their responsibilities as deputy lieutenants and committeemen. The House of Commons, however, was concerned that the number of MPs remaining at Westminster should not fall too low. In July 1643 Sir Simonds D'Ewes noted in his parliamentary journal that the House commonly dispensed with the presence of some thirty or forty MPs (out of a total of about 300) at any one time in order that 'this bloody and unnaturall civill Warre' could be carried on.[8] In fact there were many MPs who spent most of the war at Westminster, where they encountered no greater violence than the shouts and tumults of demonstrators who were anxious to prevent the opening of peace negotiations.[9] Soldiering clearly had no attraction for Sir Simonds D'Ewes who saw himself as primarily an antiquarian scholar and constitutional lawyer. But in any case he had always been of the opinion that the differences between Parliament and the king could have been satisfactorily resolved without resorting to arms and he believed that the best service he could render the nation was to persist in his efforts to persuade the Commons that the paramount need was for a negotiated settlement. In December 1643 he told the House that because of the demands which his duties as an MP had made on him he had not spent more than eight days at his house in Suffolk over the previous three years.[10] Although he had been appointed a deputy lieutenant for Kent in August 1642, Sir Henry Vane the younger would later observe that his own inclinations, nature and breeding made him ill-fitted for any military function. Vane's talents were more political than military; and he also had his duties as Treasurer of the Navy. In seeking to refute allegations that he was a man of blood, his contemporary biographer writes that

> He never affected any military employment. He was in a litteral sense free from the blood of all men, as well as in a spiritual, by his faithful performance of the duty of a Watchman, not shunning to declare unto all men the whole counsel of God.

At the same time he was at pains to stress that Sir Henry spared no effort in carrying out his parliamentary duties. So diligently, we are told, did he employ himself from early in the morning to very late at night that he scarcely had time to eat or attend to his private affairs.[11]

Vane was one of a number of leading Puritans who held offices of profit. Sir Gilbert Gerard, who had served for many years as Clerk of the Council of the Duchy of Lancaster, was appointed Treasurer of the Army in August 1642.[12] Sir Walter Erle, who was active in Dorset during the early stages of the war, became Lieutenant of the Ordnance in succession to John Pym while Sir Henry Mildmay continued to enrich himself as Master of the Jewel House, an office which he had purchased in 1618.[13] Sir Robert Harley had been deprived of his office of Master of the Mint in 1633 (when he was already in financial difficulties) but in May 1643 it was restored to him. This drew the comment from a royalist newspaper that Parliament might have made the appointment 'out of a desire of having a faithfull servant in that place, whose service and fidelity they may trust unto, in coyning money with their own stampe and impresse, when they are ready for that change.'[14] To Sir Simonds D'Ewes it was no coincidence that such men tended to be in favour of continuing the war. On one occasion when the latest set of peace proposals was narrowly rejected he declared in his journal that this had dismayed 'all religious honest men whose publique hearts were not corrupted by the enjoyment of their present employments and places.'[15]

According to Edmund Ludlow, who served as an officer in the army of Sir William Waller, there were many MPs who had always had royalist sympathies but 'their estates lying in the parliament's quarters they secured them by their presence in the house' and at the same time advanced the king's interests by their votes.[16] What is certainly true is that in the main the parliamentarian gentry (both MPs and others) of such counties as Norfolk, Suffolk, Surrey and Sussex contributed little to the war effort apart from the taxes which were compulsorily levied and regarded the protection of their own particular counties as the paramount requirement. In a petition submitted by Sir John Hobart and other Norfolk parliamentarians in September 1644 it was stressed that the county had been at great charge in supporting the army of the Earl of Manchester which had 'hetherto kept out the enimy from amungst us and may still secure us if not drawne fourth beyond the reach of our safetye.'[17] Those who appeared to be most reluctant to hazard their lives or assist financially were often strongly in favour of coming to terms with the king. As his Commons journal abundantly testifies, Sir Simonds D'Ewes came under severe pressure in the House because of his persistence in advocating the need for a peaceful settlement and his unwillingness to commit himself when others were in arms or formally pledging support for Parliament. On 23 July 1642 the Commons debated the terms of a declaration which seemed to him to be 'impertinent and dangerous'. In the course of this debate, he tells us, bitter and irreverential language was used against the king and it was clear that the militants wanted to precipitate a civil war. D'Ewes spoke against the declaration and as a result was roundly abused by William Strode, Alexander Carew, Nathaniel Fiennes and Denzil Holles. Profoundly shocked that men who 'professed religion' should be capable of such horrible ingratitude and injustice he decided to attend the House as infrequently as possible and it was not until 20 August (two days before the king raised his standard at Nottingham) that he again put in an appearance. On 27 August members of the Commons were asked, as a test of loyalty, to pledge themselves to assist the Earl of Essex, as commander-in-chief of the army, in the service of the true Protestant religion, the king's person, the laws of the land, the liberties and property of the subject and the privileges of Parliament. The official journal names a number of MPs who subscribed, among them Sir Henry Vane the younger, Sir Harbottle Grimston, Sir Samuel Luke and Sir Simonds D'Ewes. According to his own account D'Ewes indicated his willingness to declare himself on the basis that he was endorsing all these objectives 'conjunctively' and that some 'snarling spirits' criticized him for introducing such a qualification. And he adds that William Strode, with his 'profane and scurrilous witt', began to scoff at and vilify the king.[18]

On 22 September D'Ewes again found himself in an embarrassing situation when he was obliged to acknowledge that his brother was a royalist officer. Following this admission he was pressed by many MPs to declare what he would do for the defence of Parliament; and in response he chose to prevaricate. No man, he maintained, could promise more than it was in his power to fulfil and for the present he was unable to give any undertaking because his estate was in the hands of tenants who refused to pay their rents. Not surprisingly, this answer was considered unsatisfactory. Rising to his feet again, Sir Simonds offered an immediate contribution of £40 towards the war effort and intimated that this might be increased if the House would allow him to go down to Suffolk to put his estate in order. For good measure he added that he had been married two days before and wished to spend a little time with his wife (Elizabeth Willoughby) at his country seat. Some of his fellow Puritans, however, continued to harass him. While Sir Harbottle Grimston spoke in his support, Sir Robert Harley, he records, 'had soe little witt as to desire that I should declare what I would doe' and Sir William Armyne dismissed his offer as derisory. Their exasperation was perhaps understandable: after all, Harley had already provided £350 in plate and had promised £150 more, together with two horses, and Armyne, who had previously contributed in Lincolnshire, had undertaken to bring in all his plate. At one point in this quarrel among the godly the Speaker intervened to say that D'Ewes had married a fair lady (whom he had seen walking with her husband in St James's Park) and that in his view he ought to be permitted to accompany her into the country; but in the event the request for leave of absence was neither granted nor rejected.[19]

D'Ewes eventually, and no doubt grudgingly, made his contribution to the war effort. Among his papers there is a receipt which records that on 8 December 1642 he paid £100 for the defence of Parliament and the kingdom.[20]

In the Commons there were some men who took the view that Parliament should seek to obtain an all-out victory rather than enter into peace negotiations with the king. These included Sir Henry Vane the younger who in Richard Baxter's estimation was 'the Principal Man that drove on the Parliament to go too high, and to act too vehemently against the King'; Henry Marten who in August 1643 shocked the House by arguing for 'the extirpating of the royall race and the utter subverting of the monarchicall Government'; John Gurdon who is described by Sir Simonds D'Ewes as regularly acting in a turbulent manner, 'being therein onlie Mr Henry Martin's axe'; and William Strode, Miles Corbet, Cornelius Holland and Denis Bond.[21] If these violent spirits, writes D'Ewes, had not hindered attempts to bring about a happy peace

> the lives of many Thousands of Innocent men which hath since beene destroyed had beene saved, and divers Citties, Townes and almost whole shires of this kingdome which have since beene wasted or much defaced by ffire, Sieges, Mines and depopulation had now beene in a flourishing state and condition.[22]

In characterizing John Pym as one of the violent spirits he failed to grasp the point that the parliamentarian leader was not opposed in principle to the idea of making peace with the king but wished to negotiate from a position of strength.[23]

At the other extreme there were a number of MPs who considered that the whole emphasis should be on seeking a negotiated settlement and who, though seized of the need for basic safeguards to be built in, were often not unduly

71

concerned about the question of timing. During the course of the Civil War this group sustained some losses through the defection of men like Sir Hugh Cholmley but it also acquired important new recruits, among them Denzil Holles and Sir Philip Stapleton, who had initially appeared in the ranks of the militants.[24] Holles emerged as one of the leading figures in the group which also included Sir John Holland, Sir Simonds D'Ewes, Sir John Evelyn of Surrey and Harbottle Grimston. D'Ewes tells us that his associates were moderate, honest and religious men who desired a safe and honourable peace with 'the continuance of the Truth'. Although he was not unreceptive to the apocalyptic prophecies of Thomas Brightman he was in no way convinced that the Civil War was God's means of ensuring the triumph of the godly. 'God' he assured the Commons in 1643, 'is a God of peace and a God of unity.'[25]

Neither of these groups was particularly large; indeed there were many uncommitted MPs whose attitude was likely to be crucial when peace proposals were under consideration. Relations between the militants and those who were in favour of peace negotiations tended to be less than cordial. In September 1643 Miles Corbet alleged that some of the Norfolk gentry who had been named as committeemen had been slow to execute the ordinances for the weekly assessment and the sequestration of royalist estates, and singled out in particular Sir John Holland and Framlingham Gawdy. Sir John, he declared, neither attended the House nor performed any service in his county. Others joined in the criticism and the Speaker insinuated that he pretended to be ill in order to escape his obligations. Some militants felt that Holland and Gawdy ought to have their estates confiscated but in the end it was decided that they should be sent down to Norfolk for the purpose of implementing the ordinances. Shortly afterwards, however, Sir John obtained permission to travel abroad. As a royalist newspaper had put it earlier that year, he was a man who was 'not very pliable' to the desires of Parliament.[26]

On 22 December 1642 the Commons debated certain peace propositions which had been drawn up by the House of Lords. Sir Henry Vane the younger bitterly attacked them but Sir

Simonds D'Ewes offered the House a number of reasons why it was essential to enter into negotiations with the king. Whole counties had been 'impoverished and almost desolated'. Among the soldiery there was a growing practice of 'burning and spoiling and defacing the verie evidences and writings which concerne men's estates' as though it was their intention to leave things in such a state of confusion that there would be never-ending litigation. Poverty and famine were hastening upon the country with 'winged feete'. The two armies might begin to realize their own strength and 'neither permitt us to make peace when wee would nor to doe anything else but what shall be pleasing to them'. Moreover, the poor were likely to be reduced to such extreme poverty that they would be obliged 'to take some violent course for the releife of themselves and to spoile the richer and abler sort'. According to D'Ewes his speech was received with approbation and the militants held their peace.[27]

On 17 January 1643 Sir John Holland presented a Norfolk petition which called upon the Commons to inaugurate peace negotiations without further delay while on 10 February he warned the House that if no attempt was made to come to terms with the king it would occasion much discontent in the county.[28] At the end of January a parliamentary delegation which consisted of four Puritan MPs, Sir John Holland, Sir William Lytton, Bulstrode Whitelocke and Richard Winwood, arrived in Oxford but the propositions which they brought with them were wholly unacceptable to the king. In March fresh negotiations were opened at Oxford and on this occasion Parliament was represented by the Earl of Northumberland, William Pierrepont (a younger son of the Earl of Kingston), Sir William Armyne, Sir John Holland and Bulstrode Whitelocke. In his autobiography Whitelocke writes that he never became too closely associated with any faction or party; on the other hand, he diligently laboured to promote all overtures of peace and it was probably for this reason that he was frequently nominated for such missions.[29] When the Commons debated a new set of instructions for the delegation on 18 March Sir Simonds D'Ewes commented in his journal that 'The passages

73

of this day gave mee the first hopes I had received for divers moneths last past that God of his infinite mercy would bee pleased to vouchsafe a speedy peace to his almost halfed ruined kingdome.' A number of MPs, he noted, had lost their enthusiasm for the war after suffering in their estates; and although Sir Philip Stapleton, Sir Henry Vane the younger and John Hampden were opposed to the negotiations he formed the impression that above three-quarters of the members present wanted a peaceful settlement.[30] According to Clarendon the parliamentary commissioners seemed anxious to secure an accommodation. Whitelocke, for his part, had a very high opinion of his fellow MPs, which suggests that they were basically of one mind. William Pierrepont, he writes, 'acted his part with deep foresight and prudence.' Sir William Armyne was 'a gentleman of good understanding and conversation, and would give his opinion uppon good reason.' And Sir John Holland was 'a gentleman of excellent parts as well as person' who 'shewed a very good judgement and testimony of his abilities.'[31] In the end, however, it proved impossible to reach agreement and on 14 April the Commons decided to recall the parliamentary commissioners.[32]

In July, when the royalist forces were generally in the ascendant, a parliamentary delegation was dispatched to Scotland with the object of obtaining military assistance. The delegation consisted of Sir Henry Vane the younger, who was the dominant figure, and three other MPs, Sir William Armyne, Thomas Hatcher and Henry Darley, and was accompanied by two Puritan divines, Stephen Marshall and Philip Nye.[33] While they were still journeying towards Leith the House of Lords sought the agreement of the Commons to a new set of peace propositions. When the Commons debated these propositions on 5 August Sir Simonds D'Ewes emphasized the dangers involved in prolonging the war and invited the House to consider the tribulations which had befallen France and Germany. Following this speech Sir John Wray commented, with heavy sarcasm, that he was glad to hear him address the House again after he had been absent for so long. D'Ewes indignantly riposted that his absence had been solely due to a serious illness which he had contracted and expressed the hope that Wray would learn more charity.[34] The tellers who acted for the peace group were Denzil Holles and Sir John Evelyn of Wiltshire; and, according to D'Ewes, Sir William Waller and 'divers other men eminent for Religion and piety' also voted for the peace propositions. In the royalist press Lady Waller was depicted as an arch-Puritan who was 'a maine cause and encourager of her husband's Rebellion'. Sir William himself believed that the happiest outcome of the conflict would be a negotiated settlement which would be beneficial to both parties; as he put it, he would have preferred that 'the one party might not have the worse nor the other the better but such an accommodation might take effect as might be with saving of honour to King and Parliament, whereby both might have the best.'[35] On 6 August the new initiative was condemned from the pulpits of London churches and in broadsheets which suddenly appeared. The following day MPs were confronted with the spectacle of a large and unruly crowd which had gathered in Old Palace Yard with the intention of overawing those who were in favour of reopening negotiations with the king. It was a day of great tension which was further heightened by rumours that 'some seditious persons' in the City of London had resolved that if the peace propositions were approved by the Commons they would seize the Earls of Northumberland and Holland, Denzil Holles, William Pierrepont, Sir William Lewis, Sir John Evelyn of Wiltshire, Harbottle Grimston and John Maynard. In the Commons chamber Sir Simonds D'Ewes defended the right of MPs (and more particularly of Puritan MPs) to champion the cause of peace:

whosoever shall speake his conscience freely without feare or favour in this house and shall live conscientiously in his owne particular person and shall uphold the service and honor of God in his family, let all the divells in hell and all the foule-mouths on earth blast him to be noe well-affected person, yet God at the last day shall iustifie him to be soe.

When the propositions were put to the vote Denzil Holles and

Sir John Holland acted as tellers for the peace group while Sir Thomas Barrington and Sir Robert Harley performed that function for its opponents. Since Barrington and Harley miscounted it appeared at first that Holles and his associates had won by 81 votes to 79; but following a recount it was established that the propositions had been rejected by 88 votes to 81. Some MPs who had supported the peace group two days earlier were absent on this occasion, perhaps because they were alarmed by the popular agitation which had been whipped up; and others such as Sir Christopher Yelverton, Sir William Waller and William Jephson voted against the propositions, possibly for the same reason or because they accepted the logic of Pym's argument that this was not the time to be engaging in further peace negotiations when attempts were being made to forge an alliance with the Scots. In addition, Pym had the support of a number of MPs who had not attended the previous debate.[36]

As Sir Simonds D'Ewes noted in his journal, this vote brought to an end 'all our hopes of peace and tranquillity for the present'; and when the House was informed on 26 August that Sir Henry Vane the younger and Sir William Armyne had reported that the Scots were willing to provide military assistance it was clear beyond all doubt that there was no longer any immediate prospect of a negotiated peace.[37]

If many Puritan squires appeared to have little enthusiasm for the cause which they had pledged themselves to support very few of them defected to the king, though a considerable number were suspected of royalist leanings at one time or another. Although Devon was generally regarded as the most parliamentarian county in the West Country the conduct of the major Puritan landowners who served as deputy lieutenants and committeemen frequently gave cause for concern at Westminster. In March 1643 the Commons received a report that the deputy lieutenants of Devon had agreed on a ceasefire with the Cornish royalists; that they were seeking to conclude a peace treaty covering the whole region; and that for this purpose they were holding a meeting at Exeter to which some gentlemen of Somerset and Dorset had also been invited.

According to a royalist newspaper those responsible for negotiating the truce had not only taken their corporal oaths but had also had communion together. On hearing of these developments Parliament quickly put an end to what it regarded as a dangerous initiative, and on 15 March Sir George Chudleigh, Sir John Bampfield, Sir John Northcote and a number of other Devonshire parliamentarians dispatched a letter to the Speaker in which they protested that their attempts to make peace with their Cornish neighbours had been prompted only by a desire for the public good.[38]

Not long after this Sir George Chudleigh came under suspicion when his son James, a parliamentary major general, was accused of treachery following his defeat and capture by Sir Ralph Hopton and almost immediately switched his allegiance. Sir George himself resigned the commission which he held from the Earl of Stamford and in a declaration issued in May 1643 announced that he had decided to take no further part in the war:

> My lot fell to be cast on the Parliament's side by a strong Opinion I had of the goodness of their Cause, and the Royal Service I should do His Majesty in defending that his High Court from the manifest Enemies that then to my Judgment appeared against it. Religion and the Subject's lawful Rights seemed in danger and the general Interest called for the common Care to preserve it; but I believe it hath gone too far, the Destruction of a Kingdom cannot be the Way to save it. . . . I will contend no more in Word or Deed.

The following month the royalist press was reporting that James Chudleigh had not only deserted the cause himself but had sought to persuade his father to join the king and to bring over with him Sir Nicholas Martyn and Sir John Bampfield 'who depended alltogether on his Counsels'. Sir George, however, chose to reside in Exeter and was there in August 1643, along with Martyn, Bampfield and other parliamentarian gentry, when Prince Maurice began the siege which eventually resulted in the surrender of the garrison.[39]

About this time Sampson Hele, one of the wealthiest

members of the Devonshire parliamentary committee, was condemned to death by a local council of war following allegations that he had acted as a royalist spy but the sentence was never carried out and he was subsequently pardoned.[40] In March 1644 Sir Francis Drake was offered the king's pardon but declined it. In June there was a rumour circulating that he had gone over to the royalist side; in fact it was his brother Thomas, a parliamentarian major, who had defected. That same year the loyalty of Sir Samuel Rolle was brought into question because of his prolonged absence from the Commons. In August 1644, however, it was decided that he should be readmitted to the House.[41] Sir John Northcote, who had to endure a long period of captivity in the hands of the royalists, was eventually allowed to return to his house at Newton St Cyres, though he still remained under constraint. During a protracted debate on 19 March 1645 over the possibility of arranging an exchange between him and the royalist Lord Brereton some MPs claimed that Sir John was not in fact a prisoner but had received the king's pardon. The following month it was agreed that the exchange should go ahead and on 7 May Sir Samuel Rolle moved that he should be permitted to take his seat again. This proposal, writes Sir Simonds D'Ewes, met with some opposition but he and others spoke on Northcote's behalf and the motion was duly approved.[42] Doubts, however, persisted about the political sympathies of leading Devonshire parliamentarians. In July 1647 John Rushworth informed Ferdinando Lord Fairfax that many of the western gentlemen, among them Sir Samuel Rolle and Sir John Bampfield, were believed to have aided the king or to have sought or accepted pardons from him.[43]

In March 1643 Cromwell apprehended some gentlemen who were said to have been fortifying the Suffolk port of Lowestoft. Those taken into custody were mainly known or suspected royalists but they also included Sir John Wentworth, a leading Puritan patron and one of the Suffolk deputy lieutenants, who lived nearby at Somerleyton. Possibly he was simply planning to go over to the Low Countries. At all events he managed to buy his freedom (reportedly for the sum of £1,000) and was soon back in favour.[44] In August 1643 John Pym told the Commons that he had heard that the Earl of Northumberland and some MPs who were with him at Petworth in Sussex had been preparing to join the king at Oxford. As evidence for this he had a copy of an intercepted letter which Sir John Evelyn of Wiltshire (who was then at Petworth) had addressed to his uncle and fellow MP Sir John Evelyn of Surrey and which in place of a signature was subscribed 'Your freind. Burne this'. Under examination both men denied that there had been any intention of defecting but offered contradictory explanations of the letter with the result that Sir John Evelyn of Wiltshire was put under restraint. Once a prominent militant, he had undergone a change of heart and in the words of Sir Simonds D'Ewes had been 'very constant and industrious to restore this poore wasted kingdome to peace'; and for this reason D'Ewes and some of the other MPs who wanted a peaceful settlement argued in favour of clemency when his case was debated in the Commons. Eventually he was released and allowed to continue as an MP, mainly because of an undertaking which he had given to support the Independents in all particulars. On the other hand, D'Ewes testifies that Sir John Evelyn of Surrey carried himself as 'a gallant and honest man' in the Commons.[45] Sir Alexander Carew, who had been one of the most active of the Cornish parliamentarians, appears to have drawn the conclusion from royalist successes in the West Country that the king was going to win the war. In secret correspondence with the royalists he offered to surrender the fortress island of St Anthony at the entrance to Plymouth harbour in return for a full pardon but was arrested before the plan could be implemented. The House of Commons was informed of this episode on 4 September 1643 and Sir Simonds D'Ewes commented in his journal that he felt sorry for Carew, 'being my allie and descended of a most ancient familie' but added that 'he was much addicted to covetousnes which aliened the hearts of the souldiers from him'. On 22 December 1644 Sir Alexander was executed on Tower Hill after assuring the crowd which had come to witness his death that he would be received into God's everlasting kingdom.[46]

In April 1644 the editor of a parliamentarian newspaper withdrew an allegation which he had made that Sir Richard Onslow, one of the knights of the shire for Surrey, had been corresponding with 'certain great malignants'; this, he explained, had been based on a misunderstanding. Two years later Sir Richard complained in the Commons that he had been falsely accused by George Wither, in a pamphlet which he had published, of sending money to the king at Oxford. Although the House came down in favour of Onslow he may not in fact have been as innocent as he claimed. During the Commonwealth period a fellow parliamentarian would write that 'with much ado, through his policy' Sir Richard had 'steered his course between the two rocks of King and Parliament, and weathered some sore storms'.[47]

SEVEN

The Price
of War

THE impact of the first Civil War on the lives and fortunes of the parliamentarian gentry vindicated those who had predicted that it would have the most damaging consequences and shattered the illusions of those who had been convinced that the king would soon be vanquished. At one time or another there was hardly a county in England, excepting only East Anglia, where known Roundheads could feel reasonably immune from royalist attacks. In February 1645 a Hertfordshire landowner commented in a letter to his kinsman, Sir Simonds D'Ewes, that he was sorry to hear of the losses which Sir William Eliott, one of the Surrey deputy lieutenants, had recently incurred. Sir William, he recalled, had once told him that they were likely to fare better than 'many of our Countrymen for that if the miseryes of the nation did continue wee were like to bee the last in suffering'; and, he added, 'I wish it had beene so with him too.'[1] The war had hardly begun before a troop of royalist horse under the command of Sir John Byron arrived at the house of Bulstrode Whitelocke, Fawley Court in Buckinghamshire, which he had left in the care of one of his tenants, William Cooke. On hearing that the royalists were approaching, Cooke and the servants had thrown the pewter, brass and iron utensils belonging to the house into the surrounding moat and had removed some of the books, linen and furnishings but because of the short notice many of Whitelocke's possessions had been left where they were. About 1,600 soldiers were quartered in or around Fawley Court and, writes Whitelocke, 'there was no insolence or outrage usually Committed by Common soldiers on a reputed ennemy which was omitted by these brutish fellowes'. Although their officers had ordered them to exercise restraint they consumed all the food and drink in the house; broke open trunks and chests; and destroyed or carried away books and documents 'to my extreame great losse and prejudice, in wanting the writings of my estates.' They also broke down the fences around his park, killed most of the deer and allowed the rest to escape into the countryside. And, not least, they took his coach, four good coach horses and all his saddle horses.[2]

At Brampton Bryan in Herefordshire Lady Brilliana Harley had good reason to feel dangerously isolated during the summer of 1642: the royalist commissioners of array were very active and there were no visible signs of any organized opposition to them. In August Sir William Croft, who was one of the leading royalists, told her that on a personal basis he was as well disposed towards her husband as he had always been but in a public capacity he would favour no one; and in a letter addressed to Sir Robert, who was still at Westminster, he urged him to return to his allegiance to the king.[3] When Lady Harley heard that the Earl of Essex had been appointed lord lieutenant of Herefordshire she began to think it might be possible to maintain peace and good order within the county. In a letter to her husband she suggested that Sir Richard Hopton, Sir John Kyrle, Mr Vaughan, Sir Robert Whitney's son, Sir Walter Pye and her cousin Rudhall should be chosen as deputy lieutenants. It would be prudent, she stressed, to include some men from the other side (and preferably moderates) or the royalists would be extremely incensed; and if men of small estate were selected the county would take exception to them. Eventually, on 30 September, the Earl of Essex issued a commission to Sir John Kyrle, Sir Robert Harley and his son Edward, Sir Richard Hopton and others who were regarded as favourably disposed towards the cause of Parliament for the raising of troops in

Herefordshire but in the event nothing came of this. Although Sir Robert Harley was at Worcester on 8 October and at Hereford on 22 November he probably concluded that there was no real prospect of rallying support for Parliament in this predominantly royalist area; and indeed he was very soon back at Westminster.[4]

On 13 September Sir Robert Cooke, a Puritan kinsman of Harley who was seated in the neighbouring county of Gloucestershire, assured him that if his house came under attack he would hasten to the rescue of his wife, even though the way might be long and the county was 'much disaffected'. Subsequently Harley was told that Cooke and another Gloucestershire parliamentarian, Thomas Pury, were ready to relieve Brampton Castle but it would be necessary to obtain a commission from both Houses authorizing them to undertake military operations outside the county. As events turned out, however, Cooke was dead by the time that the Harley mansion first came under siege.[5]

At Brampton Castle Lady Harley and her family continued to practise their own form of religion, though they were obliged to take precautions. On 4 September she wrote in a letter to her husband that she was afraid that the house would be attacked on the Sabbath; consequently she was inclined to feel that it was better for her to remain at home on that day, in which case she would arrange for Stanley Gower, the minister of Brampton Bryan, to preach to her family. Later, on 23 September, Gower told his patron that they had lately held their quarterly fast day and for reasons of common prudence had kept it in private in the castle where they had been joined by a good company of strangers who were 'well affected'.[6]

As time went on the household at Brampton Castle came under increasingly severe pressure from the royalists. Servants who ventured out were apprehended; the tenants were prevented from paying their rents; and there were threats of armed attacks and enforced billeting of soldiers. Lady Harley felt that she and her family were in effect imprisoned and in danger of being starved into submission; and in a letter to her eldest son Edward (who was now a parliamentary colonel) she expressed the hope that God would not deliver them into the hands of the royalists 'for surely they would use all cruellty towards me, for I am toold that they desire not to leave your father neather roote nor branch.' 'Deare Ned', she added, 'desire the prayers of the godly for us at Brompton.'[7] On 4 March 1643 a royalist commander requested her to deliver up the castle but met with a blank refusal.[8]

The royalists finally began to lay siege to Brampton Castle on 26 July. In correspondence with one of the royalist officers she assured him that 'when the measure of cruelties is full the day of deliverance will soon appear to the Church of God which is now afflicted.' During the course of the siege the royalist forces destroyed the church at Brampton Bryan, Stanley Gower's parsonage house and many of the houses in the town. The inhabitants of the castle, however, held out and after six weeks the royalists moved on to Gloucester.[9] In response to a suggestion by her brother, Edward Viscount Conway, that she had been unnecessarily provocative Lady Harley stoutly defended her conduct, emphasizing that she had not been motivated by political considerations but had felt bound to hold on to what belonged to her as long as she could. In her view it was strange that the gentlemen of Herefordshire should not want her to live in the same county as them. She would, however, refrain from doing anything which might imply that she wished to make war with all the world.[10]

Writing to her son Edward on 9 October Lady Harley told him that the royalists were again threatening her and went on to say that she had been very ill for the last two or three days but she hoped that 'the Lord will be mercifull to me, in giving me my health, for it is an ill time to be sike in.' Although her husband had now belatedly agreed to her leaving Brampton Bryan she was in no position to take advantage of his change of heart. Despite the treatment which she received from her physician, Dr Nathaniel Wright, her condition grew worse. On 29 October the steward wrote in a letter to one of Sir Robert's servants at Westminster that she was dangerously ill; and in a postscript he reported that at 6pm that day (which was a Sunday) Lady Harley's soul had gone to keep the eternal

Sabbath in heaven where she could never be besieged.[11] Not long afterwards a royalist newspaper informed its readers that 'the most pious, charitable, vertuous, chast Lady, the Lady Harley (wife to Sir Robert himselfe) hath left this world.' She had been afraid that Brampton Castle would fall, it went on, and 'this beget a disease upon her'.[12]

Following the death of his wife Sir Robert entrusted the management of his estate and the defence of his house to Dr Wright and the steward, Samuel Moore. In April 1644, however, the same royalist newspaper reported that Brampton Castle had at last been taken and that among those who had been apprehended was Dr Wright the governor 'who was much fortified by the comfortable assistance of three seditious Teachers (the busie Seminaries of this bloudy warre)'. Three of Sir Robert's children also fell into the hands of the royalists but in June they were allowed to join their father at Westminster.[13]

In July 1646 Sir Robert calculated that his material losses amounted to £12,000, including £4,500 for the estate revenue which had been denied him over a period of three years; £3,000 for Brampton Castle which he described as utterly ruined; £2,500 for the furniture and household goods belonging to the castle; and £200 for his library which had contained many religious works.[14] One of his clerical associates, however, would later write of him that 'this noble Patriot would not, did not murmur and complain when brought very low.' Similarly, his eldest son relates that when he returned to Brampton Bryan after the wars and saw how ruined it was he rode up to the gate, took off his hat and said that

> God Hath brought great desolation upon this place since I saw it. I desire to say the Lord hath given and the Lord hath taken away and blessed be the name of the Lord. I trust in his good time He wil rays it up agayn.

Characteristically, he was particularly anxious that the church should be rebuilt.[15] Many years later Edward Harley recorded his thankfulness to God that throughout all the tribulations of the Civil War period 'we had allways meat to eat and raiment to put on'.[16]

In the counties to the west of London many of the parliamentarian gentry had their houses and estates plundered. During the years 1643 to 1645 Sir Thomas Jervoise's estate at Herriard in Hampshire was laid waste by soldiers from the royal garrison at Basing House. According to his computation the losses which he incurred, including sheep, cattle, corn and household goods, came to a total of £6,207. In addition, his lands in Worcestershire, which produced an income of £900 a year in normal circumstances, were sequestered and for three years he received no rents from them. In all, he estimated that his losses in the first Civil War amounted to £13,448.[17] Sir William Waller, who had estates in both Hampshire and Devon, took it as one of God's mercies towards him that through the good offices of a friend his best furniture was removed from Winchester Castle (which he had made his seat) a few hours before the arrival of royalist troops. The castle, however, was demolished and in 1645 he was in serious financial difficulties: 'my estate' he writes, 'began to fall short, part thereof lying in the King's Quarters and the rest (through the distraction of the times) affording me very litle subsistence.'[18] In March 1643 a royalist force occupied Sir Robert Cooke's house at Highnam, near Gloucester, but almost immediately capitulated when Sir William Waller appeared. In his will, which he drew up in June, Sir Robert inserted the comment that he had suffered heavy losses at the hands of those who opposed the king and Parliament; and some years later one of his daughters stated in the course of litigation that most of his personal estate had been seized and his mansion houses of Highnam and Lassington spoiled and consumed by fire.[19] In Somerset the royalists garrisoned Sir John Horner's house at Mells and ransacked Kelston Hall, the seat of John Harrington, on several occasions. Another Somerset landowner, John Pyne, complained at the time of the Restoration that he was 'really in estate some thousand pounds wourse off that att the beginning of the late unhappy warre.' He had lost all his goods both 'within Doors and without' at Curry Mallet and the house had been made uninhabitable 'by breaking down all the glass windows and taking out the iron barrs'.[20] In Devon the royalists gained possession of Stedcombe House, the principal seat of Walter Yonge, in April 1644 and took a number of prisoners who reportedly included 'a seditious lecturer'. As evidence of this exploit one of Yonge's surviving journals bears an annotation by a royalist officer which records that he found the manuscript in the study at Stedcombe House on 22 April 1644.[21] More serious was the plight of Sir Francis Drake and his mother who were deprived of their estate revenue for a period of over two years and whose mansion, Buckland Abbey, was occupied by a royalist general, Richard Grenville, who had changed sides. In a petition which they submitted in May 1645 the Drakes informed Parliament that their estates had been utterly ruined and they were now extremely poor.[22]

Although Sir Thomas Hutchinson remained loyal to Parliament he was so popular (writes his daughter-in-law) that the Nottinghamshire royalists considered it expedient to leave his tenants undisturbed. Following his death in August 1643, however, they held back no longer. His son John, who was the governor of Nottingham, 'lost the most part of his rents. . . . while the country [county] was under the adverse power, and had some small stock of his owne plunder'd, and his house, by the perpetual haunting of the enemie, defac'd and for want of inhabitation render'd allmost unhabitable.' In 1647 the Hutchinsons moved back to Owthorpe Hall but it was in such a ruinous condition that it could not be renovated 'without as much charge as would allmost build another'.[23] In the neighbouring county of Lincolnshire some royalist forces under the command of Viscount Campden appeared at Osgodby Hall, the seat of Sir William Armyne, in June 1643. Before moving on they ransacked the house, seized all the sheep and cattle, destroyed the park and killed or drove out the deer. Subsequently one of Sir William's ministers recalled that when the enemy laid waste his lands and goods it was remarkable 'how patiently and chearfully he bore it for the common good'.[24] In Yorkshire several leading parliamentarians, among them Sir Richard Darley, Sir William Lister and Sir William Strickland, sustained considerable material loss as the result of royalist activity. Lister, it was reported, had 'his estate of great value plundered by the Enimie' and his mansion at Thornton in Craven 'burnt down to the ground'. As a consequence he and his family settled in London where they were provided with a house and some furniture.[25]

Although Northamptonshire was the most strongly parliamentarian of the Midland counties there was a continuing danger of incursions from some of the neighbouring shires. In the royalist press there were reports of attacks on the houses of Sir Gilbert Pickering, 'a man most dangerously active against his Maiestie', and his fellow MP Sir John Dryden. At Titchmarsh Hall the royalist soldiers took possession of all Sir Gilbert's arms and horses 'which had been housed there for the maintainance of the Rebellion'. At Canons Ashby some of the Earl of Northampton's cavalry besieged a garrison of 50 men who were deployed in both the Dryden mansion and the church where John Dod had once been the preacher. The royalists, it was related, managed to force their way into the church

> where they tooke them all; such as fled into the steeple were instantly smoaked downe. Hereupon those in Sir John Dryden's house yeilded themselves prisoners, who with good booty and store of provision, were brought all to Banbury Castle.[26]

Whether or not their estates were situated in areas which were under royalist domination the rent revenue of the parliamentarian gentry tended to fall substantially during the Civil War period. Bulstrode Whitelocke tells us that in February 1644 he was receiving nothing from his estates (which were in Buckinghamshire and Oxfordshire) and that to make matters worse he was earning little from his legal practice.[27] Even the parliamentarian squires of East Anglia were experiencing considerable difficulties. In general, Sir Simonds D'Ewes felt it necessary to deal leniently with his Suffolk tenants when faced with mounting rent arrears. Writing to him in March 1643 one of his tenants, John Bunn, declared that

> If it would please the allmighty to sease these disturbances
> in this our kingdome I shalbe in hope to sattisfie your
> Worshipp a greate deal better then I have done heretofore. I
> have but a little to make any rent of, and that little comes
> but to a small matter, as the times are, ffor we have no
> trading but at poore rates.

Later that year he was again complaining to D'Ewes about his
lamentable condition and proceeded to add to his landlord's
anxieties by warning him that he was daily abused in his estate
'and most grosly. . . . as well'. D'Ewes, for his part, thought it
fitting to keep the Commons informed of the problems of
estate management with which he was grappling. In a speech
delivered in December 1643 he confided to the House that a
number of his Suffolk tenants 'either have or are ready to give
up their farmes into my hands'. If he found himself without
tenants, he continued, this would have serious implications
not only for him but for the public service.[28] Although Sir
Thomas Barrington's income was mainly derived from his
Essex estates he also had some valuable property in the East
Riding of Yorkshire where for a time the parliamentarians
were under severe pressure. In 1643 his Yorkshire bailiff was
reporting that the tenants were refusing to pay their rents and
demanding that they should be abated. According to the family
steward, writing in May 1645, the rents received from
Yorkshire in the previous year had not amounted to £25.[29]
That same month another Essex parliamentarian, Sir Henry
Mildmay, asked the Hampshire committee to help him collect
the rents of his estates at Wherwell and Twyford. He had no
wish, he stressed, to employ any violence against such of his
tenants as were willing to pay in a reasonable proportion of the
rents which were due from them; he was more concerned
about those who owed him large sums of money and would pay
him nothing. While the war continued it was not open to him
to seek legal redress but he hoped that the committee would
take

> such courses against such men as may be afforded in such
> tymes of warr as these are, which to my knowledge is the

practice throughout the kingdom at this tyme in all parts that lyes in such condicion as my estate lyes, being within the Enimies Quarters.

Sir Henry Mildmay was clearly of the opinion that military force should be used if necessary. He went on to say, however, that hitherto he had been prepared to let his tenants pay their rents how and when they wished; and even now he would not insist on more than they could reasonably be expected to pay in the circumstances.[30]

When a country squire was absent for long periods on military or parliamentary duty there was a danger that his estate might be impaired through neglect, mismanagement or corrupt dealing. Sir Henry Rosewell, who was seated at Forde Abbey in Devon, served as colonel under the Earl of Stamford during the first Civil War. In a Chancery suit begun in February 1649 he claimed that on the outbreak of the war he had owned a very large personal estate but James Hutchins, who had acted as his steward or bailiff while he was in arms for Parliament, had sold cattle, sheep and other goods and had declined to render any accounts. By this time Sir Henry was in grave financial difficulties and in January 1650 was forced to sell the Forde Abbey estate.[31]

In September 1643 Sir Richard Onslow and some of the other Surrey MPs complained that their county had been 'much impoverished' as a result of the activities of the Earl of Essex's forces.[32] A matter of more general concern was the high level of war taxation levied by Parliament. When it was proposed in May 1645 that a regiment of horse should be raised by the Eastern Association this met with great opposition in the Commons and Sir Simonds D'Ewes declared that

the burthens allready laid upon the Associated Counties were soe extreame as if wee should lay any more upon them it would make them even desperate ffor no Taxes laid by the king of Spaine upon any of his dominions or by the great Turke upon the Greekes in Asia ever equalled those which are now laid upon the said associated Counties.

When these taxes were first introduced, he told the House, the counties of the Eastern Association had been more willing to pay them because they were employed on the raising of an army for their own defence. Moreover, estates in this region had been generally worth one-seventh more at that time than they were at present. He, for his part, had been obliged to abate the rents of his tenants by nearly £10 in every £70 a year and to take a full quarter of his estate into his own hands with a consequential financial loss. Landowners in these counties were not much better off than those whose estates were under royalist control 'saving that our houses are not burnt downe, for we cannot receive enough to subsist.'[33]

On 14 May 1645 the Commons approved an order for providing MPs whose estates had been sequestered by the royalists or who were in such financial straits that they were unable to support themselves in the service of the House with allowances of £4 a week for their maintenance. Among those who benefited from these arrangements (which were terminated on 20 August 1646) were Bulstrode Whitelocke; Sir Samuel Rolle, Sir John Northcote, Walter Yonge and his son Sir John of Devon; Sir Walter Erle, his son Thomas and John Browne of Dorset; Sir Thomas Jervoise, his son Richard, William Jephson and Richard Whitehead of Hampshire; and Sir John Dryden and Richard Knightley of Northamptonshire.[34] In addition, it was sometimes considered appropriate that a parliamentarian landowner who had been particularly hard hit should receive some lump sum compensation: Sir William Lister, for example, was granted £1,500 and Sir Richard Darley £5,000.[35] In an account of the expenditure which he had incurred on behalf of Parliament Sir John Gell affirmed that

> I have sold my Stock, laid out my whole Revenew, which at that time was fifteene hundred pounds a yeare, borrowed money of my brother and others, married my only Sonne, received part of his Portion, all which I have spent in maintainance of the Parliament's cause.

Earlier, he had put a value of £5,000 on the losses which he had sustained through the pillaging of his Derbyshire mansion,

Hopton Hall, and the seizure of his rents. Among his private papers there is a certificate issued in 1653 which records that he had disbursed £3,000 in the public service between 1 November 1642 and 6 September 1645 and that this was to be repaid to him with interest at the rate of 8 per cent.[36]

During the course of the first Civil War several major Puritan landowners were apprehended by royalist troops who surprised them in their houses. In October 1642 Sir Richard Hawksworth, a wealthy Yorkshire squire, was seized at Hawksworth Hall and carried off to York where he remained imprisoned for 20 months. Sir Thomas Burdett, who was one of the Derbyshire deputy lieutenants, was captured by Colonel Henry Hastings in February 1643 while Sir John Rous, who lived at Rous Lench in Worcestershire, and his sons were forcibly removed to Warwick in April 1644.[37] Parliamentarian gentry who were taken prisoner while in arms included Sir John Northcote, Edmund Ludlow and sons of Sir Thomas Jervoise, Sir John Jephson, Sir Edward Ayscough and Sir John Wray. In September 1644 a royalist newspaper reported that the garrison at Basing House had secured the person of Captain Jervoise, 'sonne to Sir Thomas, who is so famous in Hampshire that when any man speake an untruth bigge enough to be voted, they presently call it Jervasing.'[38] Sir Walter Erle, on the other hand, was more fortunate. When the royalists gained the upper hand in Dorset in the summer of 1643 he managed to escape by sea to Southampton where, it was said, 'he might have the company and comfort of his deere sonne in law Colonell Norton, a man of as religious purposes as himselfe, and one that knowes how to runne away.'[39]

Of those that laid down their lives for the cause of Parliament the most celebrated was John Hampden who was described after his death in June 1643 as a man 'soe religious, and of that prudence, judgement, temper, valoure and integritie that he left fewe his like behinde him.'[40] Among other Puritans who died while on active service were Sir Robert Cooke who was never able to fulfil his undertaking to rescue Lady Harley; Sir Samuel Owfield who had been dispatched to Hull; Sir William Springett who succumbed to a fever which was rife in the regiment which he commanded; William Lister who was the eldest son of the ill-starred Sir William Lister; and Theophilus Armyne, a younger son of Sir William Armyne.[41]

For a number of Puritan squires the war or the political revolution which followed it brought material benefits which appear to have far outweighed such financial losses as they may have sustained. Some like Sir Arthur Hesilrige acquired valuable church property; others like Sir Gilbert Gerard, Sir William Roberts and Bulstrode Whitelocke improved their fortunes through office-holding. According to a hostile commentator, Sir Gilbert had been heavily in debt before the time of the Long Parliament but as Treasurer of the Army pocketed £60,000 in gratuities and when subsequently appointed Chancellor of the Duchy of Lancaster enjoyed an income of £1,200 a year in that capacity. Such was the esteem in which Sir William Brereton was held as a military commander that in December 1645 he had an estate worth £1,500 a year settled on him.[42] In the main, however, the upper-class Puritans who had thrown in their lot with Parliament fared badly during the 1640s. Some men, among them Sir Robert Harley, John Hutchinson and John Pyne, never received any compensation for their losses;[43] and even when compensation was granted it was not always easy to secure payment, particularly if it was treated as a charge on the sequestered estate of a royalist squire. The traumatic experience which the Puritan gentry, in common with their fellow countrymen, went through during the first Civil War sometimes induced a feeling that it was essential that the trials to which God had subjected the righteous should not have been suffered in vain; but for the most part it helped to fortify the more conservative instincts of men who had never considered themselves to be engaged in a rebellion against the king.

EIGHT

Presbyterianism
and
Independency

In one of his speeches on the theme of peacemaking Sir Simonds D'Ewes argued that it was Parliament's failure to undertake a thorough reformation of religion which 'hath brought all the miseries upon us under which wee now groane'. In his view it was essential that a treaty of peace should provide for such a reformation; otherwise he feared that a negotiated peace would be short-lived.[1] By the late summer of 1642 the defection of many MPs with royalist sympathies had left the House of Commons with a solid Puritan majority so that the prospects of carrying through a major alteration in religion now seemed much brighter that at any time since the beginning of the Long Parliament. On 1 September, when the House was considering a declaration from the General Assembly of Scotland, a Cornish MP, Francis Rous, brought in a motion in favour of the abolition of episcopacy. This proposition met with approval and was included in Parliament's response to the declaration together with a statement to the effect that it was the intention to seek the advice of godly and learned divines about a new form of church government.[2] At this stage in the Civil War, however, it was felt that such a radical change required statutory authority and that accordingly it would be necessary to seek the king's assent. On 30 December Edmund Prideaux introduced a bill for the abolition of episcopal government which it was intended should feature in peace propositions to be forwarded to the king; and the following day the committee responsible for the bill appointed a sub-committee (whose members included Sir Simonds D'Ewes, Sir William Armyne and Sir Thomas Barrington) with the task of considering what interim form of jurisdiction should apply until such time as the matter was resolved by act of Parliament.[3]

When the bill was debated on 20 January 1643 D'Ewes told the House that he was of the same mind as he had been from the outset: namely, that the archbishops and bishops and all their dependencies should be abolished in a parliamentary way. On 23 January Sir Robert Harley moved that the bill, which by then had received its third reading, should be carried up to the House of Lords and it was agreed that he should be entrusted with this responsibility. Since the Upper House was anxious that the peace negotiations should be put in hand without delay the bill was hurried through and by 30 January the parliamentary stages were complete.[4] There had also been some speeding up of other ecclesiastical legislation and in the propositions which were presented to the king on 1 February he was asked to give his assent not only to the bill for the abolition of episcopacy but to bills for the taking away of superstitious innovations, for the punishment of scandalous clergymen and for a process of formal consultation with godly, religious and learned divines.[5]

Following the breakdown of the Oxford negotiations it was clear that for the present at least there was no possibility of proceeding with the long-awaited reformation of the Church by the normal legislative processes. It was therefore decided to convene an assembly of divines by means of an ordinance which was formally promulgated on 12 June 1643.[6] The ordinance named 119 clerical representatives (though not all of them chose to attend) and 30 lay members who were drawn from both Houses. Among the latter were William Viscount Saye and Sele, Philip Lord Wharton, John Selden, Francis Rous, Edmund Prideaux, Bulstrode Whitelocke, Sir Benjamin Rudyerd, John Pym, Sir Henry Vane the younger, William Pierrepont, Sir Thomas Barrington, Walter Yonge and Sir John Evelyn of Wiltshire. Subsequently, following the death of Pym in December 1643, Sir Robert Harley was nominated as his successor and other Puritan MPs who eventually became members included Sir William Masham, Sir Arthur Hesilrige and Zouch Tate.[7] The clerical members had been selected by the House of Commons; and indeed many of them had appeared in the list of names which had been published in April 1642.[8]

A clear majority of the clerical members wanted a national Church without bishops and with little or no provision for nonconformity; and after an initial period of uncertainty they came down in favour of a Presbyterian form of church government, though with varying degrees of enthusiasm. According to Robert Baillie, one of the Scottish commissioners in London, the Assembly contained only ten or eleven Independent divines who were advocates of an ecclesiastical system which allowed a high degree of autonomy to gathered congregations. Of these the most prominent were the five so-called dissenting brethren, Thomas Goodwin, Philip Nye, William Bridge, Sidrach Simpson and Jeremiah Burroughes. The term 'Independency' had already begun to gain currency even before the outbreak of the Civil War: in November 1641, for example, Sir Edward Dering had referred in a parliamentary speech to 'a certain new-born, unseen, ignorant, dangerous, desperate way of Independency', though he had felt it necessary to add that he had never heard any MP speaking up for either Independency or Presbyterianism in the Commons chamber.[9] In contrast with many of the sectarian preachers (who were unrepresented in the Westminster Assembly) the dissenting brethren were university graduates and ordained ministers of the Church of England. They were also held in considerable esteem: in the opinion of Bulstrode Whitelocke, for example, Goodwin and Nye were 'persons of great judgement and parts'.[10] What marked them out from the general body of ministers in the Assembly was that they had chosen to go into religious exile during the Laudian era. In the Dutch Netherlands they had served as pastors to the English congregations at Arnhem and Rotterdam; and at Rotterdam Sidrach Simpson had quarrelled with William Bridge and formed his own congregation.[11]

The Westminster Assembly met for the first time on 1 July 1643 and initially concentrated its attention on matters of doctrine, but before long the negotiations with the Scots introduced a new factor into the situation. On 26 August Sir Simonds D'Ewes recorded in his parliamentary journal that the English commissioners in Scotland had forwarded a covenant which it was proposed should be taken by both nations. Its main provisions, he noted, were that episcopal government should be 'cleane abolished', that a Presbyterian system should be established, and that all heresies and errors should be extirpated. At the same time he was delighted to see that it emphasized the need to deal severely with great and notorious sinners, given that 'Swearing, drinking and especially Whoring were rather increased then any way diminished since the beginning of the Parliament'. D'Ewes was strongly in favour of sweeping away bishops, deans and chapters and outlawing religious beliefs and practices which were at variance with his own perception of true religion but, on the other hand, he was anxious that Parliament should not unduly restrict its freedom of choice in the matter of church government. When the Commons considered the document in detail he expressed reservations about the assertion made in the first article that the Church of Scotland had been reformed 'according to the word of God' and suggested that more information was needed about its form of discipline before this phraseology could be accepted. Since the same words were applied to the proposed reformation of religion in England and Ireland there was a danger that Parliament might be held to have committed itself to adopting the Scottish model. In anticipation of this problem Sir Henry Vane the younger had managed to persuade the Scots to agree to the addition of the words 'and the example of the best reformed churches' but there were many MPs who feared that in practice this qualification would not prove to be a sufficient safeguard. In the end, therefore, it was decided that the safest course was to delete the phrase 'according to the word of God' in the reference to the Church of Scotland.[12]

The Solemn League and Covenant was approved with relatively few amendments and on 25 September many members of the Lords and Commons subscribed their names to the document at a formal ceremony held in St Margaret's, Westminster.[13] There were, however, a number of MPs who prevaricated either because they were opposed, for one reason or another, to the whole idea of entering into an alliance with the Scots or because they were concerned that the Covenant involved too high a degree of commitment to a particular form of church government. Bulstrode Whitelocke writes that those who 'were backward to take it' were regarded as ill affected and adds that 'I was one of the last in the house that tooke it.' What worried him more that anything was the possibility that it would lead to the establishment of a rigid Presbyterian system in which the main emphasis was on clerical authority.[14] On 28 September Sir Roger Burgoyne observed in a letter to a friend that Sir John Franklin, one of the Puritan knights of the shire for Middlesex, had declined to take the Covenant and had asked for more time to consider the matter; but eventually he overcame his scruples.[15] James Fiennes, the son and heir of Lord Saye and Sele, Sir Norton Knatchbull and Sir Philip Parker were even more reluctant to signify their assent. Sir Simonds D'Ewes records in his journal that on 6 November they were asked by the Speaker whether they were now willing to subscribe and that all three replied in the negative and then withdrew. After this show of dissent the House sat in silence for a while. Finally the silence was broken by Sir Anthony Irby who to the amazement of 'all sober minded men' proposed that they should not only be expelled from the Commons but committed to prison and deprived of their estates. In the ensuing debate there were few speakers who thought that such drastic punishment was warranted. Characteristically, D'Ewes spoke up on their behalf, emphasizing that they appeared to be motivated more by theological than by political consider-ations. Since taking the Covenant he had become fully convinced of its value 'conceiving it to bee the chiefe meanes under heaven for the preserving of the outward happines of this kingdome which consists in our peace and liberty, and the inward blessings of it which consists in the maintenance of the true Religion.' Nevertheless he did not feel justified in criticizing the three dissentients since there was no offence in them other than scruples of conscience. He knew both Fiennes and Parker and could testify that they were 'men of integrity and piety who have maintained the honour and worship of God in their own persons for divers yeares past and in their ffamilies'. Indeed it was Parker's reputation for integrity which had been the main factor responsible for his election as one of the knights of the shire for Suffolk. In conclusion he suggested that they should only be suspended; and the House duly agreed that this was the most appropriate course in the circumstances.[16]

Such hesitancy was by no means uncommon among Puritan MPs. On 29 January 1645 it was noted in the Commons journal that Sir John Evelyn of Wiltshire, Sir John Potts, Sir Samuel Rolle, Sir William Drake and Colonel Ralph Assheton had taken the Covenant, apparently for the first time. Drake had been living abroad with the Speaker's permission but the others were more vulnerable to criticism. As revealed in a letter from Evelyn to Potts which was written in October 1648 both men viewed the Scots with a marked antipathy.[17]

On 12 October 1643 Parliament gave direction that the Westminster Assembly should now consider the nature of the new system of church government which, as prescribed in the Solemn League and Covenant, was to be in accordance with 'the word of God, and the example of the best reformed Churches'.[18] Although the Independent divines in the Assembly were relatively few in number they had some powerful friends in Parliament as well as growing support among the soldiery. The ministers who preached the fast sermons before the members of the Commons on 29 November consisted of a Presbyterian, William Mew (who held a living in the gift of Nathaniel Stephens, one of the Gloucestershire MPs) and an Independent, William Bridge. During the course of his sermon Bridge took the opportunity to advance the claim that individual congregations should have the right to choose their own ministers. When Sir Robert Harley moved in the House that the two sermons should be printed some MPs argued that in view of Bridge's attempt to promote the cause of Independency his sermon might cause offence but the Commons decided that it should be published without any editing.[19] This, however, was only a mild foretaste of what was to come. In January 1644 the five dissenting brethren pleaded the case for a latitudinarian church settlement in a direct appeal to Parliament and arranged for their petition to be printed, under the title *An Apologeticall Narration*, with the aim of influencing opinion outside Parliament.[20]

The debate in the Assembly over the issue of church government was to drag on for many months. In the Commons few Puritan MPs appear to have had clear-cut ideas about the kind of system which should be established in place of episcopacy; and indeed there were only a small number, among them Sir William Brereton and Sir William Constable, who could claim to have first-hand knowledge of any of the 'best reformed Churches'.[21] Richard Baxter relates that he had it on good authority that before the outbreak of the Civil War there was only one Presbyterian in the House of Commons, 'it being not then known among them'. This was Zouch Tate, a well-to-do Northamptonshire squire whose family had long been noted for its attachment to Puritanism and who numbered Edmund Calamy, one of the most influential of the Puritan divines, among his special friends. Tate was a leading parliamentary spokesman for the Presbyterian interest, as were Edmund Prideaux and Francis Rous (both of whom were younger sons of West Country squires). Prideaux was said to be 'a true professor of the Word'. Rous, who would later describe himself as a Presbyterian, was the author of numerous spiritual works and in the opinion of Sir Simonds D'Ewes a 'very religious honest' man. Robert Baillie the Scottish commissioner was on close terms with both Tate and Rous and sometimes offered them tactical advice. When he delivered a fast sermon on 28 February 1644 the Commons deputed Rous to thank him and in return he dedicated the printed version to his 'much honoured friend'.[22] Sir Robert Harley, writes his eldest son, was 'very zelous for the setling of Church Goverment'. One of his fellow MPs asked him why he was so earnest for Presbytery when it was so opposed in the Commons and in response Sir Robert told him 'Let us much rather be earnest for it, though we gayn it by Inches'. Together with Tate and Rous he was involved in the preparation of an ordinance promulgated in October 1644 which laid down interim arrangements for the ordination of presbyters or ministers within the city of London.[23] There were others who may be assigned to this group as, for example, Sir Gilbert Gerard who is characterized by Lucy Hutchinson as a 'fierce' Presbyterian and John Gurdon who according to an anonymous Puritan tract was 'a Presbyterian throughout' and who after the Restoration employed Presbyterian chaplains.[24] There is nothing to suggest, however, that more than a small handful of MPs favoured the introduction of a Presbyterian system on grounds of principle.

Far more numerous were the Puritan MPs who accepted the need for some form of Presbyterianism for essentially pragmatic reasons. Wealthy Puritan squires might be convinced that true religion would only flourish if episcopacy was abolished but in other respects they tended to be more conservative in outlook. To many of them Presbyterianism seemed to be a far from perfect system of church government but they nevertheless considered it to be much less objectionable than Independency. Presbyterianism would ensure that there was a national Church which would meet their requirements in terms of both doctrine and worship; and that this would be organized on the basis of the existing parish system in which they often had a vested interest as patrons of ecclesiastical livings. Independency, on the other hand, filled them with alarm. They were concerned that a religious settlement which assigned a substantial measure of autonomy to gathered congregations would play into the hands of the sectaries who, they believed, were enemies of godliness as they perceived it; and they also feared that religious anarchy could be the first step along the road to political and social anarchy. The consternation caused by the activity of the sectaries is reflected in the correspondence which Sir Samuel Luke, MP for Bedford, conducted while serving as the parliamentary governor of Newport Pagnell in Buckinghamshire. In November 1644 he told Stephen Marshall, who had emerged as one of the dominant figures in the Westminster Assembly, that he was having problems with persons who rejected the Church and condemned its ministers. As time went on the dissension increased and in March 1645 we find him pouring out his anxieties to a fellow MP, Cornelius Holland, who was a religious Independent. Impiety, he lamented, had now grown to such a height that his eyes could no longer endure the sight of it nor his ears the hearing. The sectaries might have the outward form of godliness but he hoped that God would infuse the power of it into their hearts. If he continued as governor of Newport Pagnell he would feel obliged to drive them out or God in his wrath might wreak vengeance on the town as he had done on Sodom and Gomorrah. For Luke and his father, Sir Oliver, it was important that the Presbyterians should prevail in their contest with the Independents.[25]

The sectaries were bitterly attacked by Thomas Edwards, a Presbyterian divine, in his polemical work *Gangraena* which appeared in three instalments between February and December 1646. Sir Simonds D'Ewes bought a copy of the original version shortly after its publication and was clearly impressed by what he had read since he subsequently added *The Third Part of Gangraena* to his library.[26] In his parliamentary journal, and particularly in some of the later insertions, D'Ewes used the term 'Independent' as a multi-purpose word which could be applied not only to those who were advocates of congregational autonomy but to sectaries of every kind, political extremists and habitual critics of peace propositions.[27]

The views of Sir Nathaniel Barnardiston on the issue of church government were probably not untypical of the attitude of those MPs who favoured Presbyterianism because they knew of no better alternative to Independency. Writing to Governor Winthrop in March 1647 he began by expressing his great regret at the religious divisions which had opened up and the fact that there was so little of that love which had once been 'the principall badge of sayntes among us'. He went on to say that he considered himself to be

a presbiterion (yet such a one as can and doe hartely love an humble and pious independant, such I meane as are with you, for ours differ much generally from them) only in this regard, in that I conceave it consisteth best with the constitution of our goverment and in that regard, if I weare with you, I should ioyne with you, for truly I cannot yet see any certayne and generall set forme of discipline set down in the word of God universally; if ther be, the Lord discover yt to us in his good tyme.

In England the Independents were prepared to shelter and countenance all opinions and blasphemy, no matter how bad. All sectaries would become Independents through the notion of a general toleration. It would be less serious if they would keep their opinions to themselves but it was a great calamity of the time that 'our differences even among those that would be estemed godly, and have beene so accounted formerly' were likely to prove more dangerous than the Civil Wars.[28]

While many MPs were willing to accept a form of church government which had Presbyterian features they were generally determined to prevent the emergence of a theocratic regime. In a parliamentary speech Sir John Holland told the House that he acknowledged that it was necessary to establish a Presbyterian system. By virtue of the Solemn League and Covenant they were obliged to reform the Church not only in doctrine but in discipline and government 'as neere as may be unto that of the church of Scotland and other reformed churches'. At the same time he had two major reservations. In the first place, he took the view that the new church government should not be unalterable. It should be open to Parliament to change it; and some latitude should be allowed in matters of worship. Secondly, it was important to guard against the danger of bringing in a tyranny of the clergy; for the clergy should not have arbitrary power.[29]

Writing in May 1644 Robert Baillie expressed the view that the Independents had 'no considerable power' either in the Assembly or Parliament or the forces of the Earl of Essex and Sir William Waller but in London and the country at large and the Earl of Manchester's army of the Eastern Association 'their strength is great and growing'.[30] In retrospect Richard Baxter described the situation in Parliament in rather different terms:

> though in the beginning of the Parliament there was scarce a
> noted gross Sectary known but the Lord Brook in the House
> of Peers and young Sir Henry Vane in the House of
> Commons; yet by degrees the Number of them increased in
> the Lower House; Major Salloway[31] and some few more Sir
> Henry Vane had made his own adherents; Many more were
> carried part of the way to Independency and liberty of
> Religion.[32]

Some of the most influential supporters of Independency were
men who had been associated with the Saybrook project for the
establishment of a Puritan colony in southern Connecticut.
One of the noblemen who had been involved, Robert Lord
Brooke, was dead before the issue of church government
became a major focus of attention but Lord Saye and Sele
emerged as a leading patron of Independency.[33] Other key
figures in the 'Saybrook group' who were Independents in
religion included Sir Arthur Hesilrige, who was a brother-in-
law of Lord Brooke, Sir Matthew Boynton, whose heir had
married a daughter of Lord Saye and Sele; and Boynton's fellow
Yorkshiremen Sir William Constable and Henry Darley.
Hesilrige was termed a 'hot-headed Schismatique' in Clement
Walker's history of Independency. During the Laudian era he
had been served by a Puritan chaplain at his Leicestershire
mansion, Noseley Hall, and had used the church adjoining his
house as virtually a private chapel.[34] The Boyntons and the
Darleys had also enjoyed some measure of religious freedom
through the employment of domestic chaplains; and indeed Sir
Matthew's chaplains had included Henry Jessey, the Independent divine. Boynton and Constable had been planning to
settle in the new colony but in the event had taken up
residence at Arnhem in the Dutch Netherlands where they had
joined the congregation which was in the pastoral charge of
Thomas Goodwin and Philip Nye. At the beginning of the
Long Parliament the religious exiles had returned to England
and it was probably no coincidence that one of Nye's first
actions had been to establish a gathered congregation in the

East Riding of Yorkshire. In July 1643 a royalist newspaper went so far as to claim that Boynton was 'a declared Anabaptist'.[35]

Among other prominent supporters of Independency were Philip Lord Wharton and, in the Commons, Sir Henry Vane the younger, Oliver Cromwell, Oliver St John, Sir Henry Mildmay and Cornelius Holland, both of whom would be later described as 'light headed Saints'.[36] Despite Baxter's opinion of him, Vane cannot readily be assigned to any particular sect; his religion was too highly personal for that. He was, however, passionately committed to the cause of religious toleration. According to his contemporary biographer, he considered that the magistrate 'ought to keep within the proper sphere of Civil Jurisdiction and not intermeddle with men's Consciences by way of Imposition and Force in matters of Religion and divine Worship.' In a testament which he prepared before his execution in 1662 Sir Henry related that he had fully assented to the Solemn League and Covenant 'but the rigid way of prosecuting it, and the oppressing Uniformity that hath bin endeavored by it, I never approved.'[37]

Sir William Armyne, who was a friend of Vane, appears to have been sympathetically inclined towards the Independents. His wife, we are told, 'was not addicted to Sects' but 'took it to be no countenancing of Schism . . . to relieve such Servants of Christ in their distress as men accuse and afflict as Schismaticks, tho she was an Adversary to real Schism.'[38] According to a Northamptonshire minister, Sir Gilbert Pickering was 'first a Presbyterian, then an Independent, then a Brownist and afterwards an Anabaptist.' His brother, Colonel John Pickering, was an Independent who had a complaint brought against him in the Commons for preaching to his regiment. The matter was debated on 25 April 1645 and it was reported in the royalist press that a Presbyterian MP had moved that the Westminster Assembly should examine him with a view to determining his ability to preach.[39]

Bulstrode Whitelocke writes that 'in all the transactions of the time I would never appear to be intirely of any faction or party butt followed the dictates of my own reason and conscience.' As a member of the Westminster Assembly he was careful not to give the impression that he was an outright opponent of Presbyterianism, though like many of his fellow MPs he was anxious to prevent the introduction of a theocratic form of church government. At a meeting of the Assembly he challenged the contention that the Presbyterian system was *jure divino*. The word 'Presbytery', he suggested, had been unknown until recently, at least in the sense that many now used it. He was not one of those 'who except against the presbiterian governement, I thinke it hath a good foundation and hath done much good in the Church of Christ'. He was not, however, convinced that it was *jure divino*; in fact it was widely held that no type of church government, including episcopacy and Independency, could truly be described as such. In his view the Assembly would be well advised to refrain from pressing this point and instead

> to present your judgements to the Parliament, That the government of the Church by presbiteries is most agreeable to the word of God and most fitt to be setled in this kingdome. . . . and I hope you may soon have a desired issue of it.

Later, when he spoke out in the Commons against the grant of unlimited disciplinary authority to the presbyteries, he was accused of being an Erastian. In practice, and certainly as time went on, he found Independency much more to his taste than any form of Presbyterianism. At one stage he was employing an Independent divine, George Cokayne, as his chaplain and it is clear from his autobiography that during the 1650s he was less concerned about a minister's denomination than about the content and quality of his preaching. He considered it indisputable, he told his children, that 'under the liberty of the Gospell any person whom our Lord Christ shall enable thereunto may in private (if not in publique) teach and instruct the people under him', whether or not he had been formally ordained; and he himself often delivered sermons for the edification of his family.[40]

For some Puritan gentry it was not simply a matter of

choosing between Scottish Presbyterianism, a more Erastian version of Presbyterianism or Independency: they felt it necessary to engage in a more extensive search for the form of religion which would most satisfy their spiritual needs. On the face of it, Sir William Springett, who served as the colonel of a regiment of foot, should have been a virtually automatic recruit for the cause of Independency: according to his wife he had 'declined bishops and common prayer very early' and before the time of the Civil War had journeyed many miles to hear the sermons of a suspended minister in preference to attending services at his parish church. Nevertheless they both came to the conclusion that for all its emphasis on the role of gathered congregations Independency had major shortcomings. As Lady Springett puts it, 'We having looked into the independent way saw death there, and that it was not that our souls sought.'[41]

NINE

A Godly
Church

On 4 February 1644 Sir John Coke, one of the knights of the shire for Derbyshire, commented in a letter to his father that the Westminster Assembly was about to address the great question which was in dispute between those who wanted a Presbyterian government and those who were called Independents.[1] By the beginning of April Robert Baillie, the Scottish commissioner, was claiming that the fortunes of the Independents were declining. The credit and reputation of Viscount Saye and Sele now amounted to nothing; Sir Henry Vane was offering them no encouragement; and, he went on: 'No man I know, in either of the Houses, of any note, is for them.' Later that month, however, he was beginning to sound rather less complacent: the Independents 'over all the land are making up a faction to their own way, the farr most part whereof is fallen off to Anabaptisme and Antinomianisme.'[2]

The first proposals on church government which the Assembly submitted to Parliament took the form of a Directory for Ordination. This was incorporated into a draft ordinance which laid down interim arrangements for ordaining ministers or Presbyters in the city of London. The Commons considered it necessary to make a number of changes in the text of the Directory and in response the Assembly forwarded its own list of proposed amendments. While the Commons accepted most of these amendments in the course of a debate on 29 August it proved less easy to reach agreement over two declaratory

108

clauses, one pronouncing that ordination was an ordinance of Christ and the other that 'ministers are set over people in the Lord'. Sir Henry Vane the younger and Sir Arthur Hesilrige took strong exception to them but it was not only the Independents in the House who felt that the Assembly was claiming too exalted a status for the clergy; as Edmund Calamy reported to the Assembly, many MPs had reservations. On 9 September the Commons decided that the first of the disputed clauses should appear in the preamble to the ordinance rather than in the main text, as the Assembly would have preferred. When the ordinance was further debated on 13 September Sir Simonds D'Ewes expressed the hope that 'in this reformation the clergie intended onlie the power and puritie of the ordinances and not to introduce. . . . such a tyrannical power as the Bishopps had.' Despite the fears of clerical domination the House assented to the other clause about the submission of the people to the minister and later that day Francis Rous and Zouch Tate were able to inform the Assembly that the ordinance as now approved accorded with its wishes in all essential particulars.[3] On 18 September the Commons discussed a list of divines whom the Assembly had nominated for the function of examining and ordaining candidates for the ministry. The list included two of the leading figures in the Assembly, Cornelius Burgess and Edmund Calamy; the authors William Gouge, John Ley and John Downame; and Stanley Gower who until recently had been one of Sir Robert Harley's ministers. The House duly approved the Assembly's recommendations and the names were inserted in the ordinance which, following the agreement of the Lords, was finally published on 4 October.[4]

Sir Simonds D'Ewes had already left the Commons chamber on 13 September when the Independents suddenly launched a carefully planned initiative which seems to have caught the House completely unawares. Oliver St John, acting with Cromwell and Vane, managed to procure an order for the setting up of a committee with the task of attempting to resolve the differences within the Assembly over the issue of church government and, failing that, of seeking to identify

109

ways of accommodating 'tender consciences'. This Grand Committee for the Accommodation, as it was commonly termed, consisted of members of the Lords and Commons together with some of the divines who sat in the Assembly. Among the politicians there were a number of Independents, including Lord Saye and Sele, Lord Wharton, Hesilrige, Vane, St John and Cromwell while, on the other hand, the Presbyterian interest was represented by such men as Sir Gilbert Gerard, Sir Robert Harley, Francis Rous, Zouch Tate and Edmund Prideaux.[5] The Independents, writes Robert Baillie, were aiming to secure a toleration from the House of Commons before any proposals for the establishment of a Presbyterian form of government had been submitted. What he found particularly disturbing was the conduct of Sir Henry Vane, once regarded as a valuable ally of the Scots, who 'twice at our table prolixlie, earnestlie and passionatelie. . . . reasoned for a full libertie of conscience to all religions, without any exceptions' and who in the House had 'opposed the clause in ordinatione that required ministers to subscribe the Covenant'.[6]

The Grand Committee first met on 20 September and at the suggestion of Oliver St John appointed a sub-committee of divines who included Stephen Marshall, Thomas Goodwin and Philip Nye and charged it with the task of producing a report highlighting the points on which the Presbyterians and Independents were agreed and those which were in dispute. With Lord Saye and Sele and Sir Henry Vane as their chief spokesmen the Independents immediately went on the offensive, their aim being to by-pass the Assembly and seek the agreement of Parliament to proposals based on the sub-committee's report. On the Presbyterian side Sir Gilbert Gerard and Sir Robert Harley appear to have taken only a limited part in the proceedings; it was Francis Rous, Zouch Tate and Edmund Prideaux who led the resistance to the Independents. At the last meeting of the Grand Committee, which took place on 25 October, the conflict reached its height but ended in deadlock; and deadlock meant defeat for those who favoured the cause of Independency.[7]

By the autumn of 1644 there was widespread concern about

the growing strength of the sects and the general lack of progress in establishing a new ecclesiastical system which would put an end to religious anarchy. In a Commons debate on 1 November a number of MPs, among them Edmund Prideaux, argued that the Assembly should be instructed to speed up its work. Sir Simonds D'Ewes suggested (presumably with his tongue in his cheek) that the only way to bring the proceedings to an early conclusion was for the Assembly to conduct its business in Latin 'as in all other Synods in the Christian world it hath been the constant practice'. He went on to say that the Directory of Worship (or Religion as he termed it) was now virtually ready and that it was therefore necessary to do no more that send for it.[8] On 4 November the Commons discussed some proposals from the Committee for Plundered Ministers[9] for the suppression of Anabaptists and Antinomians. The first proposal was that no one should expound the scriptures in any church, chapel or house except an ordained minister and this led D'Ewes to remind the Commons of the Puritan concept of the godly household. It was not presumably the intention, he observed, to prevent the masters of families from repeating a sermon or expounding a chapter of the Bible for the benefit of their families. In the time of the bishops this had been adjudged a crime if any friends or neighbours were present and it might still be brought into question should the House accept the proposals. He had

> studied too long to favour Schismatiks or Sectaries or to be
> carried away with their Tenents [tenets] but this I know that
> the persecuting Church is the Malignant Church and the
> persecuted Church maintaines the Truth, and therefore I
> would desire that wee might not under any Colour lay a
> snare for the Godly. It will be enough to restraine preaching
> and expounding of the Scripture in Churches in Publike
> Order without intermedling at all with any thing done in
> private houses.

In the end it was decided that the proposal should be referred back to the committee for amendment.[10] On 11 November the Commons received a Norfolk petition which expressed the

111

hope that as a result of the deliberations of the Westminster Assembly some rules would soon be published for the settlement of the worship, discipline and government of the Church. Such rules would 'preserve and establish quiet amongst us' and would be an effectual means of obtaining 'that blessed peace and truth which is so much wished'. Among the signatories was Sir John Hobart, a wealthy Puritan seated at Blickling Hall whose wife described herself as a Calvinist in matters of doctrine and a Presbyterian in regard to the discipline of the Church. On the same day, and clearly not purely coincidentally, Sir Nathaniel Barnardiston presented a Suffolk petition which was on similar lines.[11] The Assembly had in fact submitted a paper on certain aspects of church government on 8 November and this was followed up by two further papers on 19 November.[12] In a letter dispatched from Westminster on 11 November Ralph Assheton, who was one of the knights of the shire for Lancashire, told a fellow parliamentarian that 'The Assembly of Divines have brought in their worke to the House of Commons for Church Government and Directory of Worship. . . . which doubtless will give good satisfaction to the whole Kingdome' and in the event 'prove advantageous'. Before long his county would become a stronghold of Presbyterianism.[13]

The Commons now proceeded to consider the proposed replacement for the Book of Common Prayer. On the face of it, the Directory of Worship was likely to receive a much easier passage than any proposals for the establishment of a Presbyterian system of government since it provided for a much plainer form of public worship than the existing liturgy while at the same time allowing some measure of discretion to the minister. When the Directory was debated on 26 November there were only two specific points which engaged the attention of the House: one was the question of eligibility for admission to communion and the other concerned the inclusion of the words 'as in the Church of Scotland' in a clause relating to the administration of the sacraments of bread and wine to persons sitting at the communion table. The first issue, which foreshadowed future arguments over the disci-

plinary power of the clergy, was remitted for futher examination and it was subsequently agreed that the Directory
should stipulate in general terms that the ignorant and the
scandalous were not fit to partake of the Lord's Supper. When
the question was put whether the words 'as in the Church of
Scotland' should be retained, Richard Knightley and Walter
Long acted as tellers for the noes and Sir Robert Harley and Sir
Anthony Irby for the ayes; and it is an indication of the
antipathy aroused by Scottish Presbyterianism that the
Commons rejected the motion by 57 votes to 34. Having
delivered this rebuff to the Church of Scotland the House
resolved that the Directory should be incorporated into an
ordinance and assigned responsibility for its preparation to a
committee which included Sir Henry Vane the younger, Sir
John Holland, Sir William Strickland, Sir Robert Harley, Sir
Gilbert Gerard, Francis Rous and Zouch Tate.[14] On the day
following this debate Thomas Hill, who enjoyed the patronage
of Sir Gilbert Pickering, observed in the course of a sermon
which he preached in the presence of members of the House of
Lords that

> They who have joyned like Brethren in one practicall
> Directory for publike worship, by a prudent moderation,
> settling such an order therein as may prevent confusion in
> Church-Administrations, and withall leaving such liberty as
> may relieve tender consciences. . . . why should not they
> also as children of one Father, as Subjects of the same
> King. . . . bee brought to shake hands in lesser things,
> harmoniously concurring in matters of Church-government?

Some people, he went on, talked themselves and one another
into a passion against the Independents while others drew as
ugly a picture of the Presbyterians. By using these names
too many struck at the power of godliness.[15]

In due course the ordinance for promulgating the Directory
of Worship went up to the House of Lords where it was
approved subject to a number of alterations and additions.
When the Commons discussed these amendments on 3
January 1645 some were immediately accepted but others

which were regarded as more contentious were referred to a committee under the chairmanship of Zouch Tate which also included Sir Robert Harley, Sir Arthur Hesilrige, Bulstrode Whitelocke, Francis Rous and Edmund Prideaux. The following day there was a conference with the Lords at which the differences were speedily resolved and the ordinance was very soon in print.[16]

Most of the Puritan gentry were probably well satisfied with the Directory, not least since it prescribed a basic uniformity in matters of worship. Bulstrode Whitelocke, however, had reservations about the decision to ban all use of the Book of Common Prayer. In his view it would have been reasonable to allow it to be used in private households; to forbid this practice was contrary to that liberty of conscience which he and other MPs had claimed before the time of the Long Parliament.[17] To Lucy Hutchinson, whose sympathies lay with the Independents, the Directory was an instrument fashioned by the Presbyterians for the purpose of oppressing their religious opponents: 'such as could not conforme to it' she writes, were 'mark'd out with an evill eie, and hated and persecuted under the name of Seperatists.'[18] In April 1645 the Commons decided that further steps would have to be taken in order to secure the general adoption of the new liturgy. When a draft ordinance which had been prepared for this purpose was discussed by the Grand Committee for Religion on 31 May Sir Simonds D'Ewes objected to a clause which stipulated that anyone who criticized the Directory in speech or writing should be imprisoned for life after a third offence of this kind. In his view this was a harsh punishment for

> such persons as were both Orthodox and Godly, for that which concernes meere matter of discipline. The Truth will prevaile of itselfe and need not be established with such rigorous punishment. . . . Besides it is possible that there may be errors in the directory which if men should never write, preach or speake against them how shall they be discovered or reformed.

Banishment, he suggested, would be more appropriate than

perpetual imprisonment. Eventually, on 17 June, the Grand Committee came down in favour of a heavy fine.[19]

In a fast sermon preached at Westminster Abbey on Christmas day 1644 Edmund Calamy took the opportunity to acquaint the members of the House of Lords who were present with the anxieties of the Presbyterian divines in the Assembly and their allies among the parish clergy. The divisions over matters of religion, he told them, were delaying the happy reformation which all good people wanted to see. 'For every man drives his owne private way of Reformation and strives to hinder all other wayes that are opposite to his way.' Even the godly themselves had 'lost much of the power of godliness in their lives . . . For all their time is so much taken up with unnecessary disputation as that they have little leasure to repent, and to study to increase in holinesse.' The differences in religion were also opening a door to all forms of atheism; helping to prolong the war by giving encouragement to the enemy; and stirring up the kind of hatred which could lead to the utter ruin and destruction of the kingdom. The sectaries were casting bitter aspersions on the Assembly of Divines and on every Parliament man who opposed them. The Lords should beware of the opinion that an unlimited toleration should be granted to all religions. This was a doctrine which was in direct conflict with the Solemn League and Covenant and if it prevailed the inevitable result would be the overthrow of all church government and the end of true religion. It was incumbent on them to suppress these divisions and differences in religion by exercising their civil authority; God had made them responsible for the punishment of evil doers.[20]

On 2 January 1645 the Commons gave direction that Sir Robert Harley, Sir Gilbert Gerard, Francis Rous, Zouch Tate and Humphrey Salway should draw up an account of the proceedings of Parliament and the Assembly in ecclesiastical matters in order to satisfy a request which had been received from the Scottish commissioners. In the paper which was drafted three points in particular were highlighted. In the first place, episcopacy and its sytem of jurisdiction had been abolished by a bill which had passed both Houses and had been presented to the king for his assent (though this had not been forthcoming). Secondly, the Book of Common Prayer had been replaced by a new Directory of Worship. Thirdly, some propositions on the subject of church government had been submitted by the Assembly. One of these propositions, which was a matter of 'great concernment', was about to be debated in the Commons, namely that the scriptures held forth 'That many particular Congregations may be under One Presbyterial Government'.[21]

On 23 January the Commons recorded its approval of a petition forwarded by a number of Suffolk ministers which stressed the need for a settled government in the Church and the suppression of the sects.[22] During the course of that month the House endorsed three major concepts: that each parish should have a presbytery consisting of ministers and other public officers; that many individual congregations could be subject to the authority of one Presbyterian government, and that the Church should be governed by congregational, classical and synodical assemblies in such a manner as Parliament should determine.[23]

As yet the Commons had only come out with a broad declaration of intent: it was now necessary to put more detailed work in hand. This involved a heavy programme for the Grand Committee for Religion, a committee of the whole House which was chaired by Lawrence Whitaker, and the sub-committee which supported it. The sub-committee fulfilled a key role, liaising with the Assembly, advising the Grand Committee and producing draft ordinances. Its membership, as agreed on 17 April, consisted of Francis Rous, Sir John Coke, Sir William Masham, John Selden, Samuel Browne, John Wilde, Humphrey Salway, Zouch Tate, Alexander Rigby, Anthony Nichols, Sir Benjamin Rudyerd, Cornelius Holland, John Lisle, Sir Robert Harley, Sir Henry Mildmay and Walter Yonge. It was a mixture of zealous Presbyterians and Independents and others who were not so strongly committed, but for the most part they were agreed that there should be no question of establishing a theocratic system of church government.[24]

On 17 April Whitaker secured the agreement of the House to an initial list of sins, among them adultery, fornication, drunkenness and profane swearing, which the Grand Committee had felt should be grounds for exclusion from the sacrament of the Lord's Supper. Subsequently the Grand Committee discussed the question of whether persons accused of scandalous offences for which such a penalty was prescribed should be examined by the minister and lay elders of the parish or by a justice of the peace. Predictably, Sir Simonds D'Ewes argued strongly against clerical involvement in this process. To give such a task to the minister, he declared, would destroy the work of reformation 'for this would find him worke enough and no time to study and preach and noe minister that can either construe Latine or read Greeke would desire it.' Ministers should not take on secular employment of this kind but should tend their cures. Edmund Prideaux and others objected that 'this would destroy all presbiteriall goverment and the Minister and eldershipp would have nothing to doe.' In the end it was decided to adopt a compromise wording to the effect that anyone convicted of a scandalous offence should be excluded from the sacrament by the minister and elders of each parish.[25]

Less controversial was the ordinance on church government which received final approval on 19 August. This provided for the election of ruling elders by parochial congregations; the establishment of classical and provincial assemblies together with a national assembly; and the division of a new Province of London (which consisted of the cities of London and Westminster and adjoining parishes) into twelve classical elderships. Later, on 17 September, the Commons agreed that the Speaker should write to the local parliamentary committees about the arrangements for dividing up their counties into classical presbyteries and advising Parliament on the choice of ministers and lay elders for each *classis*.[26]

Parliament had decreed the establishment of a hierarchical system of church government which was Presbyterian in form but while the basic architecture has been settled it had still to determine the distribution of power. This fundamental question came to the surface again in the late summer of 1645. Bulstrode Whitelocke writes that on 8 August the Commons received a petition from the Westminster Assembly which plainly declared that the power to suspend from the sacrament of the Lord's Supper all such persons as were judged to be scandalous and ignorant belonged to the presbyteries by divine right. 'This', he observes, 'putt mee uppon study of that point against a further debate of it,' and he proceeded to compile some notes which revealed a marked aversion to the whole concept of ecclesiastical discipline. In his view it would be improper for pastors who were supposed to feed their flocks to suspend anyone from the sacrament; 'The more sinfull persons are, the more they have need of instruction.' In some villages the elders might not be very learned themselves 'yett the authority to be given to them is sufficiently great'. Open sins were

> punishable by the Magistrate and all matters tending to the preservation of the publique peace, which some doe thinke is noe whit promoted by the thunder of excommunication. . . . the best excommunication is for pastors, Elders and all people to excommunicate sin out of their own hearts and conversations.

He had heard many complaints about the jurisdiction formerly exercised by the prelates who had been few in number but if the Assembly's proposals were accepted there would be a great multiplication of spiritual men in government. Whitelocke drew on these notes when speaking in the debate which took place on 3 September and on subsequent occasions and in the process earned the displeasure of the rigid Presbyterians who began to describe him as a disciple of John Selden (the arch-critic of clerical pretensions) and an Erastian.[27]

On 9 September Sir Robert Honywood wrote in a letter to his father-in-law Sir Henry Vane the elder that the Assembly was pressing for an unlimited power in the matter of excommunication and the Commons did not relish the idea.[28] Subsequently Sir Peter Wentworth informed the House that in

London a petition was being organized with the aim of promoting the views of the Assembly. The petition, comments Sir Simonds D'Ewes, was so cunningly penned that it was apparent that the Assembly had been involved in the drafting. The House took strong exception to the allegation made in the petition that it had not acted sincerely over the establishment of a Presbyterian government and in a message to the Common Council of London described this criticism as scandalous and untrue. Shortly afterwards the Scottish commissioners presented a paper which also claimed that the Commons had been guilty of bad faith.[29]

During the course of the autumn the Assembly's proposals came under sharp attack from MPs who held varying opinions on other aspects of church government. As a leading Independent Sir Henry Vane the younger was no less anxious than Bulstrode Whitelocke to restrict the power of the presbyteries. Sir Simonds D'Ewes records that on 26 September he argued that it would be wrong to vest arbitrary power in any other institution than Parliament.[30] D'Ewes himself was highly suspicious of the clergy. In subsequent debates he maintained that the grant of unlimited power to the presbyteries

> would bee an occasion of infinite oppression upon the consciences and quiet of the subjects of England, of Pride, Tyranny, Insolency in the Clergy and in the issue destruction to the Church. That the offences occasioned in one year would be more than Parliament could hear and remedy in twenty. That in every parish there would be a several rule for scandals according to the humours and fancies of men.

D'Ewes rejected Sir Gilbert Gerard's assertion that in exercising its disciplinary authority the presbytery would not be judging the crime but the scandal arising from it. Nor was he impressed by John Crewe's argument that unless the eldership was granted adequate powers the minister could be forced to tender the sacrament 'against his conscience'. Indeed he was far from convinced that ministers could be safely entrusted with such powers: it was well known, he said, that clergymen were subject to great passions. No doubt he particularly had in

119

mind his bitter quarrel with Richard Davenport, a man of 'most haughty and proud spirit' who had been presented in 1625 to the D'Ewes living of Stowlangtoft in Suffolk.[31]

An ordinance which was promulgated on 20 October contained a list of sins which could be dealt with by the presbyteries. This faithfully reflected the Puritan view that the great evils of the day included swearing, drunkenness, blasphemy, idolatry and Sabbath breaking. So extreme was the Sabbatarian spirit with which it was infused that the presbyteries were even permitted to exclude from the sacrament any person who travelled on the Lord's day without reasonable cause. At the same time provision was made for a standing committee of both Houses with responsibility for considering 'the causes of suspension from the Sacrament of the Lord's Supper not contained in the Ordinance: unto which Committee any Eldership shall present such causes to the end that Parliament, if need require, may heare and determine the same.' The committee was to consist of those who were currently members of the Westminster Assembly; and this meant not only MPs with Presbyterian sympathies such as Sir Robert Harley, Francis Rous and Zouch Tate but Sir Arthur Hesilrige, Sir Henry Vane the younger and other Independents.[32]

A saving clause in the ordinance ensured that members of the Lords and Commons, together with officers of both Houses, would not find themselves exposed to the disciplinary powers of the presbyteries. Many who were denied this privilege may have thought that these powers were by no means modest but the Assembly and the Scottish commissioners considered them to be a pale shadow of what was needed if the new church government was to be more than nominally Presbyterian. Shortly after publication of the ordinance the Grand Committee for Religion was discussing proposals submitted by the Assembly for extending the catalogue of sins which carried the penalty of suspension from the sacrament of the Lord's Supper. On 14 November the committee accepted two additions to the list but hesitated over a third which was directed against those who kept images of any person of the Trinity in their own houses.[33]

TEN

A Lame
Presbyterianism

In July 1645 Thomas Hill preached a sermon at Bassishaw church in London before a congregation which included the lord mayor and other civic dignitaries. The occasion was a special day of humiliation which had been set aside for the purpose of promoting unity among the godly and one of the major themes of his sermon was the need for Presbyterians and Independents to resolve their differences over the issue of church government. While acknowledging that there were extremists on both sides he suggested that it ought to be possible for the sober Independent and the moderate Presbyterian to join together in a happy union so that the Church of England could become a glorious church without any persecuting or banishing. In seeking to work out an accommodation it was most desirable that 'Confusion (that many people fear by Independency) might be prevented' and that 'the Severity that some others fear, by their rigour of Presbytery, might be hindred.' Since 1640 there had been wonderful developments in which all the godly could rejoice: 'Your Common Prayer book is gone, and your ceremonies and Episcopacy hath its deadly blow.' If the ordinance for the punishment of ignorant and scandalous persons was passed it would be time to dispense with the word 'Independency' for 'we must be all dependent, an absolute Independency is no where to be allowed; but call it Classical and Congregational.' Every congregation should have the power to exclude the scandalous and ignorant from the sacrament of the Lord's Supper: this was what both the Independents and the Presbyterians wanted. As a first step it was essential to put an end to the war of words which was raging 'that if it were possible, they that are like to dwell in one Heaven hereafter might now dwell in one England, and might serve God together and joyntly advance Jesus Christ together in the purity of his Ordinances, and live in sweet peace and harmony together.'[1]

That same year Parliament authorized the publication of a tract entitled *Noah's Dove, or An Epistle of Peace* which also represented an attempt to mediate in the quarrel between the Presbyterians and the Independents. Its author was Sir James Harrington, a colonel of the Westminster trained bands, whose father's religious sympathies may be judged by the fact that he was named as one of the tryers who were to be responsible for the selection of elders within the Province of London.[2] Harrington believed that the advent of the millennium was now imminent and was dismayed that at this juncture the godly were so torn apart by internal dissensions. 'O be cautious that noveltie eclipse not truth,' he exhorted, 'since the last dayes foretold and fore-warned of by our Saviour are at hand, wherein iniquity abounds and the love of many waxes cold.' The whole world seemed to be on fire before its time. Jesus had said that this would be the time when many false Christs and prophets would arise. 'Let us not then be carried about with every wind of Doctrine but hold fast the Gospell delivered to us by Christ and his Apostles, in the unity of the spirit and the bond of peace.' Between the Presbyterians and the Independents there was already a considerable measure of agreement. As he saw it, they both accepted that those who were members of their churches and (excepting women) had the right to vote 'shall not only be free from just scandall, that is Prophannesse and the impenitent practise of any knowne sinne, but be indued with a sufficiencie of knowledge.' The main point of disagreement appeared to be over the question of where the 'covering power' or final authority should be vested. In his view the Presbyterians put too much emphasis on the role of the general assembly while the Independents, for their part, went too far in preferring the judgement of the individual congregation 'before the ioynt votes of all the refined Christian Churches of the Kingdome'. By contemporary standards the compromise solution which Harrington offered was surprisingly democratic. After the general assembly had initially considered an appeal arising from a local disagreement it should adjourn the case for three months. Each congregation should then vote on the issue and send up the numbers of those affirming and dissenting and at the next session of the general assembly the matter should be decided 'by the major vote, both of Churches and Members'.[3]

Such appeals for unity stood little chance of success in a situation which was charged with mutual hostility and suspicion. In a polemical work which was published towards the end of 1645 William Prynne declared that although the Independents proclaimed liberty of conscience for all sects and religions they had 'so harsh an opinion of Presbyterians and all others who submit not to their Independent Modell that they esteem them no better then Heathens, Infidels, unbelievers.'[4] In the Commons, however, there were relatively few MPs who held doctrinaire views on the issue of church government and since the dominant mood was a determination to restrict the power of the clergy it was a diluted form of Presbyterianism which emerged as the system which was the least objectionable to a majority of MPs. In a letter written on 15 January 1646 Robert Baillie identified three groups in Parliament which were holding up the establishment of an authentic Presbyterian system. The Independents, 'albeit their number in the Parliament be very small, yet being prime men, active and diligent', were seeking 'to retard all till they be first secured of a toleration for their separate congregations.' Then there were the lawyers who believed all church government to be part of the civil and parliamentary power (and here Baillie was no doubt thinking of such MPs as John Selden and Bulstrode Whitelocke and perhaps Sir Simonds D'Ewes). Finally, there was 'a third partie of worldlie profane men who are extremelie affrighted to come under the yoke of ecclesiastick discipline.' These groups, he observed, made up at least two-thirds of the total membership of Parliament.[5]

From the autumn of 1645 onwards parliamentary elections were held to fill the vacancies caused by the deaths of members since the outbreak of the Civil War and the 'disabling' of royalist MPs. On 13 October Sir Robert Honywood was writing that the House was daily admitting new members, most of them of the 'severer strain'.[6] These recruiter MPs, who numbered nearly 150 by the spring of 1646, included many representatives of the wealthier Puritan gentry, among them Sir Thomas Barnardiston, Sir Matthew Boynton, Sir John Barrington, Sir Thomas Trenchard, Brampton Gurdon, John Hutchinson, John Swinfen, Richard Norton, Hugh Boscawen, John Harrington, William Strode of Somerset and Edmund Ludlow. Harrington, who was returned as one of the knights of the shire for Somerset, was probably reflecting the attitude of a significant number of the recruiter MPs when he declared in his journal that

> members of Parliament God hath. . . . honored, advanced and called to perform services unto himself of greatest eminency and highest concernment. . . . We are called of God to be his instruments for the greatest, the more excellent and most blessed services unto him to free his Church and people from al wickednes in life and error in iudgment and to guide and order them into all truth and holines according to the glorious example of our Lord Jesus himself.[7]

Clarendon relates that the recruiter elections led to the admission of many Independent officers and gentlemen of the several counties 'who were transported with new fancies in religion and were called by a new name *Fanatics*'. The Commons considered Sir Thomas Fairfax to be 'a perfect Presbyterian in his judgment' but some New Model officers who were elected, among them Henry Ireton, Edmund Ludlow, Thomas Harrison and Charles Fleetwood, were undeniably Independents in a religious sense.[8] Other recruiter MPs who could be counted upon to support the cause of Independency included Sir Matthew Boynton who had been involved in the Saybrook enterprise; Richard Norton whose second wife was a daughter of William Viscount Saye and Sele; and Rowland Wilson who was a member of George Cokayne's gathered congregation and a close friend of Bulstrode Whitelocke.[9] As governor of Nottingham John Hutchinson 'favour'd and protected godly men that were sober, although they seperated from the publick Assemblies' and invited Independent divines to preach in his house. This indulgent attitude aroused the fury of ministers of the Presbyterian persuasion and despite the fact that the Hutchinsons continued to attend their services they were 'revil'd by them and call'd fanatick and Anabaptists, and often glanc'd at in their publick sermons'. Since Hutchinson could not stomach the 'mallitious zeale and imposing spiritt' of the Presbyterians he soon came to be regarded as an adherent of the Independent faction. His wife, however, was at pains to stress that he belonged to no particular faction as he preferred to follow the dictates of his own conscience: 'he never was any man's Sectary, either in religious or civill matters, farther than he apprehended them to follow the rules of religion, honor, and vertue.'[10]

In the third part of *Gangraena*, which was published towards the end of 1646, Thomas Edwards informed his readers that he had heard many worthy MPs testify that 'the greatest number of Members of the House by farre are no Sectaries, and though some are crept in among them yet the body of the House are neither Independents, Anabaptists, Antinomians nor such like.'[11] The number of recruiter MPs who are readily identifiable as religious Independents is not particularly large. Among the rest there were some who had a clear preference for at least a moderate form of Presbyterianism. It is apparent from his parliamentary journal that John Harrington had Presbyterian sympathies, though he might well have taken exception to Anthony Wood's description of him as 'a canting and prophetical Presbyterian'. Another Somerset MP, William Strode, was to admit in 1661, when he was being interrogated, that he was a Presbyterian and had been 'ever since I knew what religion was.'[12] John Swinfen, who was the heir to one of the largest estates in Staffordshire, was regarded as 'a strict Presbyterian'. Following his election in the autumn of 1645 Sir William

Brereton commended him as a 'very Choyce able man whoe wilbe very serviceable unto the kingdome'.[13] Two sons of Sir Robert Harley joined him in the Commons. The eldest son, Edward, would later be described by Richard Baxter as 'a sober and truly religious Man, the worthy son of a most pious father'. In 1656 he was told by his brother Robert that there were some in Herefordshire who considered him to be a rigid Presbyterian 'and soe noe good to be expected from one whoe hath not moderation'.[14]

In practice the influx of new members had no material impact on the general attitude of the Commons in the matter of ecclesiastical government. Most MPs wanted a permanent settlement which would ensure the continued existence of a national Church but few were in favour of the kind of system which would have satisfied the aspirations of the Presbyterian majority in the Westminster Assembly.

On 16 February 1646 the Commons received a petition from the Assembly which called for the speedy establishment of classical presbyteries. Two days later the Grand Committee for Religion considered a draft ordinance which laid down arrangements for the election of congregational elders throughout the kingdom but offered no satisfaction to the Assembly over the crucial matter of ecclesiastical discipline. In this latter respect the most significant change concerned the procedure for judging disciplinary cases falling outside the authority of the presbyteries. In place of the standing committee of both Houses it was proposed that this function should be performed by parliamentary commissioners in each of the new Provinces. The draft ordinance met with little opposition in the Commons and on 7 March it was taken up to the Lords by Denzil Holles, 'the whole house accompanying him' with the exception of the Speaker.[15] By this time, however, the Assembly and the Scottish commissioners were becoming thoroughly alarmed. On 6 March Robert Baillie was writing that it was the intention to establish a court of civil commissioners in every county. This, he claimed, was 'a trick of the Independents' invention of purpose to enervat and disgrace all our government, in which they have been assisted by the lawyers and the Erastian partie.'[16] Whether or not the Independents actually put forward the idea they certainly believed that the decentralization of parliamentary jurisdiction in the ecclesiastical field would work to their advantage in view of the considerable support which they enjoyed in the country at large.

On 12 March Richard Norton, who had recently been elected for Hampshire, wrote in a letter to one of his associates there that 'we are now strugling for life about the presbitery. The devines dare not call it *iure divino* and yet we have now in our house agreed it *jure humano*.' At the request of the Presbyterian ministers the City of London had sent the Lords a petition which was critical of the draft ordinance and in particular of 'that clause which we most insist upon to hold forth to the world that we hold not the government *iure divino*'. As a result it had been decided that a committee consisting of members of both Houses should meet the Common Council of London to discuss the petition. Clearly exasperated by the conduct of the Presbyterian divines, Norton went on to say that

> we may by this see the good nature of our brethren who would enforce all to submitt to the presbitery as they would have it established and yet now in one particular it doth not like them they pleade conscience; I hope this will produce a good effect in the Citty, and a little dash the wicked designes of some who I feare doe endeavor to devide us.[17]

In defiance of the external pressures Parliament declined to suspend action on the ordinance and on 14 March it was approved without any change of substance. Some provisions suggested that there was a new determination on the part of the Commons to bring the Presbyterian system into operation: in particular, it was stipulated that elders were to be elected by the congregations of the parish churches and that the classical assemblies were to meet regularly once a month. But those who wanted a thoroughgoing form of Presbyterianism were bitterly disappointed. The English, lamented Baillie, seemed inclined 'to have libertie for all religions' and 'but a lame Erastian Presbyterie'.[18] In the preamble to the ordinance it was boldly declared that one of the basic objects was 'the preventing of an indefinite and unlimited power in the Eldership'. Scandalous offences beyond the prescribed limits were to be judged by lay commissioners, acting on behalf of Parliament, in the various Provinces. In what appears to have been an attempt to pacify the Assembly by debarring sectaries from serving in this capacity it was made clear that Parliament would restrict its choice to 'men of good understanding in matters of Religion, sound in the faith, prudent, discreet, grave, and of unblameable conversation, and such as do usually receive the Sacrament of the Lord's Supper as Members of a Presbyterial congregation'.[19] The Presbyterian divines in the Assembly, however, could not be appeased so easily and on 23 March they presented both Houses with a petition in which, as noted by Lawrence Whitaker, they excused themselves that 'they could not act According to the Ordinance lately passed'. Very many scandalous sins which were frequently committed had been excluded from the scope of the disciplinary powers assigned to the presbyteries; and in their view the employment of commissioners for dealing with such offences was contrary to the way of government which Christ had appointed in his Church and at variance with the terms of the Solemn League and Covenant. The power of judging in cases not enumerated in the ordinance which had been issued belonged to the elderships 'by divine Right, and by the Will and Appointment of Christ'.[20]

The petition served notice on Parliament that it could not expect any co-operation from the Presbyterian clergy unless it was prepared to be more forthcoming over the issue of ecclesiastical discipline. 'The ministers and elders', wrote Baillie, 'are not willing to sett up and begin any action till they have a law for some power to perform; all former ordinances have been so intollerablie defective that they could not be accepted.'[21] Predictably, the petition caused a considerable stir in the Commons where it was debated at length. John Harrington records that when it was initially discussed on 1 April many MPs were of the opinion that the Presbyterian divines of the Assembly 'had greatly broken the priviledges of Parliament' and that fears were expressed that if concessions were made there would be no end to their encroaching on the civil power. Others laid stress on their learning and piety and the service which they had previously rendered Parliament and argued that they ought not to be admonished since all subjects 'may petition and shew their reasons why freely'.[22] On his copy of the petition Sir Robert Harley noted down some of the comments made by his fellow MPs, including the following:

> presbiters are evil persons
> No warrant from Christ for Commissioners
> The civill magistrate cannot make Gospel nor Sacraments
> nor adminster them Contrary to their duty and the
> priviledg of Parliament
> not to indure it that they should tell us any thing is
> against the word of God.[23]

On 11 April the Commons decided that the petition was a breach of privilege but only by the narrow margin of 88 votes to 76. The fact that the tellers on this occasion were Sir Arthur Hesilrige and Sir John Evelyn of Wiltshire for the ayes and Denzil Holles and Sir Philip Stapleton for the noes suggests that the issue had acquired strong political overtones.[24] On 16 April the House appointed a committee with the dual function of drawing up particulars of the breach of privilege and preparing a list of questions to be addressed to the Assembly about its concept of divine right. Significantly, specific responsibility for the latter task was allocated to Sir Arthur Hesilrige who was one of a number of Independent MPs on the committee. Subsequently, on 22 April, the Commons approved a list of nine questions which called for a detailed exposition of the scriptural justification for the Assembly's claims. During the course of the debate a counter-attack was staged and John Harrington summarized the outcome in terms which indicate that most MPs regarded Independency no more favourably than rigid Presbyterianism:

> The independents and not only the presbiterians to set down their government and prove it by scripture to be *iure devino*. Much ioy that the independents (*ut spes est*) be bolted out of their burrows.

In the sixth question the Assembly was asked whether the power of judging notorious and scandalous sins belonged by divine right to the congregational eldership or presbytery or 'any other Eldership, Congregation, or Persons'. In addition, the stipulation was made that every minister of the Assembly who was present when any of these questions was debated should subcribe his name to the answer forwarded to the Commons and state whether he agreed or disagreed with it. Since, however, the dissenting brethren had virtually withdrawn from the Assembly there was little prospect that this Presbyterian tactic would succeed.[25]

On 30 April a committee of MPs went along to the Assembly to inform the divines that their petition had been adjudged a breach of privilege and to communicate the list of questions to them. Sir John Evelyn of Wiltshire spoke first and told them that the House had concluded that there were some features of the petition which struck at the foundation and roots of the privileges of Parliament. 'Do not think', he declared, 'that Parliament is unwilling to submit their yoke to Jesus Christ; his yoke is easy.' But if it was 'a galling, vexing yoke' it could not be his and they would not bear it. He was followed by Nathaniel Fiennes, a zealous Independent, who harangued his audience, and Samuel Browne, a Puritan lawyer, who cited earlier breach of privilege cases. Sir Benjamin Rudyerd emphasized that the Commons expected its questions to be answered with precise scriptural quotations and not with far-fetched arguments. 'Decency and order', he maintained, 'are variable and therefore cannot be *jure divino*; discipline is but the hedge.' It was often said that the divines of the Assembly were pious and learned men but Parliament had to make laws for all sorts of men. As to the question of compliance with the terms of the Covenant he was satisfied that Parliament had done nothing which conflicted with the Word of God; nor were all the Reformed Churches agreed on every point. And he went on

The civil magistrate is a church officer in every Christian commonwealth. . . . In Scotland nobility and gentry live commonly in the country, and so the clergy are moderated as by a scattered Parliament.

In the event the Commons never received any answers to its questions.[26]

The Independent MPs were anxious to prolong the quarrel between Parliament and the Assembly, not least because they saw this as a means of further delaying the implementation of the ecclesiastical settlement which had been so laboriously worked out. Among other sections of the Commons, however, there was a growing feeling that some conciliatory gesture was necessary in order to rebuild relations with the Assembly and secure the co-operation of the Presbyterian divines in establishing an ordered form of church government. On 21 May the Commons agreed, by 110 votes to 99, that the plan to use parliamentary commissioners for the judging of scandalous offences should be further considered. With Denzil Holles and Sir William Lewis acting as tellers for the ayes and Sir Arthur Hesilrige and Sir John Evelyn as tellers for the noes, it was another occasion when political as well as religious differences played their part. The following day Samuel Browne offered the Commons an 'expedient' which involved the substitution of a standing committee of both Houses for the parliamentary commissioners; and after a lengthy debate the House decided that it should be incorporated into an ordinance.[27]

The ordinance was finally approved by the Commons on 3 June and promulgated two days later. Although the preamble records that the Lords and Commons had thought it appropriate to make further additions to the scandalous offences previously enumerated the body of the ordinance contains no such provision. In relation to the actual content of the ordinance it was explained that the delay in nominating commissioners was due to the fact that 'by reason of the present Distractions' many of those considered suitable for this role 'are absent from their habitations, and so cannot doe the service therein, which otherwise they might doe'; and that in these circumstances it had been decided that the reserved powers should be exercised by a committee of both Houses. Essentially, Parliament was reverting to the centralized system which had been prescribed in the ordinance which had been published on 20 October 1645. In the new ordinance, however, the composition of the standing committee was no longer limited to those who were lay members of the Westminster Assembly; instead it named 34 peers and 151 MPs with the proviso that any nine of them would represent a quorum. By this means Parliament assigned responsibility for judging scandalous offences which fell outside the jurisdiction of the elderships to a mixture of Presbyterians, Independents, Erastians and others with no particularly strong views on the subject of church government. Nor was it apparently regarded as unusual that this body of moral guardians should include such MPs as Sir Peter Wentworth and Henry Marten whom Robert Baillie would certainly have admitted to his category of 'worldlie profane men'.[28]

While the dispute was raging over the distribution of power within the new ecclesiastical system there was growing concern in Presbyterian circles about the designs of the Independents and the activities of the sects both in London and the country at large. William Prynne, who was a thoroughgoing Presbyterian, claimed that most of the sectaries and Independents had entered into an agreement with the aim of defending and maintaining Independency 'even to blood'. Some MPs who had reluctantly subscribed to the Solemn League and Covenant 'have adventured to plead for an exception of this meer refractory party from it, which much encourageth them in their obstinate refusall of it.'[29] The attempts of the Independent divines to secure the patronage of the rich and powerful were remarked upon by Thomas Edwards in the first part of *Gangraena* which was published in February 1646:

> some of them besides their places in the Assembly, which they seldome attend (especially this last year), and their private gathered Churches have divers Lectures and places, besides their hanging upon great men, to preach before them to ingratiate themselves, and getting to preach at White-hall, St James, Westminster, and other eminent places, where the great ones, Earls, Lords and the Grandees of the time resort.[30]

On 26 May the Common Council of London submitted a remonstrance in which it was alleged that divers sects were springing up in the capital and that some Lords and MPs were granting protections. The Council, notes Bulstrode White-locke, proposed that there should be a 'strict course for suppressing all private and seperate Congregations' and that 'all Anabaptists, Heretiques, Sectaryes &c as conforme not to the publique Discipline may be declared and proceeded against.'[31] The following day a deputation of ministers from Suffolk and Essex presented the Commons with a petition which stressed the need for a speedy settlement of religion and was assured by the Speaker that the matter was receiving urgent attention. The delivery of this petition appears to have reminded the House that as long ago as September 1645 the Speaker had written to the parliamentary committees in the various counties about the arrangements for establishing classical presbyteries; at all events it was agreed that early consideration should be given to the certificates which had been forwarded in reply to his letters.[32]

In the Commons there was continuing tension between the Independents and their opponents over matters of religion. On 27 August the House considered a draft ordinance which laid down arrangements for the ordination of ministers by the classical presbyteries and John Harrington recorded in his journal that Sir Arthur Hesilrige and Henry Marten opposed it 'a little'; that Sir Robert Harley and John Swinfen defended it; and that after it had been approved without amendment Francis Rous carried it up to the Lords.[33] More contentious was the projected ordinance for preventing the growth of heresies and blasphemies which it had been decided on 29 April should be prepared by a committee consisting of those MPs who were members of the Westminster Assembly. In part this measure was directed against the propagation of atheism (for which the death penalty was proposed) but it was also intended to be a weapon against the sectaries. The fact that it took four months to produce an initial draft suggests that the MPs responsible for its preparation, among them Sir Robert Harley, Sir Gilbert Gerard, Sir Henry Vane the younger, Sir Arthur Hesilrige and Bulstrode Whitelocke, found it difficult to reach agreement. Whitelocke tells us that those of the Presbyterian judgment were very violent and severe; and that he displeased them by arguing that the meaning of such words as 'blasphemy' and 'heresy' was far from clear.[34] When the draft ordinance was finally ready it was first discussed by the House on 2 September. John Harrington writes that it was opposed by Henry Marten (who as an atheist was hardly a disinterested party), Cornelius Holland and Sir Arthur Hesilrige but was nevertheless given a first and second reading and referred to a committee of the whole House (which in fact was Lawrence Whitaker's Grand Committee for Religion). On 16 September there was a lengthy debate in the Grand Committee over the question of whether the draft ordinance should be considered piecemeal or whether it should be shelved until the Assembly submitted proposals for a Confession of Faith. According to Harrington many MPs favoured the latter course but he took a different view, arguing that 'our charge was by making lawes and causing them to be executed to procure all men to perform the duty of Christians, that is to partake of the offices of our Saviour.' As chairman of the Somerset quarter sessions before the time of the Civil War he had been at pains to impress on his colleagues that the magistrate had a key role to play in the promotion of godliness and on this occasion he reiterated the point, emphasizing that there was a need to punish such great offences as heresy.[35] In the end it was agreed that the draft ordinance should be processed on a piecemeal basis rather than laid aside but progress continued to be painfully slow. When an ordinance was eventually published in February 1647 it was completely devoid of any penal clauses. Parliament had thought it appropriate, it was announced, 'to set forth this our deepe sense of the great dishonour of God, and perillous condition that this Kingdome is in, through the abominable blasphemies and damnable heresies vented and spread abroad therein, tending to the subversion of the Faith, contempt of the Ministry and Ordinance of Jesus Christ.' What followed, however, was merely a declaration that Wednesday 10 March was to be set apart as a day of public humiliation when God's direction and assistance would be sought for 'the suppression and preventing the same'.[36]

ELEVEN

Religion in the Provinces

AT Westminster the process of establishing a new form of church government was interminably slow but at the parish level it was generally a time of change and turmoil. In September 1641 an order had been approved for the removal of communion tables from the east end of churches, the pulling down of altar rails and the destruction of crucifixes, scandalous pictures, candlesticks and other idolatrous objects. To a large extent, however, this order had proved to be an empty gesture; in practice it appears to have been rigorously enforced only in parishes where Puritan magistrates could exert some influence.[1] On 24 April 1643 the Commons appointed a committee with power to demolish monuments of superstition and idolatry in Westminster Abbey and any other church or chapel in London. The committee included Sir Gilbert Gerard, John Gurdon and, later on, Sir John Dryden but the dominant figure was Sir Robert Harley who became its chairman. Early in May it was reported that the committee had already begun work in Westminster Abbey and St Margaret's church adjoining it and that it was not sparing the tombs of kings, queens, princes and other noble personages.[2] An ordinance which was promulgated on 26 August 1643 incorporated most of the provisions of the earlier order. On this occasion, however, it was felt prudent to include a saving clause aimed at safeguarding any image,

135

picture or coat of arms which formed part of the monument to a king, prince, nobleman or other dead person 'which hath not been commonly reputed or taken for a saint'.[3]

Before long this ordinance was superseded by a new version which was more comprehensive in scope. At a meeting of his committee on 11 March 1644 Sir Robert Harley noted in a memorandum that when reporting to the House it would be necessary to cover such points as the removal of organs from churches and the destruction or defacing of copes, surplices, altar cloths, superstitious vestments and plate 'wheron any cross, crucifixe or picture of any of the persons of the Trinity or of any that is engraven'. These requirements were duly embodied in a draft ordinance which received its first and second reading on 27 April. Sir Simonds D'Ewes records in his parliamentary journal that in the short debate which took place he expressed the hope (looking at Harley who had presented the ordinance) that there should be no question of defacing any crosses which appeared in coats of arms. He also states, with obvious satisfaction, that he was the first to be named as a member of the committee which was made responsible for processing the ordinance. Predictably, Sir Robert was a fellow member and others who were nominated included Sir John Wray, Sir Benjamin Rudyerd, Sir Henry Vane the younger, Sir Anthony Irby, Sir William Strickland and John Crewe. On 9 May Harley carried the ordinance up to the Lords where it was quickly approved. Like the earlier ordinance it provided for the exemption of secular monuments, many of which had been erected by the nobility and gentry since the accession of Elizabeth.[4]

While the Civil War was raging Harley was conducting a rather different kind of campaign. Among his private papers there are numerous receipts for payments made to workmen for services which they had performed on behalf of his committee in Westminster Abbey and the church of St Margaret's, the chapels in the royal palaces of Whitehall, Greenwich and Hampton Court, and the cathedral at Canterbury. During the years 1644 to 1646 altars and stained glass windows were taken down; wall paintings were obliterated and statues removed; and organs (which D'Ewes described as producing 'unreasonable sounds') were completely dismantled. In June 1644 a royalist newspaper carried a report that Sir Robert, 'who sits in the Chaire of Reformation, having already so reformed the Church of Westminster. . . . that it was made unfit for the service of God, betooke himselfe to the Reforming of His Majesties palace of White-hall and made it as unfit for the use of the King.' Ironically, the royalists had destroyed the church at Brampton Bryan when besieging his Herefordshire mansion in 1643.[5]

In the provinces the most severe outbreaks of iconoclasm were generally the work either of parliamentarian troops or officially appointed visitors of churches. As the colonel of a regiment Sir William Springett exhorted his soldiers to despoil all idolatrous pictures and crosses. When searching the houses of Catholics 'he destroyed all their crucifixes, reserving not one of them for its comeliness or costly workmanship'.[6] In the royalist press there were frequent allegations that parliamentarian forces were conducting themselves with great barbarity in the name of religion. During the summer of 1644 Sir William Waller and Sir Arthur Hesilrige were both castigated on this account. In Berkshire, it was related, Waller was engaged in a great and weighty work of reformation for

> having fleshed his Souldiers in the bloud and slaughter of the Crosse at Abingdon and reformed the Churches there of their Glasse and Ornaments he either would not or could not hold them from any Act of sacrilegious spoyle and rapine which ignorance and zealous Brownisme could excite them too.

Hesilrige, it was claimed, had pillaged the house of a Berkshire minister and cut his books to pieces. He was so perfect an enemy to the liturgy of the Church of England that 'with his owne hand he tore out certaine prayers'.[7] The most notorious of the parliamentary visitors was William Dowsing who in December 1643 received a letter of appointment from the Earl of Manchester in his capacity as commander-in-chief of the forces of the Eastern Association. The letter recited that in the churches of this region there still remained many crosses, crucifixes and other superstitious images and pictures and empowered Dowsing to put the ordinance of 26 August 1643 in execution. In the course of 1644 he and his deputies carried out a visitation of the Suffolk churches which had a very different purpose from the Laudian visitations. To judge from the evidence of his journal Dowsing refrained from inspecting the church at Kedington where Sir Nathaniel Barnardiston was the squire and patron and Samuel Fairclough the minister. On the other hand, he visited Assington where the patron was John Gurdon, a member of Harley's committee, and found much that was objectionable, noting that 'We brake down 40 Pictures,[8] one of God the Father, and the other very super-stitious; and gave order to levell the Chancel; and to take a Cross off the Steeple.' In contrast, the church at Rishangles, which was under the patronage of Sir Harbottle Grimston, may have been something of a disappointment to him as he records that there was 'Nothing but a Step. The Pictures were broke before.'[9]

Some Puritan patrons may have had reservations about the activities of such men as Dowsing but would certainly have acknowledged that the extirpation of idolatry was a necessary objective. For most Puritans, however, the paramount need was for the planting of godly preaching ministers in every parish. A key instrument for this purpose was the Committee for Plundered Ministers which was established by the Commons on 31 December 1642. Formally, the committee's primary concern was the relief of 'godly and well affected' divines who had suffered at the hands of the royalists; in practice it was soon heavily involved in the sequestration of church livings with the result that it came to be known in royalist circles as the Committee for Plundering Ministers. The original members of the committee included Sir Gilbert Gerard, Sir William Armyne, Sir John Holland and Richard Knightley. In January 1643 Sir Robert Harley became a member and in the course of time many other wealthy Puritan MPs were added to the committee. Essentially it was a body of godly patrons, most of them hostile to Independency, who had assumed some of the functions of episcopal government.[10]

Sir Simonds D'Ewes who, like Whitelocke, never became a member of the committee, had considerable misgivings about the way it which it treated ministers who found themselves involved in sequestration proceedings. On 22 August 1643 the chairman, John White, sought the agreement of the Commons to six draft orders for the ejection of ministers beneficed in London and Hertfordshire and their replacement by others who were regarded as godly men, among them Thomas Coleman who was one of Sir John Wray's ministers and John Conant who was then a fellow of Exeter College, Oxford. All these orders were approved, writes D'Ewes, 'although many Learned men were put out of theire places, and others of meane parts put in theire roomes'. He himself voted against them, partly because some of the ministers faced with sequestration had never had an opportunity to defend themselves but mainly because he felt that the welfare of the wives and children had received too little attention.[11]

In September 1643 Parliament empowered the county committees to examine witnesses in cases where ministers were alleged to be scandalous in life or doctrine or to have deserted their churches and joined the royalists, though this was with the proviso that the final decision would rest with the Committee for Plundered Ministers. Some of the local committees were not slow to seize the opportunity which this presented. According to a minister who was writing from first-hand experience the Northamptonshire committee secured the removal of many of the clergy in that county and the assignment of their livings to 'vile, undeserving, poor Curates, poor Schoolmasters, poor Lecturers, poor Vicars, poor New Lights'. Those members of the committee whom he described as particularly active included Sir Gilbert Pickering who was 'the principal Agent in casting out most of the Learned Clergy'; Sir John Dryden who was 'very furious against the Clergy'; and Zouch Tate who was appointed to the Committee for Plundered Ministers in November 1644.[12]

During the course of 1644 a series of ordinances which together covered half the counties of England authorized local military commanders or committees to sequester church livings where this was adjudged to be necessary and to nominate new ministers in place of the ejected clergy.[13] By virtue of an ordinance which was promulgated on 22 January the Earl of Manchester issued warrants for the establishment of committees in the eastern counties which were to initiate proceedings and submit recommendations for his endorsement. In a covering letter addressed to his nominees he emphasized that there was a need to put in orthodox and holy men in every parish and that if a general reformation failed to materialize in their particular county the blame would undoubtedly be laid on them. In the ordinance it was stipulated that the new committees should consist of men whom Parliament had previously appointed as deputy lieutenants or members of the county committees. Among those named in the warrants were Sir Thomas Honywood and Sir Richard Everard for Essex and Sir Edmund Bacon, Sir William Spring, Sir William Soame, Sir John Wentworth, Maurice Barrow and Brampton Gurdon for Suffolk. Serving MPs appear to have been deliberately ruled out on the grounds that they were normally resident in London.[14]

Neither Sir Edmund Bacon nor Sir John Wentworth seems to have played any part in the ensuing purge of the parish clergy. Others such as Sir William Spring and Brampton Gurdon displayed more enthusiasm. In April 1645 Gurdon observed in a letter to Governor Winthrop that 'The distracted times occasions of much beusines to them that are in plas to reforme. I thancke God who assists me in it.'[15]

Some of the accusations made against Suffolk clergymen offer a tantalizing glimpse of the political and religious tensions within the county. One minister was reported to have remarked in 1640 when Sir Nathaniel Barnardiston and Sir Philip Parker had been returned as knights of the shire that 'none did chuse them but leathercoats, scarecrows and squirell hunters, or words to the like effect'; and another to have ridiculed Sir Nathaniel, declaring that all he ever said was 'Sirs, shut the Doors lest we get cold.'[16] There were also allegations that Samuel Fairclough and other godly ministers had been described as rebels and men who 'did not teach the written word of god'. Nicholas Coleman of Preston, it was claimed, had commented that Fairclough preached false doctrine and on hearing that John Smith, the Puritan rector of Cockfield, 'did stirre upp and quicken his parishioners to take the Covenant. . . . made answer that the said Mr Smith would observe anythinge, and would turne as the wind and wethercocke.' Since Smith enjoyed the patronage of Sir William Spring it is perhaps not surprising that Coleman was deprived of his living.[17]

Among the parish clergy who forfeited their livings very few had been under the patronage of Puritan landowners. One of Maurice Barrow's ministers, Samuel Scrivener of Westhorpe, found himself ejected after being accused of bowing towards the altar, adultery, drunkenness and preaching against 'this present defensive war'. Scrivener had been presented to the living after the previous incumbent, Robert Stansby, had been ejected by Bishop Wren for nonconformity and he may conceivably have been forced on the patron.[18] Although Sir Simonds D'Ewes had been at loggerheads with Richard Davenport, his minister at Stowlangtoft, he nevertheless intervened on his behalf when some of the inhabitants of the parish complained about him to the Suffolk parliamentary committee. In July 1643 Davenport informed D'Ewes that the committee had criticized him 'for tolleratinge my unwarrantable dealings with yourselfe'. One of Davenport's main adversaries had blasted the reputation of his brother Richard (who had died in arms for the king) with 'dishonourable and base language' and had also spoken disparagingly of his late father who had been 'his best Maister and Maker'. Sir William Spring, he went on, was acting as chieftain of the hostile faction and had forwarded the filthy and devilish articles which had been drawn up to the Committee for Plundered Ministers before he could put in his answer. Sir Simonds's tenants were running to Pakenham Hall (the seat of the Spring family) 'as to an oracle, I pray god they be not false to you as they have bene to me'. Not long afterwards Davenport resigned the living.[19]

As time went on it became the practice to consult the people of the parish about the choice of a new minister, though this was subject to major safeguards. In the instructions which the Earl of Manchester issued to his nominees in the eastern counties he stipulated that the parishioners must be asked to choose a suitable minister to take over a sequestered living. The candidate should then bring the Earl a testimonial from the best affected gentry and ministers of the county which provided evidence of his personal qualities. Special care should be taken, he stressed, to ensure that no Anabaptists or Antinomians were nominated but only such as were orthodox in their opinions and likely to be acceptable to the Westminster Assembly.[20] In July 1643 the Commons had decided that the Committee for Plundered Ministers should not put any minister into a parsonage or benefice unless the Westminster Assembly confirmed that he was properly qualified; and in April 1645 it was further agreed that only ordained ministers should be allowed to preach in churches and other public places.[21] When Lady Dorothy Osborne, the wife of a Bedfordshire royalist, sought to present a minister to the living of Haynes Sir Samuel Luke told her that she must be aware that it was the intention of the Westminster Assembly 'to putt the choice in the maiority of voyces whereunto both your Ladyship and myselfe must submitt our inheritances for the publique good'. Later he informed her that the whole parish had made choice of a minister who was highly regarded by the Westminster Assembly and that he had accordingly agreed to sponsor a petition which sought parliamentary approval for his appointment. And for good measure he added that 'I shall ever beleeve that a single person may sooner erre in his iudgment than a whole parrish.'[22]

Since very few of the Puritan gentry sided with the king they were generally able to exercise their patronage rights when the need arose. Parliament was indeed anxious to protect the rights of godly patrons[23] and when nominations were submitted for its endorsement this process was little more than a formality. When one of his livings fell vacant a Puritan squire usually nominated a university graduate who had been ordained either before the collapse of episcopal government or under the arrangements prescribed by Parliament.[24] Some of these ministers came direct from the universities; others had already acquired experience as beneficed clergymen, curates or lecturers. During the course of the first Civil War two of Sir William Armyne's Lincolnshire ministers, John Weld of Pickworth and Matthew Lawrence of Silk Willoughby, removed to Suffolk where there was much less danger of royalist incursions. As their successors Sir William chose two Cambridge graduates, Michael Drake and Laurence Sarson. On 5 August 1647 the Commons agreed that Sarson (who was a fellow of Emmanuel College) should be instituted to the rectory of Silk Willoughby, noting that he had already been presented by the lawful patron. Although Sir William was sympathetically inclined towards Independency it is noteworthy that at least three of his ministers, Weld, Lawrence and Drake, became members of classical presbyteries while Thomas Cawton, who had served as the family chaplain during the 1630s, helped to win over the English congregation at Rotterdam to the Presbyterian discipline. On the other hand, Seth Wood of Lenton, whom Sir William had presented in 1639, would eventually be named in a list of Congregational ministers who were active in London.[25] In some cases there is evidence that in selecting a new minister a Puritan patron was heavily influenced by the wishes of the inhabitants of the parish. In 1644 Sir Simonds D'Ewes offered the rectory of Lavenham to William Gurnall, a curate or lecturer at Sudbury who, in the course of correspondence, described him as a champion of public liberty and a defender of religion. Gurnall, we are told, was completely unknown to D'Ewes who put him into the living at the request of the parish.[26]

If the Presbyterian system which had been so painfully worked out at Westminster was to be anything more than a paper project the full participation of the parish clergy would obviously be needed, but in many counties there were relatively few ministers of the Word. This deficiency was implicitly acknowledged by the Commons in April 1646 when it was decided to set up a committee to consider how a preaching ministry might be established throughout the kingdom.[27] The problem was especially acute in some of the more geographically remote counties where the king had drawn much of his support. In April 1647 Sir John Bourchier, who was seated near York, begged Ferdinando Lord Fairfax to 'take into consideracion the greate wante of mayntenance for preaching ministers in this poore blynde Countrye', by which he meant Yorkshire, and expressed the hope that he would do what he could 'that the gospell maye florishe in thes parts'.[28] There were also fears that in some counties the activities of the Independents or more radical sectaries could help to frustrate the will of Parliament in the matter of ecclesiastical government. In a letter dispatched from Lancashire in October 1646 the writer reported that there were worrying developments in the neighbouring county of Cheshire:

> We have through the mercy of God a learned and active Clergy in our County, sound and Orthodox. . . . but Cheshire is miserably become a prey to the Sectaries; they have set up already two or three Independent Churches and are setting up two or three more.[29]

Fom other counties there were reports that Puritan clergymen were being harassed by parliamentary soldiers and put under pressure to share their pulpits with sectaries who sought to win over their parishioners. At Great Hampden in Buckinghamshire, where the Hampden family had its seat, the incumbent was faced with competition from an itinerant preacher who was said to have been a blacksmith before taking up arms for Parliament.[30]

When the Speaker of the Commons wrote to the county committees in September 1645 seeking their assistance over the setting up of classical presbyteries[31] this probably led to lengthy debates not only about the merits of the new form of church government but about what was actually intended. Although the Speaker's letters were accompanied by copies of the ordinance of 19 August[32] there was no indication of the functions and powers which were to be exercised by the various types of body for which it made provision. Among the papers of a member of the Hampshire committee there is a note which records that at a meeting on 19 November it was decided to establish four *classes* (described as *classes* of the committee) each of which was to sit for three weeks at a time. No ministers were included at this stage but it is possible (though the evidence is lacking) that one of the first tasks of these new bodies was to consider the choice of clerical members. Of the men whose names appear some like Sir William Waller and Sir William Lewis are known to have favoured the introduction of a Presbyterian system while others like Sir John Evelyn of Wiltshire (who had property in the county) and Richard Norton took a rather different view.[33] By May 1646 a number of certificates had been forwarded in response to the Speaker's letters but most of the county committees appear to have procrastinated, perhaps because they were sharply divided in their attitudes to Presbyterianism or confused by the disagreement between Parliament and the Westminster Assembly or faced with such problems as an acute shortage of godly ministers.[34]

In October 1646 Lancashire became the first county to secure parliamentary authority for the establishment of con-gregational and classical presbyteries. It was a county where there was considerable enthusiasm for Presbyterianism, both among the clergy and the laity; and indeed the decision was taken in response to a petition signed by many of the 'well affected' gentry, ministers, freeholders and other inhabitants of the county which called for the introduction of a uniform discipline and government and punishment of those who frequented conventicles. The Presbyterians, writes Adam Martindale, who was himself ordained as a Presbyterian minister, were 'busie. . . . to get their government settled all over the county, and that all separate congregations. . . . might be suppressed.' Among the lay leaders nominated for the classical presbyteries were such leading Puritan squires as Ralph Assheton of Middleton, his kinsman Sir Ralph Assheton of Whalley Abbey and Richard Shuttleworth of Gawthorpe. As early as January 1645 Ralph Assheton of Middleton had obtained leave from the Commons to bring in propositions for the 'better settlement' of the county and its ministers. In the main, however, it was the clergy, men like Richard Heyricke, John Harrison and John Tilsley, who were in the forefront of the Presbyterian movement in Lancashire.[35]

In other counties the progress was more slow. In January 1647 Robert Baillie the Scottish commissioner was reporting that Parliament had passed at least four ordinances relating to church government,

> all prettie right so farr as concerns the constitution and erection of Generall Assemblies, Provinciall Synods, Presbyteries and Sessions, and the power of ordination. In the province of London and Lancashyre the bodies are sett up. That the like diligence is not used long agoe in all other places, it's the sottish negligence of the ministers and gentrie in the shyres more than the Parliament.[36]

Of the more Puritan counties Essex, Suffolk and Devon eventually adopted a system of congregational and classical presbyteries but there is no evidence that Presbyterianism ever took root in Buckinghamshire, Bedfordshire and Northamptonshire.[37]

When a list of nominees for the classical presbyteries was being compiled the inclusion of serving MPs and members of the county committee tended to be more or less automatic. Whatever their views on the issue of church government such men would generally have considered it appropriate and necessary that they should be nominated, not least since it seemed likely that the lay elders would have an important role to play in ecclesiastical matters at the local level. In view of this it is dangerous to assume that all those who were named as lay elders were necessarily committed Presbyterians; nor is it particularly surprising that some of them were men who have been described by modern historians as political Independents.[38]

Among those nominated as members of the classical presbyteries which were to be established in the East Anglian counties of Suffolk and Essex were all the leading Puritan gentry together with the ministers who enjoyed their patronage. For Suffolk the lay elders included Sir Nathaniel Barnard-

iston and his son Thomas, Sir Edmund Bacon, Sir Philip
Parker, Sir Simonds D'Ewes, Sir William Spring, Maurice
Barrow, Brampton Gurdon and his son John; and for Essex Sir
John Barrington, Sir William Masham, Sir Henry Mildmay, Sir
Harbottle Grimston and his son and namesake, Sir Richard
Everard and Sir Thomas Honywood.[39] Probably most of the
Puritan squires who were named had the same kind of attitude
as Sir Nathaniel Barnardiston and Sir Simonds D'Ewes who
were anxious that the activities of the sectaries should be
curbed and who regarded the Presbyterian system which had
been worked out as the most effective means of restoring order
and discipline. It is significant, for example, that when Sir
Edmund Bacon drew up his will in October 1648 he made
provision for an annual payment towards the cost of a
lectureship in a neighbouring market town 'soe long as the
Protestant Religion continueth that is nowe professed in the
Church of England'.[40] Although Sir Henry Mildmay champ-
ioned the cause of Independency in the Commons he also took
a close interest in the welfare of the parish clergy of his county.
His minister Humphrey Maddison, who officiated at his own
parish church at Wanstead, was certainly no Independent: not
only was he nominated as a clerical member of the same
classical presbytery but in 1648 he put his signature to a
Presbyterian manifesto.[41]

Although the Suffolk and Essex lists had originally been
prepared in November 1645 it was to be some considerable
time before any material developments took place. This
particularly disturbed the Puritan clergy of the two counties. In
the first part of *Gangraena*, which was published in February
1646, Thomas Edwards dismissed the allegation that was
sometimes levelled against Presbyterian ministers that they
'opposed the way of Independency, and stood for Presbytery,
because of great Livings'.[42] Nevertheless the fact remains that
there was an element of self-interest mixed in with the
genuinely held conviction that the sectaries were enemies of
truth and godliness. However radical they may once have
appeared the Puritan clergy, ordained and beneficed and
officiating in accordance with the Directory of Worship, had

147

now become the upholders of the established Church and as a general rule were highly antagonistic towards any interloping preacher who questioned their authority and sought to undermine the allegiance of their congregations. Edwards relates that he had been told by a learned and godly minister in Essex that the magistracy there felt unable to take any action against the leading sectaries

> for they say they have hunted these out of the country into their Dens in London, and imprisoned some, and they are released and sent like decoy Ducks into the country to fetch in more; so that they go in divers parts of Essex with the greatest confidence and insolencie that can be imagined.[43]

In May 1646 Parliament received a petition signed by ministers of both Suffolk and Essex which called for the establishment of a form of church government that was in accordance with the Word of God and the example of the best reformed Churches and for the suppression of 'schismatics, heretics, seducing teachers and soul-subverting books'.[44] It was not until March 1647, however, that the Essex committee forwarded proposals for the introduction of classical presbyteries. The joint Committee for the Judging of Scandal finally assented to these proposals on 21 January 1648 when the signatories of the authorizing order included the Earl of Warwick, who was the lord lieutenant of Essex and the patron of many livings there, Sir William Masham and Sir Martin Lumley, who had both been named as lay elders, and Sir Nathaniel Barnardiston.[45] The division of Suffolk into Presbyterian *classes* had already been sanctioned on 29 April 1647. Subsequently, on 18 February 1648, some additional names were approved by the joint Committee at a meeting which was attended, among others, by Sir Nathaniel Barnardiston, Zouch Tate and Francis Rous.[46]

The introduction of classical presbyteries in Surrey, for which parliamentary approval was obtained in February 1648, may have owed much to the influence of Sir Richard Onslow who viewed the sectaries with marked repugnance and was said to be 'totally guided' by Presbyterian ministers.[47] In

Somerset Sir John Horner was heavily involved, along with William Prynne, in the establishment of a Presbyterian system which was formally promulgated in March 1648. Besides Sir John the lay elders included John Harrington and William Strode who were both favourably inclined towards Presbyterianism and John Pyne whose sympathies lay more with Independency. In December 1648 Pyne was writing that Prynne was as much a firebrand as William Strode and Clement Walker (an arch-critic of the Independents) who had been elected as recruiter MPs for Somerset constituencies.[48] Although Sir Robert Harley was one of the leading advocates of Presbyterianism he clearly recognized that there was no possibility of introducing the system in Herefordshire. Instead he arranged for the establishment of six godly preachers (all of them orthodox in the Presbyterian sense) at Hereford, three in the cathedral and the rest in the parish churches. Yet even this proved to be a difficult undertaking and in July 1648 some of them were complaining that 'wee have toiled long with corrupt manners and perverse spirits'.[49]

TWELVE

The Growth of Faction

IN 1645 it was still possible to talk or write of the Presbyterians and Independents in terms which carried the implication that the disagreement between them was purely religious in character. Similarly, John Rushworth would later offer the view that the emergence of the Presbyterian and Independent parties was wholly attributable to the issue of church government: referring to the situation at the beginning of 1645 he relates that 'there were of the Army-Officers (especially since the coming in of the Scots) two apparent Parties, the first zealous for setting up Presbytery, the other (called Independents) endeavoured to decline that Establishment.'[1] On the other hand, Thomas Edwards declared in the second part of *Gangraena* that

> Independencie and Sectarisme in England is a meer Faction, a partie grown to this height upon particular interests, nourished and favoured all upon politike grounds and ends. Independencie now is no religious conscientious businesse but a politike State Faction, severing and dividing it selfe upon other private interests from the publike interests of this Church and State, and the interest of both Kingdoms, united by Covenant.

Many Independents, he claimed, had no knowledge or understanding of the principles of Independency. They included needy and decayed men who were hoping to advance their fortunes; ambitious and covetous men who were anxious to secure offices and places of profit for themselves; and persons of loose morals who had no wish to be subjected to a Presbyterian discipline. There was nothing, whether military, civil or ecclesiastical, which the Independents did not have designs on and in pursuing their ends they were prepared to 'discontent' the king, Parliament, 'our Brethren' of Scotland, the City of London, the Westminster Assembly, the godly ministry of the kingdom and particular worthy persons in the parliamentary forces and among the gentry. Indeed they were determined to carry all before them and 'in time to breake all that shall dare to appeare against them, or crosse their wayes'.[2]

Among the Puritan gentry there were differing views about the nature of the internal political divisions which became more pronounced as Parliament began to gain the upper hand in its struggle with the king. Bulstrode Whitelocke was markedly reluctant to use the terms 'Presbyterian' and 'Independent' in a political sense but he was well aware that there were factions in the Commons. In his autobiography he tells us that when he and Denzil Holles were accused by Lord Savile in July 1645 of committing acts of disloyalty they had the support of John Glyn, Sir Philip Stapleton, Sir William Lewis and many other noble gentlemen while the other party in the House sought their downfall. In general, those who came to their defence belonged to what he termed the Earl of Essex's party and what Clarendon called the Presbyterian party. Whitelocke also thought it worth recording that on 21 August, after they had both been exonerated, he dined with Oliver St John, Sir Arthur Hesilrige and 'others of that crue, who were very kinde to me'; and this prompted him to exhort his children to conduct themselves in public business in such a way that 'you may be esteemed by all parties, and believed (as it was truely of me) that you follow your own consciences and no factions.'[3] In the parliamentary journal of Sir Simonds D'Ewes there is no reference to a Presbyterian party as such but, on the other hand, he sometimes felt obliged to register his disapproval of

151

the Independents. In a later insertion under the date of 16 August 1643 he observed that when 'the Independent and hereticall' forces commanded by Sir Thomas Fairfax had overcome the royalist army and procured many of their own faction to be elected MPs they began to conceive hopes of carrying through their design of extirpating monarchy and changing the government of the realm. A religious work of his which appeared in 1645 under the title *The Primitive Practise for Preserving Truth* was primarily a historical survey written from a general Puritan standpoint rather than a contribution to the debate which was raging over the issue of church government. Sir Simonds, however, could not resist attacking the Anabaptists whom he described, with some passion, as 'the Devil's Master-engine in this latter age'.[4]

Lucy Hutchinson was in no doubt that the House of Commons contained both a Presbyterian and an Independent faction and that these had come into existence by the early part of 1645. In her view the leading figures of the Independent faction were William Pierrepont, Sir Henry Vane the younger, Cromwell, St John and 'some few other grandees, being men that excell'd in wisdome and utterance, and the rest believ'd to adhere to them only out of faction'. While acknowledging that there were self-seeking individuals in both parties she makes it clear that the Presbyterian faction did not figure high in her estimation. There were a number of reasons why she viewed it with disapproval. In the first place, her husband met with hostility from the Presbyterians, among them Sir Philip Stapleton and Sir Gilbert Gerard, when he was accused in 1645 of betraying his trust as governor of Nottingham. Secondly, she resented the attempts of the Presbyterians to impose a rigid uniformity in matters of religion at the expense of the sectaries with whom she and her husband were in sympathy. Finally, she regarded them as politically suspect. The Presbyterians, she writes, 'would obstruct any good rather those they envied and hated should have the glory of procuring it; the sad effects of which pride grew at length to be the ruine of the most glorious cause that ever was contended for.'[5] To Edmund Ludlow it was the Independent party, or 'army-party', which truly represented the interest of Parliament and the country; the Presbyterian party, on the other hand, sought to betray the parliamentary cause. At the same time he appears to have been firmly of the opinion that the Independent and Presbyterian parties retained the religious affiliations associated with the names which they had acquired: in writing of the events in 1648, for example, he describes them as 'these two ecclesiastical interests, one of which could endure no superior, the other no equal'.[6]

The key element in the so-called Presbyterian party in the Commons was a caucus of political activists who feared the growing power of the Independents in the army and whose prime objective was the conclusion of a peace treaty with the king which would secure the restoration of order and stability in both Church and State. Loosely associated with them were a number of MPs who were united in their abhorrence of sectaries and their desire for an ecclesiastical settlement which provided for a godly uniformity. It was certainly Edmund Ludlow's view that the Independents were faced with a coalition of this kind. In typically partisan language he relates how men with royalist sympathies who expected to benefit from a negotiated peace had joined with others who were willing to sacrifice all civil liberties to the ambition of the Presbyterian clergy and to vest them with a power as great or greater than that which had been declared intolerable in the bishops.[7] When contemporaries singled out individual MPs who in their estimation belonged to the Presbyterian party they tended to concentrate on the political activists, men such as Denzil Holles, Sir Philip Stapleton, Sir John Clotworthy, Sir William Lewis, John Glyn and Walter Long. No doubt it was the more prominent figures in this group whom Clarendon had in mind when he wrote that 'the most considerable persons who in the contest with the other faction were content to be thought Presbyterians were so only as they thought it might restore the King, which they more impatiently desired than any alteration in the government of the Church.'[8] During the years 1645 to 1647 Holles and Stapleton were generally considered to be the leaders of the Presbyterian party. From December 1644 onwards they regularly acted as tellers in opposition to the Independents when the Commons voted on matters relating to the new form of church government.[9] Neither of them, however, appears to have been a Puritan. Clarendon observes that Holles was fired with great animosity towards the Independent party and that he was 'no otherwise affected to the Presbyterians than as they constituted a party upon which he depended to oppose the other'.[10] In a eulogy published after his death in 1647 Stapleton was said to have been 'a true and zealous Protestant, though not in any way new-fangled'. Later a Puritan chronicler wrote of him that he was 'a Brave Man who Espoused not the Professors of Religion as such, though he sheltered and laid out his Interest for them'.[11] One of the few Puritans in this party caucus was Sir William Waller who provided a link between the political and religious Presbyterians in the Commons. Although he achieved some success as a military commander he had always considered that a negotiated settlement would be preferable to an outright victory for Parliament. In terms of his religious loyalties he was a moderate Presbyterian who abominated 'a promiscuous toleration of all sects and professions. . . . as inconsistent either with purity or unity, the beauty and bands thereof; and as indeed the principal cause of atheism in this our age'.[12]

In 1645 there were a significant number of Puritan MPs whose hostile attitude towards religious Independency made them potential allies of the Holles-Stapleton group when ecclesiastical matters were being debated. Among others, these included Sir Gilbert Gerard, Sir Robert Harley, Sir Anthony Irby, Sir Oliver Luke and his son Sir Samuel, Sir Nathaniel Barnardiston, Sir Simonds D'Ewes, Sir John Holland, Harbottle Grimston, Zouch Tate, John Gurdon, Francis Rous and Edmund Prideaux. There is no evidence that such men saw themselves as owing any particular allegiance to Holles and Stapleton but they could normally be counted on to support the kind of measures which upheld the principle of uniformity in doctrine, worship and discipline. On the other hand, their political views were more varied. Some like Sir Simonds D'Ewes and Sir John Holland had always been strongly in favour of peace negotiations and less than wholehearted in their commitment to the cause of Parliament. In contrast, John Gurdon was one of those whom D'Ewes had characterized as 'violent spirits'; and Zouch Tate, Francis Rous and Edmund Prideaux also had little in common with the Holles-Stapleton group in political terms.[13] Even the apparent unanimity on ecclesiastical questions had a certain fragile quality since there were many who were prepared to join with the Independents in resisting proposals which appeared to them to confer too much power on the ministry.

To judge from the correspondence of Sir Samuel Luke as governor of Newport Pagnell neither he nor his father regarded himself as belonging to a party or grouping which was engaged in a political contest with the Independents. Sir Samuel deplored the activities of the Independent faction within the army and remained steadfastly loyal to the Earl of Essex who had appointed him governor. On the other hand, his attitude to the war was very different from that of the Holles-Stapleton caucus. When news came through that the Uxbridge peace negotiations had broken down he expressed the hope that Parliament would now prepare for war. His distrust of the Independents appears to have owed more to religious than to political considerations and in particular to his detestation of the sectaries. Writing to his father in March 1645 he referred to the danger which threatened the kingdom

> and this place in particular by reason of the severall Sectaries which begin to bee soe bold and peremptory amongst us, it being farr easier to breed people up to wickednesse and licentiousnesse then to Godlinesse and Holinesse, espetially when under profession of the Latter they may with allow-ance practise the former.

That same month he was involved in an argument with his friend Cornelius Holland, who in religion favoured the cause of Independency, over the conduct of an army surgeon whom the latter had recommended to him. In responding to Luke's criticism Holland put it to him that the godly should avoid such quarrelling. 'Sir', he wrote, 'lett not us who are all for

155

heaven parte in our way thither upon differences in opinions upon things that if well considered will noe wayes hinder us to our Jorney's end, but lett love cover the multitude of all our infirmities and faylings.' Sir Samuel in turn rebuked Holland for his lack of judgment and made it clear that he was not prepared to tolerate a man who refused to subscribe to the Solemn League and Covenant or to conform to the ecclesiastical regime which had been established at Newport Pagnell. In conclusion, however, he assured Holland that he would be heartily glad that 'our ends and endeavours should iump together, espetially in these things which most of all concernes us, the salvacion of our soules.'[14]

In Clarendon's view, a major reason why the Independent faction was patently more effective than the Presbyterian faction was that it was dominated by two or three individuals to whom the others 'resigned implicitly the conduct of their interest'.[15] In fact the 'Independent party' was merely a loose association of MPs with a small political caucus at its centre which consisted of such men as Cromwell, Vane, Hesilrige, Sir Henry Mildmay and Henry Marten. As in the case of the Presbyterian faction the degree of support which this junto was able to command tended to vary according to the particular issues which were under consideration. A belief that only the Independents were genuinely committed to the cause of Parliament helped to promote a sense of unity but in political terms there were both radical and moderate groupings. The Independent party, observes Clarendon, 'comprehended many who were neither enemies to the State or to the Church but desired heartily that a peace might be established upon the foundations of both, so their own ambitions might be complied with.'[16] One Puritan squire who who may be assigned to this group was John Crewe who was generally regarded as a man of great moderation, though Clarendon tells us that during the course of the Uxbridge peace negotiations he displayed 'more bitterness and sourness than formerly'. Before the time of the Civil War he had argued for a modified form of episcopacy in preference to total abolition.[17] Sir John Evelyn of Wiltshire was certainly no ideologue; indeed he appears to have joined with the Independents for no other reason than self-preservation. At first he had been one of the most militant of the parliament-arian MPs but within a short while had become an advocate of peace negotiations. However, this shift in his political stance did not long survive his arrest in August 1643 on the grounds that he had been planning to defect to the king. According to Sir Simonds D'Ewes he eventually managed to extricate himself from this predicament by promising the Independents that if they helped to secure his release he would fully support them in the future. Subsequently, writes D'Ewes, he did everything possible to forestall peace negotiations and 'to kindle a fire alsoe and to raise a warre betwixt the two Nations of England and Scotland and to hinder the Reformation of Religion which was intended and desired to be effected by setting up the Presbiterian Goverment.' Evelyn frequently acted as a teller for the Independents but was secluded at Pride's Purge.[18]

The Independents, complained Thomas Edwards, had appro-priated to themselves the name of the godly and well affected party, calling themselves the saints.[19] Sir William Waller, however, was emphatic that there were saints among both the Presbyterians and the Independents. So far as the Independents were concerned he was convinced that

> all are not of the godly party that wear that badge and cognizance; all are not burning that are shining lights among them. . . . I am sorry to see how small a piece of religion will serve to make a cloak; and ashamed to think how some have worn it to cousin others.[20]

Contemporary commentators were generally agreed that the objective of securing liberty of conscience was one of the main distinguishing features of the Independent faction in Parlia-ment. This was not only a product of genuine conviction but an important factor in the forging of the alliance between the Independent faction and the New Model Army with its variety of sects or, as Sir Arthur Hesilrige would later call it, the 'saint-like army'.[21]

Both before and after the recruiter elections there were many

MPs who remained uncommitted in the sense that their views on major political and religious issues could never be taken for granted; in the words of Clement Walker, these were 'the middle and disingaged men in the House'.[22] Bulstrode Whitelocke was in favour of some measure of toleration within the framework of a national Church but, on the other hand, he consistently supported peace propositions and clearly regarded himself as a political moderate. Some of his friends were major figures of the Presbyterian faction such as Denzil Holles, Sir Philip Stapleton and John Glyn; and indeed Holles told him in 1645 that he had been 'as a brother to him, and a most faithful and constant friend in all his trouble'. Notwithstanding these connections, however, he was still able to maintain good relations with Vane and other Independents.[23]

In his parliamentary journal Sir Simonds D'Ewes recorded a number of events which appeared to foreshadow the internal political divisions of the late 1640s. One of the most important of these was the quarrel which broke out in August 1643 between the Earl of Essex and Sir William Waller. Both generals, writes D'Ewes, were 'firme and cordiall to the Presbiterian goverment' but the dispute was 'nourished' by the Independents who considered that their interests would best be served by supporting Waller.[24] Looking back on this episode, Waller maintained that the Independents had only given him their backing for tactical reasons: 'they were willing enough to foment these differences between his Lordship and me (to the prejudice of the public service) that they might make their ends upon us both.'[25]

Denzil Holles claims that the Self Denying Ordinance, which was eventually passed on 3 April 1645, was the outcome of a plot which the Independents had conceived long before, that is 'to have an Army composed of those of the Independent Judgment, to interpose if there were like to be a Peace'.[26] The proposition that members of the Lords and Commons should voluntarily resign their commands and offices was first put forward on 9 December 1644 in a motion introduced by Zouch Tate and seconded by Sir Henry Vane the younger. In a subsequent debate Bulstrode Whitelocke emphasized that he personally had no office or employment of the kind under discussion but went on to express strong reservations about the projected ordinance. Its effects, he warned the House, would be far-reaching for many persons of standing would be laid aside, among them the Earls of Denbigh, Warwick and Manchester, Sir William Waller, Oliver Cromwell and Denzil Holles.[27]

The proposals for a Self Denying Ordinance and the plans for the establishment of a New Model Army did much to open up divisions between the Presbyterians and the Independents. In February 1645 John Pyne, who was then at Westminster, sent his cousin Alexander Popham an account of the latest political developments and rumours. Pyne was a radical Independent MP who was described by Bulstrode Whitelocke as an enemy of his. Apparently referring to the Earl of Essex, he wrote that, 'the Great One lookes very bigge and blacke, and obstructs all good motions from us; But I hope to see him and his accomplices laid aside, and then I trust God will blesse and further our proceedings.' Progress in the Uxbridge peace negotiations was slow and this seemed to him to offer grounds for optimism that little would come out of them. On his return to London he had found 'so great an alteration that it startles me to see it, yet I trust God will carry on his owne worke in despight of all Counter-working, and wicked plots whatsoever.' Enclosed with his letter was a note which, he told Popham, would acquaint him with the great mystery of the times. According to this note the Scottish commissioners had joined in a 'seeming confederacy' with Sir Philip Stapleton and his associates who included Denzil Holles, John Glyn, Sir John Clotworthy, Robert Reynolds, Bulstrode Whitelocke and John Maynard. As yet it was unclear what was intended but it was hoped that they had nothing more in mind than the advancement of the Presbyterian form of church government.[28]

Later that month the Commons agreed with the Lords that all officers and men of the New Model Army should subscribe to the Solemn League and Covenant but rejected a proposal that they should also be required to submit to the new type of ecclesiastical government which had recently been approved on the grounds that the details had still to be settled. The Independents, Sir Oliver Luke told his son, were not 'well pleased' by the first of these decisions. In reply Sir Samuel expressed his delight that the House had done what was most fitting and just. At the same time he had no doubt that many of the greatest Independents would be prepared to conform to the Presbyterian government rather than forfeit their military commands. Few of them, he went on, would refuse to take the Covenant so long as they could interpret it in their own way.[29]

In the event the requirement to take the Covenant proved to be no real impediment and some of the New Model regiments soon began to acquire a reputation for religious extremism. As a result the Commons decided on 25 April to rush out an ordinance which debarred anyone from preaching unless he was an ordained minister or had specific authority from Parliament. This, reported a royalist newspaper, 'mightily inflamed' the Independent MPs.[30]

Following the breakdown of the Uxbridge peace negotiations, writes Clarendon, the Independent party, as it was 'now contented to be called', renewed its efforts to secure the adoption of the Self Denying Ordinance and met with strong opposition from the Presbyterian party. The leading Presbyterians believed that their party was much stronger in numbers but the Independents 'spake more and better'.[31]

By February 1645 Sir Samuel Luke was beginning to realize that he might soon be forced to surrender his governorship. When, however, attempts were made to organize a petition on his behalf he actively discouraged them since, as he explained to a fellow officer, he had no wish to be beholden to the people's clamours for an appointment which Parliament might no longer consider him worthy to hold. The following month his father warned him to expect the worst and in response he was at pains to show that while he remained governor of Newport Pagnell he would advance the public good to the best of his ability and if necessary at the expense of his own private interests.[32]

As a consequence of the Self Denying Ordinance many MPs, among them Sir William Waller, Sir Philip Stapleton and Sir

Samuel Luke, relinquished their military appointments.[33] There were, however, some exceptions. On 10 June the Commons accepted a proposal which had been received from Sir Thomas Fairfax and other senior officers of the New Model Army that Cromwell should be appointed commander-in-chief of the horse; and, as Sir Samuel Luke put it a few days later, Cromwell was 'willing to kepe himselfe in imployment'.[34] After the Restoration Sir Arthur Hesilrige would claim that he had never been in the field since 1644; on the other hand, he was named as governor of Newcastle in 1647.[35] Sir William Brereton, who was commander-in-chief of the parliamentary forces in Cheshire, was told that in future his powers would be exercised by a committee of which he would be a member. By his autocratic conduct he had antagonized many of his fellow deputy lieutenants and officers but in the autumn it was decided that he should be reinstated.[36] Although the Self Denying Ordinance applied to offices of profit as well as military commands it had very little impact in this respect. Sir Robert Harley, Sir Gilbert Gerard and Sir Henry Mildmay were able to retain their offices; Sir Walter Erle was forced to surrender his office of Lieutenant of the Ordnance but in May 1647 the Commons agreed that it should be restored to him.[37]

Sir William Waller was engaged in military operations in the west of England when the Lords finally consented to the Self Denying Ordinance and had only recently gained a victory over the royalists in Wiltshire. As he would later acknowledge it was a development which was not unwelcome to him:

> I was so little fond of the trade of a souldier (notwithstanding those temptations of honour and profitt that accompany it) that I gladly gave my vote to the self-denying ordinance and the new modell; and when the Committee at Darby House signify'd their desire to me that I would continue for some time in my command. . . . I was so perfectly tired with the drudgery of it that I demanded as a right (by vertue of that ordinance) to have leave to deliver up my charge.[38]

Sir Simonds D'Ewes records in his journal that on 16 April the House was informed of a letter from Waller in which he reported that his soldiers were extremely discontented through lack of pay and concluded with the request that the parliamentary authorities should call him home 'to serve them in the house since he had been soe unfortunate in theire service abroad'. By the beginning of May Sir William was back in London where he now settled with his family. 'Itt was just with God', he writes, 'to lay me by all employment, as a broken vessel, in regard of the corruption of my heart, in my first engagement, and neglect of reformation in the officers and souldiery under me.' In the Commons he very soon emerged as a leading opponent of the Independents. In explaining his political views he relates that during the early stages of the Civil War he sided with the Independent party but later went over to the Presbyterians. This, he stresses, was not because of any change of outlook on his part but because of the growing radicalism of the Independents. Many Independents had ceased to walk uprightly in accordance with the truth and simplicity of the Gospel and had become incendiaries, 'putting the whole state into combustion and confusion'. On seeing them deviate into 'impious, disloyal, antimonarchical ends' he had come to the conclusion that it was time to part company with them. Nor was he alone in his disenchantment: very many members of both Houses, 'of eminent reputation for piety and integrity', also turned away from them.[39]

Although Sir Samuel Luke was a capable military commander[40] there was never much prospect that he would be granted a new commission in view of his close association with the Earl of Essex and his belligerent attitude towards the sectaries. To the Committee of Both Kingdoms he wrote that 'The great misfortune which is now fallen upon mee cannot be exprest with greife sufficient' but emphasized that any further orders which he might receive would be faithfully executed. On 14 April Richard Cokayn, whom he had recommended as his successor, told him that he was confident that the Lord General and his party were prepared to support his candidature, though he added that if only the Independent party would come down on their side 'wee could assure you more; there is much excepicions taken against you and all the officers of the

Garrison for not favouring the good party as they call them.' In the event the Commons declined to endorse Cokayn's appointment and as a stop-gap measure it was agreed that Sir Samuel should retain the governorship until 25 June. In a letter written on 16 June to a nobleman who was clearly regarded as an ally[41] Luke stressed the need to take care over the choice of his successor 'that he may be such a one whose estate may bee lyable for restitution, his person fitt for action and his heart sound to the Parliament, his affections right to the Nobility and Gentry of the kingdome.'[42]

As a parting gesture Sir Samuel apprehended two captains belonging to the New Model regiment of Colonel Charles Fleetwood who had been preaching within the area of his military jurisdiction. In his estimation these men, whom he described as taylor Hobson and druggist Beamont, were Anabaptists and therefore held views which were hostile to magistracy and government. The treatment meted out to them angered Sir Thomas Fairfax and led to a sharp exchange of letters between Fleetwood and his kinsman Luke which tells us much about the conflicting attitudes of the Independents and Presbyterians. Writing on 21 June Fleetwood argued the case for religious toleration:

> I feare your Honour may bee much eclipsed by the harsh dealeings of your officers not only with these but with others whose tendernesse of conscience will not give them leave to doe as others and truly in these tymes wherein wee expect light from God our duty is not to force men but to bee tender of such as walke conscientiously and rather to give then deprive them of Liberty for wee know not but those who discent from us may bee in the right.

In reply Sir Samuel expressed surprise that Fleetwood should have authorized the two men to preach about the working of miracles and the unlawfulness of fighting for the cause of Parliament. He assumed that Fleetwood was aware of 'the Covenant that I have taken and, God willing, will with my life and estate endeavour to maintaine'; and that he had heard of the parliamentary ordinance which prohibited anyone from preaching who was not in orders or approved of by the Westminster Assembly. Finally, he warned him that the toleration of sectarian radicalism could have the most dangerous consequences: 'I pray God the light you speake of. . . . proves not the darknesse which hath plunged Germany in to all her miseryes.'[43]

THIRTEEN

Revolution

ONE of the most striking points about the recruiter MPs who took their seats in the Commons from the autumn of 1645 onwards is the degree of continuity in terms of the family ties which linked them with the original members of the Long Parliament. Sir Christopher Wray was succeeded by William Wray, Sir Thomas Hutchinson by John Hutchinson, Sir Samuel Owfield by William Owfield and Sir Henry Ludlow by Edmund Ludlow.[1] In addition, a number of sitting MPs, among them Sir William Armyne, Sir Nathaniel Barnardiston, Sir Robert Harley and Sir Thomas Pelham, were joined in the Commons chamber by their eldest sons. Edmund Ludlow had considerable reservations about his fellow recruiter MPs, claiming that most of them were men of a neutral spirit or such who, though they had been actively engaged against the king, were in favour of entering into an accommodation with him.[2] According to Denzil Holles it seemed at first that the elections had mainly benefited the Independents but their expectations proved to be ill-founded. At the time of their admission, he observes, the new members were heavily prejudiced against the moderate party, as he termed it, which was reputed to consist of 'persons ill affected, not faithful to the Parliament, obstructing all businesses that were for the good of the Kingdom'. Before long, however, they came to realize that 'all these aimed at was but to get a good Peace, see the Government settled both in Church and State, and make no advantages to themselves.'[3]

Although Holles was a highly partisan commentator it is clear from the evidence of parliamentary divisions that during the years 1646 and 1647 there was a major shift of opinion in favour of the Presbyterian faction after it had suffered some initial setbacks. Bulstrode Whitelocke writes that many sober men in the Commons were anxious to accept the peace propositions which the king forwarded from Newcastle in May 1646 but they were outvoted, mainly because the newly elected MPs came out in opposition. When there was a division on 29 May Sir John Holland and Sir William Lewis acted as tellers for the Presbyterians and Sir John Evelyn of Wiltshire and Sir Arthur Hesilrige as tellers for the Independents. The result was a decisive victory for the Independents by 145 votes to 103.[4] By the end of 1646, however, the situation was very different. On 22 December the Commons decided, by 156 votes to 99, to take into consideration a London petition which called for the disbandment of the New Model Army and the suppression of heresy. Subsequently, on 31 December, the House approved the terms of a declaration which announced its intention to proceed against such persons as should preach or expound the Scriptures unless they had been ordained in the Church of England or another Reformed Church; and against any ministers or others who should dare to criticize the new form of church government which had been established by Parliament. When the House divided over the question of whether the words 'or expound the Scriptures' should be included in the declaration Sir Walter Erle and Sir Anthony Irby acted as tellers for the ayes and Sir Arthur Hesilrige and Cromwell as tellers for the noes. By 105 votes to 57 the Commons agreed that the public exposition of biblical passages was a function which only ordained ministers should be entitled to perform.[5]

With England now at peace many of the Puritan gentry who had supported Parliament considered that the New Model Army should be disbanded with all possible speed. In part this reflected their growing concern about the heavy taxes which they had to pay for the maintenance of such large forces. At the same time they were repelled by the religious extremism which was so much in evidence in the New Model Army. As Sir William Waller put it in explaining why he had joined the Presbyterians,

They that claim no less then to be GOD's host, an army of
Saints . . . .are becom the men that have given great occasion
to the enemies of the LORD to blaspheme, by introducing a
general confusion in the Church, fomenting Popery, tolerat-
ing Heresy, contenancing Schisme, prophaning Holy Ordinances, persecuting good Ministers, and indeed the Ministry.[6]

The possibility that the army might seek to become a political
force in its own right was perhaps less readily appreciated even
in the early months of 1647. In the view of some commentators such as Bulstrode Whitelocke the antagonism which the
leaders of the Presbyterian faction displayed towards the army
was largely the product of personal rancour occasioned by the
Self Denying Ordinance. Confident that they would be able to
carry the House with them they embarked on a campaign for
the disbandment of the army. Whitelocke writes that in
private discussions with Denzil Holles, Sir Philip Stapleton,
John Glyn and others of 'that party' he warned them of the
potential dangers of adopting this course of action but his
advice went unheeded.[7] On 28 May 1647 the Commons agreed
that Sir Gilbert Gerard, Harbottle Grimston, Richard Knightley and Sir John Potts, together with representatives of the
Lords, should assist Sir Thomas Fairfax in the disbanding of
those regiments which had not been detailed for service in
Ireland. It was soon apparent, however, that the army was
unwilling to co-operate.[8]

In June the army responded to the challenge which Parliament had thrown down by taking over custody of the king and
pressing for the impeachment of eleven members of the
Commons for high treason. These MPs included all the leading
figures of the Presbyterian faction, among them Denzil Holles,
Sir Philip Stapleton and Sir William Waller. That Edward
Harley found himself in this company was due to the fact that
he had been communicating intelligence to the House about
the army's deliberations on matters of political import.
Eventually the Commons decided that the eleven members
should be granted leave of absence for a period of six months.[9]

On 26 July the two Houses came under siege from a London

mob which demanded, among other things, the resumption of negotiations with the king and the restoration of the eleven members. Shortly afterwards some peers and MPs assembled at Syon House in Middlesex where they conferred with Sir Thomas Fairfax and other senior officers. Many of these MPs, who included Sir Arthur Hesilrige, Sir John Evelyn of Wiltshire and John Hutchinson, are readily identifiable as Independents or their associates. On the other hand, most MPs, among them Sir Robert Harley, Sir Walter Erle and Sir Simonds D'Ewes, remained at Westminster; these, Lucy Hutchinson tells us, were the Presbyterian members.[10] On 6 August Sir Thomas Fairfax arrived at Westminster and the MPs who had sought the protection of his army returned to the Commons. Some of the members who were faced with the threat of impeachment proceedings now took ship for Calais where Sir Philip Stapleton died of the plague. Sir William Waller journeyed on to Holland and sojourned for a time first at Leiden and then at the Hague.[11] On 16 August a correspondent of Framlingham Gawdy, one of the Norfolk MPs, was writing that 'I perceive the Presbyterian party do again prevail in the House' but as Edmund Ludlow remarks it was seriously weakened by the departure of its leaders.[12]

During the weeks that followed a strikingly large number of MPs absented themselves from the Commons, sometimes with prior permission but often without. On 9 October a total of 235 members were recorded as absent, of whom 80 were immediately excused for one reason or another. Among other things, the House noted that Sir Samuel Luke and Sir Harbottle Grimston were both ill; that Sir John Holland was employed on official business; and that Sir William Drake was abroad. Sir William had spent much of his time on the Continent since the outbreak of the Civil War and on 6 July had been granted leave to return there for the recovery of his health. Possibly he had arranged to travel with Grimston who on the same day had obtained permission to go to the Belgian health resort of Spa along with two servants and a chaplain.[13] One of the absent MPs, Sir Francis Drake, was full of pessimism about the future. Writing from his Devonshire seat, Buckland Abbey, on 10

September he lamented that England now seemed to 'languish towards death. The universal high discontent which I find everywhere appearing is a sad pressage of further troubles.'[14] Many MPs were clearly apprehensive about the political designs of the army. In November a royalist observed that all rich men were alarmed by the possibility of a general moulding of the kingdom into a paity. The Presbyterian party, he went on, had never been so passionate against the Cavaliers as it was against the army.[15]

Looking back at the events of the summer, Edward Harley recorded his gratitude

> That my God delivered mee when I prayed unto him, in my journey to London, June 1647, from falling into the hands of the Army though I came through their quarters. That my Sicknes in London August 1647 was not the plague, my recovery out of it so gracious, and the very sickness a deliverance from other evills.
>
> That God very graciously preserved mee from the malice of many Enemies, Specially from the Army in their Accusation.[16]

Although a pass had been obtained from the Speaker his illness led him to abandon any thought of going abroad; instead he took up residence with his relatives the Smiths at Theydon Mount in Essex. On 19 October Timothy Woodroffe, one of the preachers whom his father had established at Hereford, assured him that he was praying daily that God would give him a rich spirit of holiness, wisdom and patience. God was imposing his will through the whirlwind and the storm. It was a time of great earthquakes and commotions in which the great Antichrist was pushing with his horns against kings and kingdoms. Even among Christians there were major divisions and sad distractions, 'nay the sword halfe, yea quit drawen'. He was in no doubt that God was preparing the way for Antichrist's downfall, the drying up of the Euphrates, the calling of the Jews and the fulfilment of the Gentiles which they might both live to see. He was inclined to feel that God 'did Arest you in your late sickenes Least pusillanimitie, I had almost said Coward-

169

ize, should have surprized your noble publique spirit, as I believe it did many Others.' He thanked God who made him stand his ground when so many turned their backs. Harley, he went on, should be of good cheer and recollect his sacred principles. For he was confident that God would establish Jerusalem.[17] The MPs who had been staying away from Westminster gradually drifted back but Edward Harley had to wait until June 1648 before the charge of high treason which had been brought against him was formally expunged by the House and he was allowed to take his seat again.[18]

On 3 January 1648 Sir Arthur Hesilrige moved in the Commons that no further attempt should be made to negotiate a settlement with the king. He was supported by Sir Thomas Wroth who seized the opportunity to call for the abolition of monarchy. 'From divells and Kings', he declared, 'Good Lord deliver me. It's now time, up and be doing. I desire any government rather than that of Kings.'[19] According to his Commons journal Sir Simonds D'Ewes intervened in the debate to deliver an *ex tempore* speech in the defence of the monarchy. When Parliament had first assembled above seven years since, he told the House, it had been inconceivable that 'wee should ever live to have seene the deposing of the king to have beene the subiect matter of the debate of this House.' Parliament had no right or power to depose him or to alter the government of the kingdom. There was no scriptural authority for his subjects to do more than assert their just liberties. In his view these proceedings would not only fill the godly orthodox party in England with grief and amazement but prove to be a scandal to the true Protestant religion throughout the whole of Christendom.[20]

In view of the king's recent conduct the decision, by 141 votes to 92, that there should be no further negotiations with him was not altogether surprising.[21] During the second Civil War which broke out shortly afterwards the wealthy Puritan gentry tended to remain loyal to Parliament or at least passive, though there were a few defections to the royalists. One of the counties in which there was heavy fighting was Essex which had hitherto escaped lightly. In June Sir William Masham and

170

other members of the Essex committee were captured by Lord Goring's forces and imprisoned at Colchester. The same month royalist troops plundered the house of Sir Harbottle Grimston, who had recently succeeded to his father's estate and title, and turned out his wife. Following the release of the Essex committeemen Samuel Fairclough preached a sermon at Romford as an act of gratitude for their deliverance.[22]

Lucy Hutchinson claims that the victories achieved by the New Model Army displeased the Presbyterian party which resolved to join with the common enemy in order to destroy the Independents.[23] What is certainly true is that there was a growing solidarity among the more conservative elements in the Commons which for a time enabled the Presbyterian faction to further its own objectives. One manifestation of this closing of ranks was the readmission of Denzil Holles, Sir William Waller and the other suspended members; another was the issue on 29 August of a consolidating ordinance on church government.[24] Most important of all, there was a series of decisions which led to the opening of peace negotiations at Newport in the Isle of Wight. Among the MPs who were appointed as commissioners for this purpose were Sir Henry Vane the younger and Denzil Holles; in the main, however, they were moderates, men such as Sir Harbottle Grimston, Sir John Potts and John Crewe. Grimston, it was subsequently related, 'was lookt upon as one heartily affected to the King.'[25]

At Newport the king made important political concessions but was much less willing to endorse the changes which had been introduced in the ecclesiastical field. This posed a major dilemma for the many MPs who wanted both a formal agreement with the king which would ensure a lasting peace and a church settlement on the lines already prescribed by Parliament. On 13 October John Swinfen, who was responsible for liaising with the commissioners, informed John Crewe that Parliament was not satisfied with the king's initial response over the issue of church government. He prayed to God that the king would be more forthcoming in his next answer to the proposition for taking away episcopacy; otherwise the consequences would be very serious indeed. By subscribing to the

Covenant the two Houses had sworn publicly and solemnly to secure the extirpation of bishops; and this had been put forward as a main point of reformation. The king, on the other hand, was under no such obligation to preserve episcopacy.[26] In contrast, Sir John Evelyn of Wiltshire was telling Sir John Potts a few days later that he had never attached much importance to the abolition of bishops.[27] On 21 October Sir Harbottle Grimston wrote in a letter to his friend Sir Robert Harley that the king's second answer to the proposition on the future of the Church was somewhat better than the first yet he feared that it would not give full satisfaction to the two Houses. If, however, Parliament was to break off negotiations with the king over this issue when agreement had been virtually reached on all other matters he could not tell 'how we shall be able to answere it to god, the world or our owne Consciences'. He went on:

> beleeve it, there is not a man amongst us that thinke it worth endangeringe the kingdome for . . . .
> Pray desyre all our freinds to attend the house diligently and lett not a shipp richly laden after a long voyage full of hazards be cast a way within sight of land.[28]

Grimston, however, had underestimated the degree of antipathy with which episcopal government was regarded by many of his fellow MPs. When this question was further debated on 26 October the Commons agreed, without a division, that the king's latest answer was inadequate and that the reasons for refusing to accept it should be set down in writing by a committee which included such zealous advocates of Presbyterianism as Zouch Tate and John Swinfen. This was done in the form of draft instructions to the commissioners which Swinfen presented to the House on the following day. As the committee put on record, the king was not prepared to sanction the abolition of the functions and powers of the bishops and he would only accept a Presbyterian form of church government for a three-year trial period.[29]

On 6 November John Crewe, who like Grimston had once argued in favour of a limited episcopacy,[30] sought to impress on Swinfen that it was necessary to compromise in the interest of securing a permanent settlement. No man knew, he declared, what would become of either religion or Parliament if the negotiations were to break down; and in the event of further troubles it was likely that the people would blame their miseries on Presbytery. In a further letter which was dispatched on the same day he told Swinfen that if the king's latest offer on church government was set out in specific terms in a parliamentary statute the bishops would be able to do nothing, even in the matter of ordination, without the consent of the two Houses.[31] On 11 November, however, the Commons agreed that the commissioners should be instructed to press the king to accept without qualification that episcopal government should be replaced by a Presbyterian system.[32]

When a report on the Newport negotiations was debated on 4 December Sir Robert Harley, Sir Benjamin Rudyerd, Sir Simonds D'Ewes, Sir Harbottle Grimston and other MPs argued that the king's concessions satisfied all the main objectives which Parliament had been striving to achieve when first resorting to arms. A number of Independent MPs voiced their opposition to any settlement which was unacceptable to the army and Sir Henry Mildmay was insistent that the king could not be trusted. On 5 December, however, the Commons decided, by 129 votes to 83, that the answers of the king to the propositions of both Houses provided a basis for the settlement of the peace of the kingdom.[33] Faced with the possibility that this might be the last opportunity to conclude a peace treaty with the king the Puritan moderates had convinced themselves that political considerations mattered more than any doubts which they had about the adequacy of his proposals on church government.

The vote on 5 December angered such radical MPs as Sir James Harrington, Sir Thomas Wroth, John Hutchinson and Edmund Ludlow who subsequently felt obliged to register their dissent.[34] Hutchinson considered that 'both the cause, and all those who had with an upright honest heart asserted and maintain'd it, were betray'd and sold for nothing.' When he remonstrated with some of the Newport commissioners they acknowledged that the king's propositions did not offer as much security as they would have liked but argued that in view of the growing power and insolence of the army it would be prudent to accept them.[35]

According to a modern computation the purge conducted by Colonel Thomas Pride, which began on 6 December, resulted in the seclusion of 231 MPs.[36] These included all the leading figures of the Presbyterian party and many other MPs who are known to have been in favour of accepting the king's propositions. Most of the wealthy Puritan members now ceased to sit in Parliament. All four Bedfordshire MPs, Sir Beauchamp St John, Sir Roger Burgoyne, Sir Oliver Luke and his son Sir Samuel, found themselves excluded and the parliamentary representation of such Presbyterian counties as Lancashire and Suffolk was heavily depleted. On the other hand, there were a considerable number of major Puritan squires in the Rump Parliament.[37] Some were political radicals like Sir Henry Vane the younger, Sir Arthur Hesilrige, Sir John Bourchier, Sir Thomas Wroth and Sir Gilbert Pickering. Others, among them Sir William Armyne, had leanings towards the Independent party but such men as Sir Thomas Jervoise, Sir William Strickland and Bulstrode Whitelocke belonged to no particular faction. Lucy Hutchinson writes that those MPs who were either of the Independent faction 'or of none att all, but look'd upon themselves as call'd out to manage a publick trust for their country, forsooke not their seates while they were permitted to sitt in the House.' Some of them, however, were profoundly disturbed by what had happened. Although John Hutchinson was generally regarded as an Independent he 'infinitely disliked the action of the Armie.'[38] In contrast, John Pyne, who was the dominant figure in Somerset, was convinced that the purge was fully justified. Writing to John Rushworth on 16 December he told him that for the last two or three years the predominant party in the Commons had been pursuing unworthy ends 'insoemuch that had not god in providence enabled the Armye to give check unto theire sinister designes we had longe ere this bin delivered upp the most absolute slaves in the Christian wourld.' Probably it was a matter of particular satisfaction to him that William Strode, a fellow Somerset landowner, had fallen victim to the purge. Earlier in the year it had been alleged that Strode had declared that all those in the Independent party were rogues; that he would never take up arms again except against the Independents; and that as for Pyne 'I make noe doubte but wee shall have him hanged'.[39]

For some at least the most scandalous feature of Pride's Purge was the arrest of 47 of the secluded members. These MPs, who are described by Edmund Ludlow as 'the most suspected', included many of the leading Puritan gentry, among them Sir Robert Harley and his sons Edward and Robert, Sir William Waller, Sir Walter Erle, Sir Samuel Luke, Sir Richard Onslow, Sir Gilbert Gerard and his son Francis, Sir Harbottle Grimston, Sir Anthony Irby, Sir Simonds D'Ewes, Sir William Lytton, Richard Knightley, John Swinfen, John Crewe, Francis Buller and William Strode.[40] Lytton was quickly released but most of the arrested MPs were put under guard in two inns on the Strand, the King's Head and the Swan. Waller, who was eventually moved to Windsor Castle, writes that he was imprisoned 'because I voted for a new peace'.[41] Except for the leading figures of the Presbyterian faction who had been apprehended the prisoners were gradually set at liberty over a period of some two months. On 22 December Stanley Gower informed Sir Robert Harley that he would preach on the next Sabbath day as he had requested. The ministers of London, he assured him, 'have bene this day praying hartily for yow and the rest of those worthys which beare testimony to God's cause with yow.' On 27 January Edward Harley (who like his father was still under restraint) sent the Lord General some papers in which the secluded MPs defended themselves against the accusations of disloyalty which had been levelled against them. In the accompanying letter he told Fairfax that he was confident that they would convince him that 'no respect to our particular advantage, nor Envy, or revenge against your Army but the powerfull ties of the greatest trust from men and solemne Covenant to God have caused myselfe and others my fellow-sufferers to oppose your Army in their late and present actings.' Four days later Fairfax gave order that Sir Robert Harley should be allowed to return to his house at Westminster on the understanding that he would continue to reside there and on 12 February authorized the release of Edward Harley and two of his fellow prisoners.[42]

Writing to a friend on 2 January Sir Roger Burgoyne, who though secluded had escaped imprisonment, expressed his concern about the political situation:

> I could be content to be a monke or hermit rather than a statesman at the present conjunction of affairs . . . .What will become of us in England God only knowes. The passages of late presage the saddest of times.[43]

For those MPs who were no longer allowed to sit in the Commons there was at least the consolation that they could completely dissociate themselves from the proceedings against the king which Parliament initiated under pressure from the army. Sir William Waller's views on the institution of monarchy were probably not untypical. 'I am the rather inclined on the side of this forme of government', he observes, 'because it is, and from all antiquity hath been, the most agreeable to the complexion and genius of this nation'; but his preference was for a monarchy which was circumscribed by good laws.[44] Even among the Rumpers there were many who had grave misgivings about the course of action on which Parliament had embarked. Bulstrode Whitelocke writes that although he was named as a member of the committee which was responsible for drawing up the charge against the king he deliberately absented himself from its meetings since he was determined not to meddle in the business. On 26 December 1648 he persuaded Sir Thomas Widdrington, another lawyer MP, to accompany him on a journey to his country house in Buckinghamshire where he proposed that they should live quietly until the trial was over. He was resolved, we are told, 'to hazard or lay downe all, how beneficiall soever, or advantageous to me, rather then to doe any thing contrary to my judgement and conscience.' Whitelocke's name was omitted from the list of MPs and others who in an act dated 6 January 1649 were empowered to serve as the king's judges; this, he explains, was because the House was well aware of his views.[45] In the event a considerable number of the judges who were appointed, among them Sir William Armyne, Sir William Masham and his nephew Sir John Barrington, took little or no part in the proceedings which culminated in the execution of the king on 30 January. In Lucy Hutchinson's estimation most of those who declined to take part did so 'not for conscience, but for feare and worldly prudence'.[46]

Those who signed the king's death-warrant on 29 January mainly consisted of men of small or middling estate. Many wealthy MPs who had acquired a reputation for political radicalism remained inactive or displayed great caution. Sir Henry Vane the younger, who had strongly disapproved of Pride's Purge, was absent from Westminster between 3 December 1648 and 7 February 1649 and when subsequently elected as a member of the new Council of State refused to take the oath which required him to endorse 'what had been done to the late King'. Some years later he reacted angrily on hearing the Richard Baxter had written that he had been involved in the king's death.[47] Although Sir Arthur Hesilrige had been named as one of the judges he failed to attend any of the sittings of the court. In 1659, however, he would attribute the king's execution to the 'wonderful hand of God' and in a reference to the political revolution which had taken place entreat his parliamentary colleagues not to set up what God had pulled down 'lest we be said to build against God'.[48] Others such as Sir James Harrington, Sir Henry Mildmay and Sir Thomas Wroth withdrew at various stages between the first session of the court and the session on 27 January at which sentence was pronounced.[49] Not all the regicides with large estates were Puritans but Sir John Bourchier, John Hutchinson and Anthony Stapley are readily identifiable as such. Lucy Hutchinson testifies that in signing the death-warrant her husband acted 'according to the dictates of a conscience which he had sought the Lord to guide'. Both he and others who took this step felt that they could not do otherwise 'without giving up the people of God, who they had led forth and engaged themselves unto by the oath of God, into the hands of God's and their enemies'.[50]

In a pamphlet entitled *The High-Way to Peace* which had appeared in 1647 Sir Edward Peyton, a Puritan baronet of decayed estate, had offered the view that 'Monarchy must not infringe the liberty of the people, nor people destroy Monarchy'. Five years later, however, he published a very different work, *The Divine Catastrophe of the Kingly Family of the House of Stuarts*, in which he sought to justify the execution of the king and the abolition of the monarchy by depicting these actions as the working of God's will. In the preface, which he addressed to the Purged Parliament, he referred approvingly to the 'divine Revolution' which 'God hath brought to pass instrumentally by your wisdom and discretion, and his heavenly Providence'. The body of the work mainly consists of a catalogue of the alleged sins and misdoings of the Stuart kings interspersed with assertions aimed at establishing the thesis that the revolution had been not only necessary but inevitable. God, he assured his readers, had decreed that there should be a change from an autocratic to an aristocratic or plebeian form of government which would more readily ensure the advancement of the kingdom of Jesus Christ. Indeed it was probable that God intended to destroy all monarchy in Christendom. Kings, he stressed, were no longer the anointed of God as David had once been; as the scriptures made clear, every saint was anointed.[51] It is noteworthy that both Peyton and the regicide Edmund Ludlow were heavily influenced by apocalyptic beliefs; yet apocalyptic beliefs of one kind or another helped to colour the thinking of Sir Henry Vane the younger and Sir James Harrington whose political radicalism fell short of regicide and even of moderates like Sir Robert Harley and Sir Simonds D'Ewes whose preference for continuing negotiations with the king had led to their seclusion.[52] For a postscript on the king's execution we have the last recorded words of Sir John Bourchier, a wealthy Yorkshire squire who was a long-standing opponent of the Crown. When he was dying in December 1659 some of his relatives pressed him, for reasons of self-interest, to admit that he had been mistaken in signifying his agreement to the king's execution but they met with a defiant response: 'I tell you it was a just act, and God and good men will owne it.'[53]

FOURTEEN

The Twilight of Godliness

A royalist intelligence report which Sir Edward Nicholas received in 1650 depicted an England in which the Independents had possession of all the forts, towns and treasure while the Presbyterians, for their part, had a 'silent power' which owed much to the clergy and some of the nobility and gentry. Among the Presbyterians, it went on, there were zealots who considered that the system of church government which they favoured was divinely ordained but the great majority were weary of the trouble and the rod which was hanging over them and would be willing to repent and serve the king.[1] During the Commonwealth period most of the leading Puritan gentry were excluded from power, both at Westminster and in their counties. Many of them were removed from the commission of the peace in the early 1650s[2] while on the other hand large numbers of men of inferior social status were exercising responsibility as members of the county committees, sheriffs, justices of the peace and commissioners of the militia. Not long after the establishment of the republic several of the secluded MPs were forced to relinquish the offices of profit which they held. Sir Gilbert Gerard, who had been appointed Chancellor of the Duchy of Lancaster in March 1648, was deprived of the office in July 1649 and Sir Walter Erle was replaced as Lieutenant of the Ordnance by Major General

Harrison.[3] On 16 May 1649 the Commons was informed that a letter had been received from Sir Robert Harley which indicated that 'he doth decline further meddling with the Making of Money for the present'. Faced with this act of defiance, which was occasioned by plans for redesigning the coinage, the House decided to relieve him of his Mastership of the Mint. Sir Robert was now without any kind of employment and his loss of office immediately exacerbated the financial difficulties which had been brought on by the seizure of his estate during the first Civil War. In June his kinsman Sir William Waller, who was then imprisoned in Windsor Castle, was writing to him that it was the chemistry of a true Christian 'to extract good Spiritts out of the evills of this world. The Lord sanctify his hand to us all, and teach us to learne righteousness out of his iudgments.' In 1652 Harley took up residence in a rented house at Ludlow in Shropshire after being refused permission to settle in Shrewsbury.[4]

In the memoirs which he wrote during his imprisonment Sir William Waller inserted the heartfelt comment that 'under the notion of a freedom we live like slaves, enforced by continual taxes and oppressions to maintein and feed our own misery'.[5] In general there was little prospect that the Presbyterian gentry would abate their hostility towards a regime based on military power which had imposed its will on Parliament, executed the king and abolished monarchy, and shown from the outset that in matters of religion its sympathies lay firmly with the sectaries. Not only had they witnessed a political revolution which thoroughly alarmed them but they sensed that there was a growing danger of a major social upheaval. As a possible foretaste of what might be in store for the upper classes the Purged Parliament gave its approval in February 1652 to an act for making void all titles of honour which had been granted by Charles I since 4 January 1642, the day on which he had attempted to arrest the Five Members. The act was mainly directed against the many royalists who had been recipients but several parliamentarian gentry were also caught in the net. Sir John Gell, who had been created a baronet on 29 January 1642, found himself stripped of his title; and in Chancery litigation in 1653 he had to suffer the humiliation of being described as 'John Gell of Hopton, Derbyshire, esquire, lately called Sir John Gell, baronet'. Subsequently he joined with other baronets in petitioning Cromwell for permission to retain their titles but apparently without effect.[6] In August 1653 it was proposed in a document submitted to the Parliament of Saints that 'the tytles of Duke, Marquess, Earle, Lord, Knight, Esquire, and such like should be layd asyde as a vaine glorious thinge; for God's people should be under but one name, viz Christians, or for distinction in the Commonwealth, Freemen of England'. It was a proposal which was unlikely to have had much appeal for the handful of upper-class members of the assembly, men such as Sir Gilbert Pickering, Sir William Roberts and Richard Norton.[7] In the event nothing came of it but men of high social rank had good reason to feel apprehensive about the spread of levelling influences. In London, writes Sir John Reresby, the people could scarcely endure the sight of a gentleman and cries of 'French dog' or some similar expression would be hurled at any man who was well dressed. The nobility and gentry, he adds, 'lived most in the country'.[8] Even among the gentry who supported or were regarded as loyal to the Cromwellian regime there was serious concern about the tendency for traditional social values to be openly challenged. When MPs debated the problem of the Quakers in December 1656 the fears which they expressed were not solely a product of their religious outlook. 'They are a growing evil', declared Sir William Strickland, 'and the greatest that ever was. Their way is a plausible way; all levellers against magistracy and propriety.'[9] Significantly, Edmund Ludlow was alleged to have betrayed his own class: in his history of Independency Clement Walker described him as 'once a Gentleman, but since by himself Levelled into the plebeyan rank'.[10]

Some of the Presbyterian gentry such as Sir Samuel Luke and Sir Roger Burgoyne decided to travel abroad for a time.[11] For the most part, however, they lived at home in the country, improving their estates, repairing or rebuilding their houses and not infrequently engaging in litigation. Although they tended to remain quiescent until the death of Cromwell in 1658 they were regarded with a great deal of suspicion by the authorities. In November 1649 John Pyne wrote of the dangers which threatened the Commonwealth:

.... but now the soldier begins to grow discontented, being apt to turn leveller, and the old deceitful interest under the notion of the Presbyterian party begins to rejoice and practise their old designs .... We must submit unto God, who hitherto hath protected his people, though but a very small remnant comparatively with the multitude of enemies they are environed with.[12]

In March 1650 it was reported that in Lancashire two of the leading gentry, Ralph Assheton and Richard Holland, were intending to organize a party which would join with the Scots against the republican government; and that the Presbyterian clergy were the chief cause of the new war which was now imminent.[13] That same month Sir John Gell was committed to the Tower. The charge which was brought against him was that he had been privy to a conspiracy aimed at subverting the Commonwealth, delivering up forts to the enemy and proclaiming the young Charles Stuart king of England. In September he was found guilty of misprision of treason and as a result incurred the penalty of forfeiture of his personal estate and the rents of his lands for life. In April 1652, however, he was released from his imprisonment and a year later managed to obtain a full pardon.[14] In view of his past conduct it was inevitable that Edward Harley should be suspected of disloyalty. In August 1650, when he was living at Wigmore in Herefordshire, he received a letter which required both him and his brother Robert to appear before the commissioners for the militia at Hereford in order to be questioned about the allegations that they were disaffected to the present government. Shortly afterwards some soldiers arrived and after searching through his papers took him away to Hereford. Almost immediately, however, he was set at liberty and he would subsequently record his gratitude to God for delivering him 'from restraint at Hereford August 1650 unexpectedly and without any prejudice to the peace of my Conscience'. On the other hand, his brothers Robert and Thomas were imprisoned for a time at Bristol.[15]

In April 1651 the government was informed that Sir Richard Onslow 'appears fierce upon the Presbyterian score and also upon the King's', though the Cavaliers were unwilling to trust him; that Francis Buller, one of the secluded Cornish MPs, had said that 'hee would never serve the Parliament againe, and did appear to serve the King'; and that Sir Harbottle Grimston, Sir John Gell and Bulstrode Whitelocke all had royalist leanings.[16] According to an eighteenth-century account of the Onslow family, Sir Richard was one of those MPs 'who were not for carrying things to extremities against the King but only to restrain his power, and to preserve the constitution upon its true basis; and was besides a great enemy to the wild and enthusiastic principles of religion that prevailed during these times.' In the Commonwealth period 'he acted in the country upon frequent occasions with great zeal and resolution against the then powers, but with so much prudence. . . . that he never subjected himself to any prosecution or public censure, though he was more than once very near it.' As the colonel of a Surrey regiment he was ordered to join Cromwell at Worcester but he took care to arrive only after the battle was over. This led Cromwell to remark that 'he should one time or other be even with that fox of Surrey'.[17]

Meanwhile, Sir William Waller had been moved to Denbigh Castle in north Wales where the conditions were not particularly to his liking. Writing to his cousin Edward Harley in October 1651 he observed that although there was 'some conformity between these ruinous walls and my decaied body yet I have reason to doubt (as you do) how they will agree together this winter, especially in an aire so penetrative as this.' Nevertheless he was ready to endure all things through Jesus Christ. If he petitioned the Council of State for his liberty it would be necessary to employ a form of address which would imply acknowledgement that it was 'a Parliamentary authority'. This put him in some difficulty since 'before this late blow itt was the generall opinion of our ministers, and all the zealants of our party, that this way of address was utterly uniustifiable.' His object was to preserve a conscience which was devoid of offence, both towards God and man. If, he went on, 'the aims of these Gentlemen that have gotten the power be only to secure the peace of the kingdome I do not see but itt might be a faire way for them, and most agreable to what they have held out before God and the world in favour of liberty of conscience, to grant Passes to go beyond Sea unto those that cannot perswade themselves to come upp to their principles.' Despite his scruples he eventually submitted a petition and in January 1652 was granted his freedom.[18]

In 1649 many of the Presbyterian clergy of London had publicly declared their revulsion over the execution of the king and in 1651 a number of them had been arrested on the grounds that they had been involved in a royalist conspiracy.[19] Subsequently, in January 1656, Simeon Ashe (who was one of the most prominent of these ministers) was lamenting to his friend Robert Baillie that attempts were being made 'to overthrow the power and practise of Presbyteriall government and to advance Independencie' and that indulgence was being shown towards the Anabaptists 'and other erroneous persons'. Even so, all was not lost. 'Through God's mercy', he assured Baillie, 'many act presbyteriallie in London, and in many counties, both in reference to ordination and admission to the sacrament.'[20]

In February 1654 Edward Harley told his father that it was the opinion of great lawyers that all the ecclesiastical benefices in England had now become donative cures since, following the extirpation of the bishops, there was no one authorized to receive presentations or give institutions.[21] On 20 March Cromwell issued an ordinance which, as explained in the preamble, was intended to remedy a situation in which there was no settled procedure for filling vacant places with godly preachers and as a result the rights of patrons were being prejudiced. Accordingly it was decreed that any person who was nominated for a benefice or public lectureship would require the approval of commissioners whose grant of admission would constitute an institution and induction. The

185

commissioners named in the ordinance included Stephen Marshall and Samuel Fairclough but in the main they were Independent divines, men such as Thomas Goodwin, Philip Nye and Sidrach Simpson. There is, however, no evidence of any discrimination against Presbyterian nominees.[22] In a further ordinance which was promulgated on 28 August 1654 the government appointed lay commissioners in each county for the purpose of ejecting 'scandalous, ignorant and insufficient ministers and schoolmasters'. Some of these commissioners were religious Independents such as Sir Arthur Hesilrige and Sir William Constable; others were religious Presbyterians such as Sir Robert Harley and his son Edward and Sir John Horner. And among the ministers chosen to assist them there was a similar mixture of Independents and Presbyterians.[23]

In September 1656, following his election to Parliament, Edward Harley sought guidance from Richard Baxter on what should be done 'for the service of the distressed Church'. In his response Baxter emphasized that it was important to avoid extremes in the matter of toleration and to 'helpe the Orthodoxe unanimous ministers to as many Advantages as you can'. There was a need to 'settle' the committee for the approbation which had done 'much good' and to ensure that the arrangements for ejecting scandalous ministers extended to every county. At the same time he was convinced that standards of morality would never be improved until there were more zealous magistrates than most of those who were currently serving. Finally, he considered that an attempt should be made to secure a reconciliation between the Presbyterians, the Independents and the prelatical party which would bring them together in a comfortable communion without requiring them to abandon any of their principles.[24]

During the 1650s most counties had both Presbyterian congregations which continued to use the Directory of Worship and Independent congregations which might dispense with any kind of formal liturgy. Some Puritan squires were strongly attached to Independency. When William Bridge published an edition of his collected works in 1657 he inserted a dedication to Sir John Wittewronge, William Owfield and other members of his London congregation or, as he termed it, the family which God had made one. Owfield, who had been secluded from the Long Parliament in 1648, may possibly have been influenced by Christopher Feake, the Fifth Monarchy preacher, whom his father had once employed as a household chaplain.[25] In the main, however, the Puritan county families had a marked preference for ministers of the Presbyterian persuasion. In January 1653 Sir Robert Harley was informed that in a pamphlet which had recently appeared he had been violently attacked for countenancing Presbyterian ministers. These ministers included the preachers who had been established at Hereford through his influence and such leading figures among the London clergy as Edmund Calamy and James Nalton.[26] Another of the secluded MPs, Nathaniel Stephens, was the patron of William Mew, a Presbyterian divine who officiated at Eastington in Gloucestershire. In July 1653 we find Mew writing to his friend Richard Baxter that he had been attempting to promote an association of godly ministers but added that 'Our Common dilapidations need more Cyment then stones for the repayringe of our Breaches; wee have to many rough and hardy dissenters that will not Easyly be brought to Lye Square and Even'.[27] In Derbyshire, Samuel Charles, who had been ordained as a Presbyterian divine in 1655, served for a time as Sir John Gell's domestic chaplain and was subsequently presented to the living of Mickleover by Sir John Curzon. The Gell mansion, Hopton Hall, was situated in the extensive parish of Wirksworth which had a functioning classical presbytery.[28] In Devon the Bampfields of Poltimore had a Presbyterian chaplain and tutor, Humphrey Philips, while another 'orthodox' minister, Ambrose Clare, held the living which was in their gift.[29] When it became necessary to fill a vacant living a wealthy Puritan patron would usually nominate a university graduate who had already been ordained (either before or after the abolition of episcopal government) or who was willing to be ordained in accordance with Presbyterian usage.[30]

During the Commonwealth period many Puritan squires

who had been active in the cause of godliness before the time of the Civil Wars were finally laid to rest. In June 1649 Brampton Gurdon observed in a letter to Governor Winthrop which he was obliged to dictate that

> Age much impaires both my sight and heareing which enforceth mee thus to make use of helpes. God hath vouchsafed mee a long pilgrimage in this world. God enable mee to stand out His tyme to His glory and my comfort. Yf God spares mee but an other month I shall be 83 yeares of age.

Before the end of the year, however, he was interred in his parish church of Assington.[31] His friend Sir Simonds D'Ewes who, like him, was seated in Suffolk, died on 8 April 1650 at the age of 48. After a brief period of imprisonment in December 1648 he had retired to his estate and devoted much of his time to intellectual pursuits. For two years or so before his death (we are told) he had enjoyed the company of Louis de Grand who was 'skilfull in the languages, mathematicks and other learnings' and whose functions had taken the form of 'Conversing with him. . . . in Latine and doeing and performinge such other Scholasticall things as he desired'. In the absence of a published funeral sermon the last word on D'Ewes should perhaps be left to a fellow antiquarian, Sir Roger Twysden, who had once described him as 'a person never wearyed in doing courtesies'.[32]

Writing to Cromwell in September 1650, following his victory at Dunbar, Sir William Armyne told him that all honest men were praying that God would 'add a second blessing, in directing us to make a right use of what he hath now done for us, to the glory of his great name and the good of his church and people.'[33] For Sir William, however, time was running out. In May 1651 he died in London while serving as a member of the Council of State and his body was taken home to Lincolnshire for burial. If he had made a will he might well have stipulated that his funeral should be without ostentation; in the event, however, it was on a scale which was in keeping with the status of a man who had a landed income of £4,000 a year. To judge from some accounts which have survived, the total expenditure arising from the funeral arrangements amounted to nearly £1,000. At the interment, which took place at Lenton, the sermon was preached by Seth Wood, the Puritan minister there, who received the sum of £5 for his pains. After referring to Sir William's ancient and honourable extraction Wood praised him for the holiness of his life, his patronage and protection of godly ministers, the qualities which he had displayed both as a landlord and an MP and his defence of public liberty.[34]

When Sir Nathaniel Barnardiston, the most celebrated Puritan patron in Suffolk, drew up his will in September 1651 he stressed in a reference to his sons that 'I had need rather they should be good men then greate men'. To his long-serving minister Samuel Fairclough he bequeathed £10, desiring him to afford to the children 'his best helpe and assistance in the waies of God'.[35] Sir Nathaniel lived for nearly two years after this but in failing health. While residing at Hackney he sent for Fairclough who conversed with him about such matters as the immortality of the soul, the joys of heaven and the vanity and emptiness of all worldly things. At their parting he told his friend that there was little likelihood that God 'hath any more work or service for me to do, except it be to suffer for keeping a good Conscience, in witnessing against the Apostacys and Impieties of the Times'. Sir Nathaniel died in London on 25 July 1653 but the body was taken down to Kedington for burial in his own parish church. For the funeral sermon Fairclough took as his text the passage 'Of whom the world was not worthy' and in that general spirit commended the deceased for his zeal in religion, his strict personal morality, his defence of public liberty and his charity towards the poor.[36] In a collection of elegiac verse which was subsequently published there was general agreement that he had been a true saint. As one contributor put it:

Thou stately Top-bough of a noble Stem,
One of God's Jewels, and thy Country's Gem,
That help'd to bless the Land wherein thou wast
Lately a Saint: but now those joyes are past.[37]

189

According to his eldest son Sir Robert Harley bore the ailments which afflicted him in his latter years with exemplary fortitude. Not long before his death, which occurred at Ludlow on 6 November 1656, he received a visit from his friend Edmund Calamy who ventured to ask him what comfortable evidences he had that he was assured of salvation and was informed that he had nothing to rely upon but Jesus Christ. After his death one of the female servants wrote that he was a man 'that had not Converse with the Corruptions of the tymes' but had been an instrument for propagating the Gospel in his generation. God had enabled him faithfully to keep his Covenant and to walk in his commandments 'and rather to part with estate then a good Conscience'. He had, moreover, been eminent in charity. A memorandum about the arrangements for the funeral, which took place in the newly rebuilt church at Brampton Bryan, lists a number of matters requiring attention, among them escutcheons for the hearse; meat and wine for the entertainment of relatives and friends; mourning ribbons, hatbands and gloves; and a seating plan for the church. In the funeral sermon Thomas Froysell singled out, among other things, Sir Robert's achievement in bringing the Gospel into Herefordshire through the planting of godly ministers; his determination as a magistrate to preserve the sanctity of the Sabbath; and his enthusiasm for a Presbyterian form of church government.[38]

At the Restoration the Puritan gentry who had been associated with the republican government experienced varying fortunes: Sir Henry Vane the younger was beheaded on Tower Hill; Sir Arthur Hesilrige and John Hutchinson both died while in confinement; Sir Henry Mildmay was required to suffer the humiliation of an annual act of penance; Sir Gilbert Pickering and Bulstrode Whitelocke managed to avoid any kind of punishment; and Sir James Harrington and Edmund Ludlow fled abroad. During his long exile Harrington drew some solace from the spiritual meditations which he committed to paper, though he came round to the view that the inauguration of Christ's rule on earth was not as imminent as he had once believed.[39] In September 1661 some of the deputy

190

lieutenants for Somerset informed the lord lieutenant that they had apprehended two eminent persons of 'Notorious sedicious spiritte, and Ringleaders in disaffecion and opposicion of his Majesty's Governmente and the lawes of this land'. These were both major Puritan squires, John Pyne the Independent and William Strode the Presbyterian. Pyne, it was reported, had recently held a conventicle in his house and had openly declared that he was unable to conform to the discipline of the Church of England. Strode, for his part, had stated flatly that he could not consent to the orders and government of the Church. In the event both men escaped lightly.[40]

Generally, however, the Puritan squires who had taken the side of Parliament in the first Civil War either supported or readily acquiesced in the restoration of the monarchy. In their judgement a restored monarchy which would guarantee social and economic stability was far preferable to a regime which was dependent on military force, which imposed heavy taxes on the landed interest and which allowed too much freedom to sects which persistently challenged the privileged position of the upper classes. In 1657 a wealthy Yorkshire MP, Sir William Strickland, had spoken up on behalf of many of his fellow gentry in complaining that the country had for too long been subject to the burden of a land tax and in calling for the punishment of those who refused to pay tithes on the grounds that 'The same levelling principle will lay waste properties and deny rents'.[41] The general mood of disenchantment with the 'good old cause'[42] was reflected in the will which Sir Francis Drake, whose loyalty to Parliament had cost him dearly, drew up in April 1661, not long before his death. He was under an obligation (he observed) to render an account to the Lord of what he had done with those talents which had been lent to him,

> which worldly troubles with the late Civill or rather barbarous and uncivill wars for my greate sins have lessened the increase and much diminished and I confesse in all humillity I have not improved that temporall Estate left mee

after the late sad troubles nor my spirituall as it ought to god's glory.[43]

Whatever their political views the Puritan gentry were saddened by the realization that all the high expectations about the advancement of godliness had proved illusory. During the Protectorate, writes Lucy Hutchinson, 'True religion was now allmost lost, even among the religious party, and Hipocrisie became an epidemicall disease.'[44] The general decline in moral standards which was often commented on owed much to the socially disruptive effects of the Civil Wars but there were many who considered that it was also a product of such factors as the fragmentation of the godly party, the toleration of heterodox religious opinions and the difficulties encountered over the establishment of a new kind of national Church. Looking back on these turbulent years Richard Baxter expressed his contempt for the 'sin of separating principles' which had corrupted Cromwell's army 'and cast the greatest dishonor on Religion that ever was done in England'.[45]

Among the Puritan gentry there is evidence that some of the younger generation were rejecting the values of their parents. William Wray, the eldest son of Sir Christopher Wray, was described by John Evelyn, who met him on the Continent in 1646, as 'a good drinking gentleman' and 'our mad Captain'.[46] During the Civil War period Richard Baxter had been given shelter by Sir Thomas Rous, a Worcestershire Puritan, and his wife Lady Jane whom he characterizes as a godly, grave and understanding woman. In September 1657 Baxter wrote in a letter to the heir, Edward Rous, that he had heard that 'you were quite given up to drinkinge, sportinge, idle company and courses, in flatt licentiousness, in your disobedience to your father to the greife of his heart'; indeed he understood that his father was even thinking of marrying again in order to disinherit him. 'O Sir', he told him, 'Remember sin is deceitfull, the flesh is base, the world is worthless; pleasures here are short.' Holiness, on the other hand, was 'sweet and amiable; the life of Godlynes is clean and safe and pleasant.'[47] Sir William Armyne's son and namesake also failed to live up to his father's expectations despite a strict upbringing. In his will, which was drawn up in December 1657, he expressed the hope that if God was pleased to add any more days to his life he would be able to spend them, in a spirit of repentance, 'to the glory of his holy name and the eternal comfort of my own poor immortal soul'. The following month the preacher at his funeral declared in the course of a sermon which was unusually frank that he had lived a sinful life but had come to loathe his former vanities.[48] In October 1661 Sir William Waller told his kinsman Edward Harley that he now had only one son 'whome I can own with the affection of a father'. His elder son, William, had gone away in a rebellious manner and he was afraid that he might seek to debauch his brother, as indeed he had already attempted to do.[49]

Many Puritan squires had no strong objection to bishops provided they were sympathetically inclined towards the godly and had their powers curtailed. After Bishop Thomas Morton, who had always been well regarded in Puritan circles, had been turned out of the see of Durham Sir Christopher Yelverton took him into his household at Easton Mauduit in North-amptonshire and employed him as a tutor to his son Henry. To judge from his will, which was drawn up shortly before his death in 1654, Sir Christopher remained a thoroughgoing Puritan but through Morton's influence Henry became 'a true Son of the Church of England'. In 1670 a posthumous work of Morton entitled *The Episcopacy of the Church of England Justified to be Apostolical* was published with a preface written by his former pupil who claimed that John Dod was 'none of those who disliked the Liturgy' or 'despised our Ecclesiastical Government.'[50]

In the case of some Puritan gentry there appears to have been a close link between the emergence of royalist sympathies and a decline in religious fervour.[51] More striking, however, is the continuing attachment of many wealthy families to the cause of godliness in spite of the constraints imposed by the ecclesiastical legislation of the Pension Parliament and the influences at work in what Sir Willian Waller termed 'this corrupt age'.[52] While some of the younger generation failed to maintain the Puritan tradition in their families there were others who faithfully upheld it. Sir Thomas Strickland, who was the only son of Sir William Strickland, is said to have been a 'serious and religious person' who was in favour of reformation.[53] Arthur Onslow, who succeeded his father Sir Richard in 1664, was 'a man of great plainness and sincerity and of most remarkable sobriety of life' who was active in 'support of the liberties of the people and the Protestant interest'.[54] Sir John Gell's heir and namesake was probably a stricter Puritan than his father. In March 1659 we find him writing to his wife, who was in poor health, that the best course was to rely on God for

> hee sends deliverance, you have had great experience of his love, he chastizes you but as a father. . . . use meanes, do your duty, and trust him, who is all sufficient. The lord I hope hath mercyes in store for you, draw them forth by faith and fervent prayer.[55]

Edward Harley took over his father's role as the chief patron of Puritan ministers in Herefordshire. In 1664 he was expressing concern about the amount of drinking in Brampton Bryan and in 1678 he wrote in a 'retrospect' of his life 'O Lord!. . . . Fashion this house of clay to be thy temple. . . . make me holy, as my God is holy, in all manner of conversation and godliness.'[56]

On 13 May 1661 the Commons decided that all MPs should take communion at St Margaret's Westminster in the form prescribed in the liturgy of the Church of England. A Lancashire member, Sir Ralph Assheton of Whalley, asked to be excused on grounds of conscience; and according to Edmund Ludlow two other Puritan MPs, Richard Norton and Richard Hampden, the son of John Hampden, declined to receive communion in a kneeling position.[57] Many of the Puritan gentry gave shelter to ministers who were forced out of their livings as a result of the Act of Uniformity. Among the chaplains employed by Sir Anthony Irby there were at least three nonconformist divines, Thomas Cawton, William Bruce and Thomas Clark. When the plague broke out in London in 1665 the Irby family went back to Lincolnshire and Cawton joined the household of Lady Mary Armyne. In a sense this was highly appropriate since his father had served as chaplain to the Armyne family before the time of the Civil Wars.[58] Some Puritan magistrates were considered to be too well disposed towards nonconformist ministers and their lay associates. In 1664 it was alleged that there were fourteen justices of the peace in Devon who were 'arrant Presbyterians', among them Sir John Davie, Sir Walter Yonge (a grandson of the diarist), Sir Edmund Fowell and Matthew Hele. Similarly, there was a report in 1669 that through the indulgence of Sir John Curzon a number of Presbyterian ministers were regularly holding conventicles at Little Ireton in Derbyshire.[59]

By virtue of the Act of Uniformity the patrons of church livings were obliged to nominate ministers who were episcopally ordained and willing to give an undertaking to conform to the Book of Common Prayer. For a Puritan squire this could mean a lengthy search for an able preacher who was both godly and conformable.[60] Some of the gentry were regularly visited by nonconformist divines who helped to satisfy their need for edifying preaching; and, more significantly, many of the leading Puritan families, among them the Barringtons, Hampdens and Stricklands, were able to worship in a way which suited them through the employment of domestic chaplains.[61] Where there was a chaplain it was sometimes the practice for conventicles to be held: in Devon, for example, Sir John Davie's house, Creedy in Sandford, was said to be the 'chief place of resort' for the Presbyterians of the neighbourhood.[62] With the issue of the Declaration of Indulgence in March 1672 there was a brief period of toleration and arrangements were introduced for the licensing of nonconformist ministers and the houses in which their congregations were to meet. Some of the Puritan gentry who applied for licences opted for a Presbyterian form of worship: these included Sir John Stapley, John Gurdon and Thomas Hutton of Yorkshire. Others such as Lady Frances Vane, the widow of Sir Henry Vane the younger, and Lady Eleanor Roberts, the widow of Sir William Roberts, declared a preference for Independent or Congregational ministers.[63] At Titchmarsh in Northamptonshire Sir Gilbert Pickering's widow was to have had a Presbyterian divine, Henry Searle, as her licensed minister but he died early in 1672 and she then chose Nathaniel Whiting who was of the Congregational persuasion.[64]

If the Puritan gentry were to retain their religious identity it was clearly imperative that they should take particular care over the education of the children. In some cases nonconformist ministers acted as tutors to the sons of Puritan squires during their travels on the Continent. In 1660 William Trevethick, the Presbyterian minister of Petrockstow in Devon, preached the sermon at the funeral of his patron Robert Rolle, and two years later, following his ejection, went abroad with the young heir, Samuel Rolle. Other Presbyterian divines who took on the same kind of employment included Humphrey Philips who travelled to Holland with a younger son of William Strode and Francis Tallents who accompanied Richard Hampden's heir and one of the sons of Hugh Boscawen.[65] Many of the children of Puritan gentry were educated by nonconformist divines either at home or in private schools such as the establishment of Samuel Birch at Bampton in Oxfordshire which was attended by Edward Harley's sons.[66] In his autobiography Adam Martindale relates that in Lancashire he was employed as a tutor first by Sir Richard Hoghton of Hoghton Tower and then by Lady Anne Assheton of Middleton.[67]

In November 1668 a Presbyterian minister, George Primrose, wrote in a letter to Edward Harley that he was praying that

> the seeds of grace and of pious education sowne in the hearts of your hopefull children may budd and yeeld their pleasant and wholesome fruit in their seasons, that the name of Harley may still send forth a sweet and fresh perfume in the Churches of Christ.[68]

Such expectations were not always fulfilled yet it would be a long time before the strange phenomenon of upper class Puritanism became no more than a memory.

APPENDIX

A CATALOGUE OF LEADING PURITAN GENTRY FAMILIES

List A represents an attempt to compile a complete list of those Puritan gentry families which on the outbreak of the Civil War had an estate revenue of £1,000 a year or more.

List B consists of other Puritan gentry families which feature in this study. In most cases the family had an estate revenue of £500 a year or more, though under £1,000 a year, on the outbreak of the Civil War.

List A

Armyne of Osgodby Hall, Lincolnshire and Orton Longville, Huntingdonshire
Ashe of Freshford, Somerset
Assheton of Middleton, Lancashire
* Assheton of Whalley Abbey, Lancashire
Ayscough of South Kelsey, Lincolnshire

Bacon of Redgrave, Suffolk
Bacon of Shrubland Hall, Suffolk
Bampfield of Poltimore, Devon
Barkham of Tottenham High Cross, Middlesex and South Acre, Norfolk
Barkham of Wainfleet, Lincolnshire
Barnardiston of Kedington, Suffolk
Barrington of Hatfield Broad Oak, Essex
Barrow of Barningham, Suffolk
Bindloss of Borwick Hall, Lancashire
Booth of Dunham Massey, Cheshire
Boscawen of Tregothnan, St Michael Penkevil, Cornwall
Bourchier of Beningbrough, Yorkshire
Bowyer of Knypersley, Staffordshire
Boynton of Barmston, Yorkshire
Boys of Fredville in Nonington, Kent
Brereton of Handforth, Cheshire

Brooke of Cockfield Hall, Yoxford, Suffolk
Browne of Betchworth Castle, Surrey
Browne of Frampton, Dorset
Buller of Shillingham, Cornwall
Burdett of Foremark, Derbyshire and Bramcote, Warwickshire
Burgoyne of Sutton, Bedfordshire and Wroxall, Warwickshire

     Cheke of Pirgo, Essex
SR Chudleigh of Ashton, Devon
SR Cooke of Highnam, Gloucestershire
U   Cope of Hanwell, Oxfordshire
     Crewe of Steane, Northamptonshire
     Cutts of Childerley, Cambridgeshire

Dacres of Cheshunt, Hertfordshire
Darley of Buttercrambe, Yorkshire
Davie of Creedy in Sandford, Devon
SR D'Ewes of Stowlangtoft, Suffolk
     Doddington of Breamore, Hampshire
SR Drake of Buckland Abbey, Devon
     Dryden of Canons Ashby, Northamptonshire
     Dunch of Little Wittenham, Berkshire

     Earle of Stragglethorpe, Lincolnshire
U   Elmes of Lilford Hall, Northamptonshire
     Erle of Charborough, Dorset
     Evelyn of Lee Place, Godstone, Surrey
     Evelyn of West Dean, Wiltshire

Franklin of Willesden, Middlesex

SR Gee of Bishop Burton, Yorkshire
     Gell of Hopton Hall, Derbyshire
     Gerard of Flambards, Harrow on the Hill, Middlesex
     Goodwin of Over Winchendon, Buckinghamshire
     Grantham of Goltho, Lincolnshire
     Grimston of Bradfield, Essex
     Gurdon of Assington, Suffolk

Hampden of Great Hampden, Buckinghamshire
Harley of Brampton Bryan, Herefordshire
Harrington of Ridlington, Rutland
Hartopp of Buckminster, Leicestershire
SR Hawksworth of Hawksworth, Yorkshire

PR   Hele of Gnaton Hall, Newton Ferrers, Devon
       Hesilrige of Noseley, Leicestershire
       Hobart of Blicking Hall, Norfolk
       Holland of Quidenham, Norfolk
       Holman of Markworth, Northamptonshire

R   Holt of Stubley, Lancashire
       Honywood of Marks Hall, Essex
       Horner of Cloford and Mells, Somerset
       Hungerford of Corsham, Wiltshire
       Hutchinson of Owthorpe, Nottinghamshire

       Ingoldsby of Lenborough, Buckinghamshire
       Irby of Boston and Whaplode, Lincolnshire

SR   Jackson of Hickleton, Yorkshire
       Jephson of Froyle, Hampshire
       Jervoise of Herriard, Hampshire

       Knightley of Fawsley, Northamptonshire

       Leman of Northaw, Hertfordshire
       Lister of Coleby, Lincolnshire
       Lister of Linton on the Wolds, Yorkshire
       Lister of Thornton in Craven, Yorkshire
       Lucy of Broxbourne, Hertfordshire
       Ludlow of Maiden Bradley, Wiltshire
       Luke of Wood End in Cople, Bedfordshire
       Lumley of Great Bardfield, Essex
       Lytton of Knebworth, Hertfordshire

       Mainwaring of Whitmore, Staffordshire
       Masham of Otes Hall, High Laver, Essex
       Mildmay of Wanstead, Essex
       Moundeford of Feltwell, Norfolk

       Norcliffe of Langton and Nunnington, Yorkshire
       Northcote of Hayne in Newton St Cyres, Devon
       Norton of Southwick, Hampshire

       Onslow of Knowle in Cranleigh, Surrey
       Overbury of Bourton on the Hill, Gloucestershire
       Owfield of Gatton, Surrey and Elsham, Lincolnshire

       Pelham of Laughton, Sussex

*   Peyto of Chesterton, Warwickshire

Pickering of Titchmarsh, Northamptonshire
Pile of Compton Beauchamp, Berkshire
* Popham of Littlecote, Wiltshire and Hunstrete, Somerset
Purefoy of Wadley, Berkshire
SR Pye of Farringdon, Berkshire
Pyne of Curry Mallet, Somerset

Rivers of Chafford in Penshurst, Kent
Roberts of Neasden House, Willesden, Middlesex
Rolle of Heanton Satchville, Devon
Rosewell of Forde Abbey, Devon
Rous of Rous Lench, Worcestershire

Scott of Scot's Hall, Smeeth, Kent
R Slingsby of Red House, Moor Monkton and Scriven, Yorkshire
Soame of Little Thurlow, Suffolk
Spring of Pakenham, Suffolk
Stapley of Patcham, Sussex
Strickland of Boynton, Yorkshire
Strode of Barrington Court, Somerset
Strode of Newnham, Devon
* Swinfen of Swinfen, Staffordshire

Tate of Delapré Abbey, Northamptonshire
U Townshend of East Raynham, Norfolk
Trenchard of Wolfeton House, Charminster, Dorset

* Vane of Fairlawne, Kent and Raby Castle, Durham

Waller of Winchester Castle, Hampshire
Walrond of Bradfield House, Devon
Wentworth of North Elmsall, Yorkshire
Wentworth of Somerleyton, Suffolk
Whitehead of West Tytherley, Hampshire
Whitelocke of Fawley, Buckinghamshire
SR Wilbraham of Woodhay, Cheshire
Wilson of Gresegarth, Westmorland and London
Winch of Everton, Bedfordshire
Windham of Felbrigg, Norfolk
Winwood of Denham in Quainton, Buckinghamshire
Wise of Sydenham Hall, Marystow, Devon
Wodehouse of Kimberley, Norfolk
Wray of Barlings Abbey, Lincolnshire
Wray of Glentworth, Lincolnshire

Wroth of Petherton Park, Somerset

Yelverton of Easton Mauduit, Northamptonshire
Yonge of Stedcombe House, Axmouth, Devon

List B

Alston of Odell, Bedfordshire

Bond of Dorchester
Bosvile of Gunthwaite, Yorkshire
Browne of Arlesey, Bedfordshire

SR * Carew of Anthony, Cornwall
Cobb of Adderbury, Oxfordshire
Constable of Holme on Spalding Moor, Yorkshire
Corbet of Yarmouth, Suffolk
Curzon of Kedleston, Derbyshire
Cutler of Stainborough, Yorkshire

Drake of Shardeloes, Buckinghamshire

Eliott of Busbridge, Surrey
Everard of Langleys in Much Waltham, Essex

Fowell of Fowelscombe, Devon

Harrington of Kelston, Somerset

Ireton of Attenborough, Nottinghamshire

Kemp of Spains Hall, Finchingfield, Essex

Legard of Anlaby, Yorkshire
Lisle of Wootton, Isle of Wight

Martyn of Oxton in Kenton, Devon
Marwood of Nun Monkton and Little Busby, Yorkshire

Nichols of Faxton, Northamptonshire
Nichols of Penvose in St Tudy, Cornwall

Parker of Erwarton, Suffolk
SR Peyton of Isleham, Cambridgeshire
Potts of Mannington, Norfolk

Rigby of Goosnargh, Lancashire
Rodes of Great Houghton, Yorkshire
Rudyerd of West Woodhay, Berkshire

Salway of Stanford, Worcestershire
Shuttleworth of Gawthorpe, Lancashire
Sleigh of Ashe, Derbyshire
Springett of Langley, Kent
Stephens of Eastington, Gloucestershire

Wittewronge of Rothamsted, Hertfordshire

NOTES

1 The main sources of information which have been used in the calculation of annual income are estate papers, journals and correspondence; the records of Chancery proceedings; and Court of Wards records.
2 In the case of families marked * the heir was a Puritan but the father cannot be readily identified as such.
3 In the main the families listed supported Parliament during the first Civil War. The exceptions are annotated as follows:

U   uncommitted (in such cases there was a minority)
R   the family supported the king
PR   the head of the family at first supported Parliament but later went over to the king
SR   the heir or younger son supported or went over to the king.

In addition, several Puritan gentry, including Sir John Evelyn of Wiltshire and Sir John Northcote, were suspected of royalist leanings.

NOTES

CHAPTER 1   REFORMATION DEFERRED

1 Edmund Calamy, *England's Looking–Glasse*, 22 December 1641, *Fast Sermons*, ii, 48, 49, 65.
2 BL, Portland MSS, BL Loan 29/119.
3 Samuel Fairclough, *The Troublers Troubled*, 4 April 1641, epistle dedicatory and 28, 34, 35, 38, 47, 52–3.
4 Sir Simonds D'Ewes, *The Journal of Sir Simonds D'Ewes. From the First Recess of the Long Parliament to the Withdrawal of King Charles from London* (ed. W. H. Coates), 343–4.
5 Thomason Tracts, 669 f. 4(65). *Camden Society*, lviii, 227. BL, Portland MSS, BL Loan 29/173, f. 243.
6 Sir Simonds D'Ewes, *The Journal of Sir Simonds D'Ewes. From the Beginning of the Long Parliament to the Opening of the Trial of the Earl of Strafford* (ed. W. Notestein), 204, 373, 485. *C.J.*, ii, 84, 279, 283. BL, Portland MSS, BL Loan 29/173, f. 165. *Hutchinson Memoirs*, 54.
7 Dorothy Gardiner (ed.), *The Oxinden Letters, 1607–1642*, 257.
8 *Puritan Gentry*, 218, 220, 226, 228–31. Shaw, i, 78.
9 BL, Additional MSS 53, 726, f. 32. Bristol Record Office: Ashton Court MSS. 36074 139a.
10 Speech at a conference of both Houses, 20 July 1641, Thomason Tracts, E.199(2).
11 BL, Harleian MSS 7162, ff. 240, 256–7. *Puritan Gentry*, 227.
12 BL, Harleian MSS 164, f. 217. Dr Williams's Library: Morrice MSS, I, 373(16).
13 Both D'Ewes and Pyne testify to the strength of the episcopalian party in the Commons. *The Journal of Sir Simonds D'Ewes* (ed. W. H. Coates), 149. Bristol Record Office: Ashton Court MSS, 36074 139b.
14 *The Journal of Sir Simonds D'Ewes* (ed. W.H. Coates), 290. BL, Harleian MSS 163, f. 80.
15 *The Journal of Sir Simonds D'Ewes* (ed. W. H. Coates), 151–2.
16 *Hutchinson Memoirs*, 51. See Anthony Fletcher, *The Outbreak of the English Civil War*, 136–45.

17 W. M. Brady, *Annals of the Catholic Hierarchy in England and Scotland 1585–1876*, 83.
18 William Prynne, *Hidden Workes of Darkenes*, 189–94.
19 *The Journal of Sir Simonds D'Ewes* (ed. W. H. Coates), 146.
20 Thomason Tracts, E.200(9).
21 *HMC, Fifth Report*, Appendix, 7. G. W. Johnson (ed.), *The Fairfax Correspondence*, ii, 367–72.
22 *C. S. P. Dom., 1641–3*, 241.
23 For a detailed account of the petitioning campaign see Fletcher, *op.cit.*, 191–227.
24 Thomas May, *The History of the Parliament of England*, 85.
25 Thomason Tracts, E.135(36). *HMC, Duke of Buccleuch MSS*, i, 290.
26 *Camden Society*, lviii, 146. BL, Harleian MSS 386, f. 199. *HMC, Duke of Buccleuch MSS*, i, 291.
27 G. W. Johnson (ed.,), *The Fairfax Correspondence*, ii, 362, 373. House of Lords Library: House of Lords MSS, 15 February 1642. See also BL, Egerton MSS 2546, ff. 23–4.
28 The Bishops' Exclusion Act (17 Charles I, cap.xxvii) banned all persons in holy orders from exercising any temporal jurisdiction or authority.
29 Thomason Tracts, E.200 (33).
30 BL, Harleian MSS 163, f. 31, and 164, f. 226. House of Lords Library: House of Lords MSS, Derbyshire petition (date given as 26 February 1642).
31 BL, Harleian MSS 163, f.31. For the published version of the petition see Thomason Tracts, E.138(32).
32 Thomason Tracts, 669 f. 4(82).
33 See *Puritan Gentry*, 224–5.
34 BL, Harleian MSS 386, f. 197.
35 BL, Portland MSS, BL Loan 29/173, ff. 207, 228–9, 239–40.
36 PRO, S. P. Dom., Charles I, S.P.16/cdxxxii/34. BL, Harleian MSS 164, f. 226. Thomason Tracts, 669 f. 4.
37 BL, Harleian MSS 163, f. 24. *C. J.*, ii, 471.
38 *C. J.*, ii, 515, 518, 534, 535, 539–41. BL, Harleian MSS 164, f. 253. Thomason Tracts, E.144(23). *Camden Society*, lviii, 158.
39 Clarendon, ii, 70.
40 Clarendon, ii, 71. Shaw, i, 124–7.

CHAPTER 2   DRIFTING INTO WAR

1 *A. & O.*, i, 1–4.
2 The official journals of the Commons and the Lords (*C. J.*, ii and *L. J.*, iv and v) give the names of most but by no means all of the deputy lieutenants who were appointed.

3 *C. J.* ii, 483, 609, 618, 637, 655. *L. J.*, v, 94. *HMC, Duke of Buccleuch MSS*, i, 304.

4 BL, Additional Charter 29, 277 and Additional MSS 33, 147, f. 101. Hampshire Record Office: Jervoise of Herriard Park MSS, 44 M69/F9.

5 BL, Additional Charter 29, 276 and Additional MSS 21, 922, ff. 20, 38, 186.

6 *C. J.*, ii, 498. *HMC, Coke MSS*, ii, 309. BL, Harleian MSS 163, f. 130.

7 BL, Additional MSS 37, 343, ff. 247–9, 253.

8 *Yorkshire Archaeological Journal*, vii, 74.

9 *HMC, Eighth Report*, Appendix, pt i, 211.

10 Rushworth, iv, 615–17. House of Lords Library: House of Lords MSS, 6 June 1642.

11 BL, Harleian MSS 163, f. 121.

12 *C. J.*, ii, 589, 593, 600, 606, 608, 609, 616, 618, 619, 622, 627, 629, 632, 633, 637, 639, 641–2, 651, 653, 658, 659, 668, 698, 706. See Anthony Fletcher, *The Outbreak of the English Civil War*, 348–56.

13 BL, Harleian MSS 163, f. 146.

14 *A. & O.*, i, 6–9.

15 *C. J.*, ii, 630. BL, Harleian MSS 163, f. 162.

16 *C. S. P. Dom., 1641–3*, 345. Northamptonshire Record Office: Finch-Hatton MSS 133 (no pagination).

17 Clarendon, ii, 319–22. John Milton, *Complete Prose Work of John Milton*, iii, 236, 243. See John F. Wilson, *The Pulpit in Parliament*, *passim*, and Lawrence Stone, *The Causes of the English Revolution 1529–1642*, 139–40.

18 See *The English Revolution. I. Fast Sermons to Parliament*.

19 *Puritan Gentry*, 183, 207–8, 214–15. *C. J.*, ii, 473. BL, Harleian MSS 163, f. 71.

20 BL, Egerton MSS 2650, f. 214.

21 *C. J.* ii, 497. *A. & O.*, i, 621.

22 BL, Harleian MSS 163, ff. 291, 292, 319, 354, 383; 164, ff. 233, 241, 248, 271, 273, 277, 281, 295, 308, 334, 367; and 165, ff. 122, 132, 135, 152, 167, 190.

23 Lady Alice Macdonald of the Isles, *The Fortunes of a Family*, 64.

24 BL, Harleian MSS 163, f. 153; 164, f. 257; 374. ff. 69–71; and 379, f. 96.

25 BL, Harleian MSS 165, f. 258. *Hutchinson Memoirs*, 61–2. A. C. Wood, *Nottinghamshire in the Civil War*, 33. Clarendon, ii, 228. *HMC, Coke MSS*, ii, 309.

26 Rushworth, iv, 753–4.

27 BL, Additional MSS 37, 343, ff. 251–2.

28 BL, Harleian MSS 163, f. 261.

29 Rushworth, iv, 755.
30 *C. J.*, ii, 579, 619, 623, 627, 628, 642, 646, 650, 657. BL, Harleian MSS 163, ff. 160, 161, and Additional MSS 11, 331, f. 4.
31 *C. J.*, ii, 618, 633. BL, Harleian MSS 163, ff. 153, 163. Bedfordshire County Record Office: St John of Bletsoe MSS, DDJ 1410.
32 John Walker, *Sufferings of the Clergy*, pt i, 91.
33 BL, Harleian MSS 163, f. 294. *Fast Sermons*, iii, 291, 320, 323, 325. *C. J.*, ii, 694.
34 *C. J.*, 634–6, 645, 646, 650, 653, 658–9, 664, 669. *L. J.*, v, 139, 145, 147–9, 190–2, 202–3.
35 *Puritan Gentry*, 90–1.
36 PRO, Chancery Proceedings, Six Clerks' Series, C.6/139/72 and C.7/405/45. *C. S. P. Dom, 1635–6*, 395. *C. J.*, ii, 651, 698, 710, 732–3. Northamptonshire Record Office: Finch-Hatton MSS 133 (no pagination). W. D. Christie (ed.), *Memoirs, Letters and Speeches of Anthony Ashley Cooper, First Earl of Shaftesbury*, 26–8. *C. S. P. Dom., 1637*, 400.
37 *C. J.*, ii, 632. *L. J.*, v, 246. *DNB* (Sir Samuel Luke).
38 *C. J.*, ii, 695. *L. J.*, v, 251–2. Bodleian, Tanner MSS 63, ff. 121, 126. BL, Harleian MSS 164, f. 257, and 386, ff. 206, 233. Clive Holmes, *The Eastern Association in the Civil War*, 55–7.

CHAPTER 3   AN UNNATURAL WAR

1 *HMC, Thirteenth Report*, Appendix, pt i, 43.
2 *C. J.*, ii, 686, 695, 696. BL, Harleian MSS 163, f. 285. *Puritan Gentry*, 162. *Oxford Royalist*, iv, 195–6.
3 BL, Harleian MSS 163, f. 152.
4 *HMC, Thirteenth Report*, Appendix, pt i, 44–6. Puritan Gentry, 21. Rushworth, iv, 687–8.
5 Richard Baxter, *Reliquianae Baxterianae* (ed. Matthew Sylvester), 41.
6 BL, Portland MSS, BL Loan 29/173, f. 252. *Camden Society*, lviii, 169, 170,176, 179, 181, 182. *HMC, Fourteenth Report*, Appendix, pt ii, 88, 90, 92, 93.
7 *Hutchinson Memoirs*, 60–1, 64, 67.
8 Thomason Tracts, 669 f. 6(27) and (53). *Cobbett's Parliamentary History of England*, ii, columns 1450–1. See Brian Manning (ed.), *Politics, Religion and the English Civil War*, 91–4.
9 PRO, Chancery Proceedings, Six Clerks' Series, C.10/9/49. T Tindall Wildridge, *The Hull Letters*, 161–3. *C. J.*, iv, 61.
10 BL, Additional MSS 37, 343, ff. 253, 254, 258.
11 *C. J.*, ii, 723,731,738.
12 Sir William Waller, *Vindication of the Character and Conduct of Sir William Waller*, 7, 108–9.
13 *HMC, Thirteenth Report*, Appendix, pt iv, 462.

14 Edmund Ludlow, *Memoirs of Edmund Ludlow*, 18–19.

15 BL, Additional MSS 37,343, f. 292.

16 BL, Harleian MSS 163, f. 163. Clarendon, ii, 460–1. *A Reall Protestation of Many and Very Eminent Persons in the County of Yorke*(Thomason Tracts, E.116(17)).

17 BL, Althorp Papers, B3. Clarendon, ii, 461–3. J. Hunter, *South Yorkshire*, i, 131. *HMC, Thirteenth Report*, Appendix, pt i, 64. See Anthony Fletcher, *The Outbreak of the English Civil War*, 390–1.

18 *England's Memorable Accidents*, 12 to 19 September 1642 (Thomason Tracts, E.240). *The Several Accompts of Sir John Gell . . . . and . . . . Thomas Gell* (Thomason Tracts, E.273(15)).

19 Derbyshire Record Office: Gresley MSS, D803 M/Z9, pages v to xvii. *VCH, Derbyshire*, ii, 126–7.

20 Bodleian, Tanner MSS 63, f. 126. BL, Harleian MSS 386, f. 234.

21 Bodleian, Tanner MSS 64, ff. 8, 10, 30–1, 50–1, 97, 102–4, 106. Clive Holmes, *The Eastern Association in the Civil War*, 56–60.

22 BL, Harleian MSS 163, f. 381.

23 *L. J.*, v, 245. BL, Harleian MSS 163, f. 257, and 165, f. 167. *C. J.*, ii, 718.

24 See, for example, B. G. Blackwood, 'The Cavalier and Roundhead Gentry of Suffolk', *The Suffolk Review*, New Series Nos. 5 and 7.

25 *C. J.*, ii, 740. *Camden Society*, lxvi, 121–2. Bodleian, Tanner MSS 63, f. 146.

26 BL, Harleian MSS 163, f. 325; and 164, f. 278. *A Perfect Diurnal of the Passages in Parliament*, 12 to 19 September 1642 (Thomason Tracts, E.240). Holmes, *op. cit.*, 48, 50–2.

27 Holmes, *op. cit.*. 68, 69, 226–8.

28 The Commons agreed that the Militia Ordinance should be executed in Surrey on 9 June 1642 but he appears to have taken no action (*C. J.*, ii, 606).

29 *HMC, Fourteenth Report*, Appendix, pt ix, 476, 483.

30 *C. J.*, ii, 707, 794–5. *VCH, Surrey*, i, 405.

31 BL, Harleian MSS 382, f. 37, and 386, f. 207.

32 *A. & O.*. i, 94. *VCH, Surrey*, ii, 142.

33 Clarendon, ii, 448–9. Eugene A. Andriette, *Devon and Exeter in the Civil War*, 56, 58, 72. *Camden Society*, cv, 229.

34 *HMC, Tenth Report*, Appendix, pt vi, 93.

35 *HMC, Thirteenth Report*, Appendix, pt i, 106.

36 *HMC, Seventh Report*, Appendix, 550.

CHAPTER 4 A NATION DIVIDED

1 Richard Baxter, *Penitent Confession*, 18–19.

2 J. T. Rutt (ed.), *Diary of Thomas Burton*, iii, 187–8.

3 Derbyshire Record Office: Gresley MSS, D803 M/Z9, pages v, xi.

4 *Hutchinson Memoirs*, 57.

5 *Oxford Royalist*, i, 492.

6 Clarendon, ii, 248.

7 *HMC, Thirteenth Report*, pt i, 70.

8 Sir Hugh Cholmley, for example, used this term (*State Papers Collected by Edward Earl of Clarendon*, ii, 185).

9 Sir Henry Slingsby, *The Diary of Sir Henry Slingsby* (ed. D Parsons), 3, 8, 19, 67–8, 121, 275, 318. J. T. Cliffe, *The Yorkshire Gentry*, 267.

10 *A. & O.* i, 91, 148.

11 BL, Harleian MSS 163, f. 376; 164, f. 377; and 646, f. 149. *Oxford Royalist*, i, 270.

12 *C. J.*, iii, 300.

13 R. N. Dore, *The Civil Wars in Cheshire*, 8, 15. BL, Additional MSS 33, 498, f. 69. *C. J.*, iv, 530.

14 West Devon Record Office: Strode MSS, 72/215. PRO, Exchequer, Depositions, E.134 1654 Easter No. 2 Devon.

15 Sources of information which have been used include estate papers, correspondence, memoirs and diaries; records of legal suits; Court of Wards papers; and papers of the Committee for the Advance of Money, the Committee for Compounding and the sequestration committees.

16 Clarendon, ii, 468 and iii, 527–9. Dr Williams's Library: Morrice MSS, J, no pagination. Sir Simonds D'Ewes, *The Journal of Sir Simonds D'Ewes. From the First Recess of the Long Parliament to the Withdrawal of King Charles from London* (ed. W. H. Coates), 152.

17 J. T. Cliffe, *The Yorkshire Gentry*, 349.

18 *Ibid.*, 138, 300–1, 303, 343. Dr Williams's Library: Morrice MSS, J, no pagination.

19 David Underdown, *Pride's Purge*, 223. PRO, Chancery Proceedings, Six Clerks' Series, C.6/18/26 and 28. BL, Harleian MSS 6395, f. 82.

20 BL, Harleian MSS 165, f. 152. John Aubrey, *Aubrey's Brief Lives* (ed. Oliver Lawson Dick), 353–4.

21 BL, Harleian MSS 165, f. 144.

22 Aubrey, *op. cit.*, 406. BL, Harleian MSS 164, f. 332.

23 See, for example, *Hutchinson Memoirs*, 57.

24 Samuel Clark, *The Lives of Sundry Eminent Persons*, pt i, 172. BL, Additional MSS 4275, f. 184. Thomas Fuller, *The Church-History of Britain*, xi, 220.

25 BL, Additional MSS 19,098, f.364. Thomason Tracts, E.43(9).

26 Ralph Josselin, *The Diary of the Rev. Ralph Josselin 1616–1683, Camden Third Series*, xv, 26.

27 *C. S. P. Dom.*, *1641–3*, 388, 391, 397, 398. Richard Baxter, *Reliquiae Baxterianae* (ed. Matthew Sylvester), 42, 51.

28 H. G. Tibbutt (ed.), *The Letter Books 1644–45 of Sir Samuel Luke*, 42, 77, 86.

29 *Oxford Royalist*, i, 643 and ii, 18, 444–5. *Puritan Gentry*, 170, 189–91. *C. S. P. Dom., 1631–2*, 402.

30 *Bibliotheca Gloucestrensis*, 172.

31 Anthony Fletcher, *A County Community in Peace and War: Sussex 1600–1660*, 284. Tibbutt, *op. cit.*, 434.

32 *Fast Sermons*, iv, 172, 173, 175, 176.

33 *Fast Sermons*, x, 265. *Oxford Royalist*, iv, 285.

34 Edmund Calamy, *The Noble-man's Patterne of True and Reall Thankfulnesse*, 20, 30, 44, 47, 50–1, 55.

35 *Puritan Gentry*, 25, 188–9, 226. BL, Portland MSS, BL Loan 29/88; 119; and 175, ff. 77–8, 79–80. *Fast Sermons*, xii, 38.

36 Calamy, *op. cit.*, 46.

37 *Oxford Royalist*, iv, 141, 145–6.

38 See above, p. 28.

39 *Life and Death of Mr Henry Jessey*, 5. HMC, *Seventh Report*, Appendix, 551. See *Puritan Gentry*, 172–3.

40 *Hutchinson Memoirs*, 89.

CHAPTER 5   FOR LIBERTY AND RELIGION

1 Derbyshire Record Office: Gresley MSS, D803 M/Z9, pages iii and iv. This is a commonplace book which belonged to Sir George Gresley.

2 J. T. Rutt (ed.), *Diary of Thomas Burton*, iii, 95. See Lawrence Stone, *The Causes of the English Revolution 1529–1642*, 51.

3 *L. J.*, v, 259.

4 Clarendon, ii, 149. BL, Additional MSS 18, 777, f. 54.

5 BL, Egerton MSS 2646, f. 193.

6 Sir William Waller, *Vindication of the Character and Conduct of Sir William Waller*, 241, 243, 244.

7 Richard Baxter, *The Autobiography of Richard Baxter* (ed. J. M. L. Thomas), 34–5.

8 *L. J.*, v, 259.

9 BL, Additional MSS, 37, 343, f. 280.

10 Edmund Ludlow, *Memoirs of Edmund Ludlow*, 45.

11 H. G. Tibbutt (ed.), *The Letter Books 1644–45 of Sir Samuel Luke*, 52. BL, Egerton MSS 786, f. 25. Bodleian, MS Top. Beds., d.4, f. 88.

12 HMC, *Ninth Report*, Appendix, pt ii, 494.

13 *Somers Tracts*, vi, 306–7. George Sikes, *The Life and Death of Sir Henry Vane, Knight*, 98, 102, 106. *The Tryal of Sir Henry Vane, Knight*, 90.

14 *Puritan Gentry*, 152–3, 195–6.

15 Rushworth, i, 473. Seth Wood, *The Saint's Enterance into Peace*

and Rest by Death, 22. Samuel Fairclough, *The Saint's Worthinesse and the World's Worthlesnesse*, 18.

16 W. Knowler (ed.), *The Earl of Strafforde's Letters and Despatches*, ii, 138. BL, Additional MSS 37, 343, f. 269.

17 J. T. Rutt (ed.), *Diary of Thomas Burton*, iii, 57 and iv, 77. *Harleian Miscellany*, iii, 487.

18 Sir Edward Peyton, *The Divine Catastrophe of the Kingly Family of the House of Stuarts*, 84–5.

19 *HMC, Portland MSS*, v, 641.

20 *Hutchinson Memoirs*, 53.

21 *Ibid.*, 107.

22 *Camden Society*, lviii, 179. BL, Portland MSS, BL Loan 29/176, ff. 177–8. Timothy Woodroffe, *A Religious Treatise upon Simeon's Song*, epistle dedicatory.

23 *C. S. P. Dom., 1634–5*, 250.

24 Luke Norton, *Elegies on the Death of That Worthy and Accomplish't Gentleman Colonell John Hampden, Esquire*, 2–3. Bodleian, Carte MSS 103, f. 92.

25 BL, Additional MSS 37,343, f.280. Obadiah Sedgwick, *Christ the Life and Death the Gain*, 31.

26 *Hutchinson Memoirs*, 67–8. Josiah Ricraft, *A Survey of England's Champions*, 79. Derbyshire Record Office: Chandos–Pole–Gell MSS, Boxes 41/31, 56/25 and 58/18. Edmund Calamy, *Account*, ii, 182.

27 John Prestwich, *Prestwich's Respublica*, 33, 34, 37,42.

28 *C. S. P. Dom., 1644*, 31.

29 BL, Additional MSS 37, 343, f. 259.

30 Rushworth, v, 125–7.

31 BL, Harleian MSS 384, f. 183. *HMC, Fourteenth Report*, Appendix, pt ii, 117.

32 See, for example, J. T. Cliffe, *The Yorkshire Gentry*, 344 and B. G. Blackwood, *The Lancashire Gentry and the Great Rebellion 1640–60*, 65.

33 P. R. Newman, 'Catholic Royalists of Northern England, 1642–1645', *Northern History*, xv, 89.

34 See Bryan W. Ball, *A Great Expectation. Eschatological Thought in English Protestantism to 1660* and Katharine Firth, *The Apocalyptic Tradition in Reformation Britain 1530–1645*. Apocalyptic influences at the upper levels of society are discussed in *Puritan Gentry*, 206–11.

35 Sir James Harrington, *Noah's Dove*, 2–3. Sir Edward Peyton, *The Divine Catastrophe of the Kingly Family of the House of Stuarts*, 6, 125.

36 Edmund Ludlow, *A Voyce from the Watch Tower* (ed. A. B. Worden), *Camden Fourth Series*, xxi, 144.

37 *Puritan Gentry*, 206, 209–10.
38 *The Tryal of Sir Henry Vane, Knight*, 115–16.
39 For an important article on this general subject see A. B. Worden, 'Providence and Politics in Cromwellian England', *Past and Present*, no. 109, 54–99.
40 BL, Additional MSS 34, 253, f. 23 and Harleian MSS 166, f. 186.
41 BL, Additional MSS 37, 343, f. 376.
42 *The Poetry of Anna Matilda*, 111–12.
43 *HMC, Thirteenth Report*, Appendix, pt i, 92.
44 *Fast Sermons*, xii, 35, 36, 37, 39.
45 *HMC, Fourteenth Report*, Appendix, pt ii, 113.
46 *Hutchinson Memoirs*, 106–7.
47 *The Poetry of Anna Matilda*, 109, 110.
48 *BL, Portland MSS, BL Loan 29/176, f. 201.*
49 BL, Harleian MSS 165, f. 165. *Oxford Royalist*, i, 139. Edmund Calamy, *The Noble–Man's Patterne of True and Reall Thankfulnesse*, 57.

CHAPTER 6   DEGREES OF LOYALTY

 1 Rushworth, v, 100–1. *Cheshire's Successe* (Thomason Tracts, E.94(6)). R.N. Dore, *The Civil Wars in Cheshire*, 14–16, 25.
 2 Derbyshire Record Office: Gresley MSS, D803 M/Z9, pages xx and xxi.
 3 M. F. Keeler, *The Long Parliament, 1640–1641*, 160. *C. J.*, ii, 960.
 4 *C. J.*, iii, 58, 149, 159, 251, 374, 669. *HMC, Seventh Report*, Appendix, 446.
 5 *C. J.*, ii, 899 and iii, 161, 198, 200, 207. BL, Additional MSS 33, 084, f. 48 and 33, 145, f. 157. H. G. Tibbutt (ed.), *The Letter Books 1644–45 of Sir Samuel Luke*, 20, 126, 206, 208, 607–8.
 6 Sheffield Central Library: Wentworth Woodhouse Collection, Bright MSS, BR 84.
 7 *C. J.*, iii, 390 and iv, 99, 127. *HMC, Seventh Report*, Appendix, 450.
 8 BL, Harleian MSS 165, f. 143.
 9 BL, Harleian MSS 165, ff. 145–8, 150.
10 BL, Harleian MSS 165, f. 243.
11 *C. J.*, ii, 728. *The Tryal of Sir Henry Vane, Knight*, 32, 49. George Sikes, *The Life and Death of Sir Henry Vane, Knight*, 9,105.
12 *C. S. P. Dom., 1641–3*, 369.
13 *C. J.*, iii, 65, 196. BL, Additional MSS 37, 343, f.283. N. E. McClure (ed.), *The Letters of John Chamberlain*, ii, 125.
14 *Puritan Gentry*, 194–5. *HMC, Fourteenth Report*, Appendix, pt ii, 110. *Oxford Royalist*, i, 264.
15 BL, Harleian MSS 165, f. 148.
16 Edmund Ludlow, *Memoirs of Edmund Ludlow*, 80. See Robert

Ashton, *The English Civil War*, 190–1.

17 *HMC, Eleventh Report*, Appendix, pt vii, 101.

18 BL, Harleian MSS 163, ff. 291–2, 304, 307. *C. J.*, ii, 744.

19 BL, Harleian MSS 163, ff. 376, 381–2. *C. J.*, ii, 776.

20 BL, Harleian MSS 378, f. 12.

21 Richard Baxter, *Reliquiae Baxterianae* (ed. Matthew Sylvester), 75. BL, Harleian MSS 163, ff. 291, 319, 354; 164, ff. 233, 273, 295, 308; and 165, ff. 132, 135, 138, 142, 167, 180, 190.

22 BL, Harleian MSS 165, f. 148.

23 BL, Harleian MSS 165, ff. 146, 147. See Robert Ashton, *The English Civil War*, 194, 196–7.

24 BL, Harleian MSS 163, f. 292; 164, f. 334; and 165, ff. 142, 151.

25 BL, Harleian MSS 163, ff. 139–40; 164, ff. 277, 294, 295; and 165, ff. 139, 147. *Puritan Gentry*, 210–11.

26 BL, Harleian MSS 165, f. 190. *C. J.*, iii, 58, 149, 159, 251. *Oxford Royalist*, i, 390.

27 BL, Harleian MSS 164, ff. 271–3.

28 Clive Holmes, *The Eastern Association in the Civil War*, 61. BL, Harleian MSS 164, f. 294.

29 Clarendon, ii, 438–45. BL, Additional MSS, 37, 343, ff. 263–4.

30 BL, Harleian MSS 164, f. 334.

31 Clarendon, iii, 1, 9, 10, 13. BL, Additional MSS 37, 343, ff. 265–8.

32 Clarendon, iii, 9.

33 Clarendon, iii, 116. BL, Harleian MSS 165, f. 194.

34 BL, Harleian MSS 165, ff. 139, 141–2.

35 BL, Harleian MSS 165, ff. 142, 145. *Oxford Royalist*, iii, 192, 204, 222, 249. Sir William Waller, *Vindication of the Character and Conduct of Sir William Waller*, 8.

36 BL, Harleian MSS 165, ff. 145–8.

37 BL, Harleian MSS 165, ff. 148, 158.

38 BL, Harleian MSS 164, ff. 331, 333, 362–3. *Oxford Royalist*, i, 156, 237. *C. J.*, iii, 57. Eugene A. Andriette, *Devon and Exeter in the Civil War*, 82.

39 Rushworth, v, 271–2. *Calendar of the Proceedings of the Committee for the Advance of Money*, 1248–9. *Oxford Royalist*, i, 321.

40 *Calendar of the Proceedings of the Committee for the Advance of Money*, 1248–9.

41 Lady Eliott-Drake, *The Family and Heirs of Sir Francis Drake*, i, 321, 327. *HMC, Fourth Report*, Appendix, 296. *C. J.*, iii, 575.

42 BL, Additional MSS 31, 116, f. 199 and Harleian MSS 166, f. 207. *C. J.*, iv, 101, 133.

43 R. Bell (ed.), *Memorials of the Civil War*, i, 367.

44 B. Schofield (ed.), *The Knyvett Letters (1620–1644)*, 109–11. BL, Harleian MSS 164, ff. 337, 340.

45 BL, Harleian MSS 165, ff. 152, 156–9.

46 BL, Harleian MSS 165, ff. 165, 167. Rushworth, v, 742–3.
47 *The Spie*, No. 12, 95 (Thomason Tracts, E44(18)). BL, Additional MSS 10, 114, f. 17. *C. J.*, iv, 639–40. *Harleian Miscellany*, iii, 486. C. E. Vulliamy, *The Onslow Family, 1528–1874*, 14.

CHAPTER 7   THE PRICE OF WAR

1 BL, Harleian MSS 387, f. 20.
2 BL, Additional MSS 37, 343, f. 259.
3 *Camden Society*, lviii, 176. *HMC, Fourteenth Report*, Appendix, pt ii, 96, 97.
4 *HMC, Fourteenth Report*, Appendix, pt ii, 97, 100, 102. *HMC, Fifth Report*, Appendix, 161.
5 *Ibid.*, 98.
6 *Ibid.*, 97, 99.
7 *Camden Society*, lviii, 185–8. *HMC, Fourteenth Report*, Appendix, pt ii, 103, 104, 106.
8 *HMC, Fourteenth Report*, Appendix, pt ii, 105.
9 *Ibid.*, 114–15, 131. *HMC, MSS of Marquis of Bath*, i, 1–23.
10 *C. S. P. Dom., 1641–3*, 486–7.
11 *Camden Society*, lviii, 209. *HMC, Fourteenth Report*, Appendix, pt ii, 117–18. *HMC, MSS of Marquis of Bath*, i, 27–8.
12 *Oxford Royalist*, ii, 192.
13 *HMC, MSS of Marquis of Bath*, i, 28, 32–5. *HMC, Fourteenth Report*, Appendix, pt ii, 122–3. *Oxford Royalist*, iii, 36–7.
14 *Camden Society*, lviii, 230. See also *HMC, MSS of Marquis of Bath*, i, 40.
15 Timothy Woodroffe, *A Religious Treatise upon Simeon's Song*, epistle dedicatory. BL, Portland MSS, BL Loan 29/88.
16 *Camden Society*,, lviii, 247.
17 Hampshire Record Office: Jervoise of Herriard Park MSS, 44M 69/F9 and F10. PRO, Chancery Proceedings, Six Clerks' Series, C.5/384/76. *C. J.*, vi, 296.
18 Sir William Waller, *Vindication of the Character and Conduct of Sir William Waller*, 202–3, 207. *The Poetry of Anna Matilda*, 128, 130.
19 I. G. Philip (ed.), *Journal of Sir Samuel Luke*, i, 33, 51. PRO, Wills, PROB 11/194/142 and Chancery Proceedings, Six Clerks' Series, C.8/101/47 and 104/34.
20 David Underdown, *Pride's Purge*, 57. BL, Additional MSS 46, 381, f. 145. *HMC, Ninth Report*, Appendix, pt ii, 494.
21 *Oxford Royalist*, iii, 47. BL, Additional MSS 35, 331, f. 3. *HMC, Tenth Report*, Appendix, pt vi, 151.
22 Lady Eliott-Drake, *The Family and Heirs of Sir Francis Drake*, 330, 331, 334–5, 345. Clarendon, iv, 66, 70. *C. J.*, iv, 141.

23 *Hutchinson Memoirs*, 91–2, 173.
24 *HMC, Seventh Report*, Appendix, 1. Seth Wood, *The Saint's Enterance into Peace and Rest by Death*, 22.
25 *C. J.*, v, 693. House of Lords Library: House of Lords MSS, 18 October 1644 and 7 May 1646. *HMC, Thirteenth Report*, Appendix, pt i, 102.
26 *Oxford Royalist*, i, 210 and iii, 40–1.
27 BL, Additional MSS 37, 343, f. 286.
28 BL, Harleian MSS 165, f. 243; 387, ff. 21, 23; and 7658, f. 1.
29 *HMC, Seventh Report*, Appendix, 569, 570. BL, Egerton MSS 2648, f. 85.
30 BL, Additional MSS, 24, 860, f. 114.
31 PRO, Chancery Proceedings, Six Clerks' Series, C.5/628/57. Dorset County Record Office: MSS deposited by G. D. Roper, D55/T60. Forde Abbey is now in Dorset but at that time was in a detached part of Devon.
32 BL, Harleian MSS 165, f. 178.
33 BL, Harleian MSS 166, f. 210.
34 *C. J.*, iv, 141, 161, 649.
35 House of Lords Library: House of Lords MSS, 7 May 1646. *C. J.*, v, 693.
36 *The Severall Accompts of Sir John Gell . . . and . . . Thomas Gell* (Thomason Tracts, E.273(15)). *HMC, Ninth Report*, Appendix, pt ii, 396. Derbyshire Record Office: Chandos-Pole-Gell MSS, Box 30/16.
37 Sheffield Central Library: Wentworth Woodhouse Collection, Bright MSS 83 and 84. *HMC, Coke MSS*, ii, 331. W. Hamper (ed.), *The Life, Diary and Correspondence of Sir William Dugdale*, 64.
38 Edmund Ludlow, *Memoirs of Edmund Ludlow*, 42–8. *Oxford Royalist*, i, 284 and iii, 256, 266, 354. For Sir John Northcote see above, 78.
39 *Oxford Royalist*, i, 464–5.
40 *The Kingdome's Weekly Intelligencer*, week ending 4 July 1643 (Thomason Tracts, E.59, 61).
41 Thomas Nash, *History and Antiquities of Worcestershire*, ii, Supplement, 87. PRO, Chancery Proceedings, Six Clerks' Series, C.8/104/34. M. F. Keeler, *The Long Parliament, 1640–1641*, 292. *C. J.*, iv, 432. *Gentleman's Magazine*, New Series, xxxvi, 368–71. *Yorkshire Archaeological Journal*, xxiii, 387. *DNB* (Sir William Armyne). The deaths of Arthur Goodwin (1643) and Sir Thomas Barrington (1644) cannot readily be attributed to military activities.
42 *DNB* (Sir Arthur Hesilrige). *C. S. P. Dom., 1641–3*, 369. Clement Walker, *The Compleat History of Independency*, 168. G. E. Aylmer, *The State's Servants*, 251–2. *Harleian Miscellany*, iii,

459, 480. *HMC, Seventh Report*, Appendix, 65. *C. J,*, vi, 51. Bulstrode Whitelocke, *Memorials of the English Affairs*, ii, 275, 279.

43 BL, Portland MSS, BL Loan 29/88. *Hutchinson Memoirs*, 90. *HMC, Ninth Report*, Appendix, pt ii, 494.

CHAPTER 8   PRESBYTERIANISM AND INDEPENDENCY

1 BL, Harleian MSS 165, f. 125.
2 Shaw, i, 134.
3 BL, Additional MSS, 18, 777, ff. 107, 108, 109.
4 BL, Harleian MSS 164, ff. 279, 280. *C. J.*, ii, 942, 951.
5 Clarendon, ii, 441. BL, Additional MSS 37, 343, f. 264.
6 *A. & O.*, i, 180–4.
7 A. F. Mitchell and J. Struthers (eds), *Minutes of the Sessions of the Westminster Assembly of Divines*, lxxxii.
8 See above, 13.
9 Baillie, ii, 110. Thomas Fuller, *The Church-History of Britain*, xi, 208, 212. John Nalson, *An Impartial Collection of the Great Affairs of State*, ii, 665.
10 BL, Additional MSS 37, 343, f. 286.
11 Fuller, *op. cit.*, xi, 211. *DNB* (Goodwin, Nye, Bridge, Simpson and Burroughes).
12 BL, Harleian MSS 165, ff. 158–9. Robert Ashton, *The English Civil War*, 202–3.
13 BL, Additional MSS 37, 343, f. 275. *HMC, Seventh Report*, Appendix, 445. Rushworth, v, 478–81. Fuller *op. cit.*, xi, 200–6.
14 BL, Additional MSS 37, 343, f. 269.
15 *HMC, Seventh Report*, Appendix, 445. Rushworth, v, 480.
16 BL, Harleian MSS 165, ff. 222–3. *HMC, Seventh Report*, Appendix, 445–6. *C. J.*, iii, 374, 389, 390.
17 *C. J.*, iv, 35. Henry Cary, *Memorials of the Great Civil War in England*, ii, 36. For Sir William Drake see above, 66.
18 *C. J.*, iii, 275.
19 *Fast Sermons*, ix, 13–50 and 53–106. BL, Harleian MSS 165, f. 221. *C. J.*, iii, 324. William Mew was rector of Eastington (Sir Robert Atkyns, *The Ancient and Present State of Glocestershire*, 219). For evidence of his Presbyterian sympathies see below, 187.
20 See William Haller, *Liberty and Reformation in the Puritan Revolution*, 116–19.
21 During the 1630s Sir William Brereton visited both Holland and Scotland (*Travels in Holland, United Provinces, England, Scotland and Ireland*, ed. Edward Hawkins, *Chetham Society*,i). Sir William Constable spent some time in voluntary exile in Holland (J. T. Cliffe, *The Yorkshire Gentry*, 307–8).

22 Richard Baxter, *Penitent Confession*, 30. PRO, Wills, PROB11/ 215/41. Baillie, i, introduction, xciii; ii, 237, 333, 393; and iii, 345– 6. John Prince, *The Worthies of Devon*, 508. *DNB* (Rous). *Past and Present*, no. 47, 131. BL, Harleian MSS 164, f. 287.

23 BL, Portland MSS, BL Loan 29/88. *C. J.*, iii, 625, 630, 631–3.

24 *Hutchinson Memoirs*, 153. BL, Harleian MSS 166, f. 267. *Vindiciae Veritatis*, 138. A. G. Matthews, *Calamy Revised*, 268, 293. Lyon Turner, i, 451.

25 H. G. Tibbutt (ed.), *The Letter Books 1644–45 of Sir Samuel Luke*, 77, 197, 435, 438–9.

26 A. G. Watson, *The Library of Sir Simonds D'Ewes*, 264, 266.

27 BL, Harleian MSS 165, ff. 152, 157, 179, and 166, f. 218.

28 *Massachusetts Historical Society Collections*, Fourth Series, vi, 549–50.

29 Bodleian: Tanner MSS 321, ff. 11–12.

30 Baillie, ii, 186.

31 This was Richard Salway who was returned MP for Appleby in the recruiter elections.

32 Richard Baxter, *Reliquiae Baxterianae* (ed. Matthew Sylvester), 63.

33 BL, Harleian MSS 165, f. 157. Baillie, ii, 117, 146, 236. *Oxford Royalist*, ii, 405.

34 *Massachusetts Historical Society Collections*, Fifth Series, i, 482– 3. BL, Egerton MSS 2648, f. 1. *Puritan Gentry*, 164–5, 202–3. George Gillespie, *Notes of Debates and Proceedings of the Assembly of Divines (The Presbyterian Armoury*, ii), 67. Clement Walker, *The Compleat History of Independency*, i, 29. Richard Baxter, *Penitent Confession*, 30. George Yule, *Puritans in Politics*, 129. Clarendon maintains that Hesilrige was 'perfectly Presbyterian' in matters of religion and that his primary concern was to secure the abolition of episcopacy (Clarendon, vi, 148). Hesilrige, however, was very active on behalf of Independency in the House of Commons.

35 J. T. Cliffe, *The Yorkshire Gentry*, 272–3, 306–8. M. Tolmie, *The Triumph of the Saints. The Separate Churches of London 1616– 1649*, 105. *DNB* (Philip Nye). *Oxford Royalist*, i, 375.

36 Baillie, ii, 117, 153, 226, 229, 235, 236. Gillespie, *op. cit.*, 67, 107. Walker *op. cit.*, ii, 10.

37 George Sikes, *The Life and Death of Sir Henry Vane, Knight*, 98. *The Tryal of Sir Henry Vane, Knight*, 91.

38 George Yule, *Puritans in Politics*, 129. *C. J.*, v, 179. Samuel Clark, *The Lives of Sundry Eminent Persons*, pt ii, 195.

39 John Walker, *Sufferings of the Clergy*, pt i, 91. BL, Harleian MSS 166, f. 205. *Oxford Royalist*, iv, 42–3.

40 BL, Additional MSS 37, 343, ff. 263, 315–16; 37, 344, f. 12; 37, 345,

ff. 277, 278, 280 (and *passim* for Whitelocke's churchgoing); and 53,728 (Whitelocke's lectures or sermons). A. G. Matthews, *Calamy Revised*, 124. George Yule, *The Independents in the English Civil War*, 126.

41 *Gentleman's Magazine*, New Series, xxxvi, 367, 371, 586, 587. Sir William's mother was an Independent (*ibid.*, 366).

CHAPTER 9   A GODLY CHURCH

1 *HMC, Coke MSS*, ii, 342.
2 Baillie, ii, 146, 157, 168.
3 George Gillespie, *Notes of Debates and Proceedings of the Assembly of Divines* (The Presbyterian Armoury, ii), 53, 67, 69–71. BL, Harleian MSS 166, ff. 110, 113. *C. J.*, iii, 610–11, 622, 625.
4 *C. J.*, iii, 630–3. *A. & O.*, i, 521–6.
5 BL, Harleian MSS 166, ff. 113–14. *C. J.*, iii, 626. Gillespie, *op. cit.*, 103–7. Baillie, ii, 236–7.
6 Baillie, ii, 229, 235.
7 Gillespie, *op. cit.*, 103–7. Baillie, ii, 236–7. See Shaw, ii, 37–43.
8 BL, Harleian MSS 166, f. 151.
9 For the Committee for Plundered Ministers see below, 138–9
10 BL, Harleian MSS 166, ff. 151–2.
11 *C. J.*, iii, 642. *HMC, Eleventh Report*, Appendix, pt vii, 101. John Collinges, *Par Nobile*, treatise on the life of Lady Frances Hobart, 4.
12 *C. J.*, iii, 691, 699.
13 *HMC, Tenth Report*, Appendix, pt iv, 74.
14 *C. J.*, iii, 705, 709.
15 Thomas Hill, *The Right Separation Incouraged*, 30.
16 *C. J.*, iv, 9–10. *A. & O.*, i, 582–607.
17 Bulstrode Whitelocke, *Memorials of the English Affairs*, ii, 118.
18 Hutchinson *Memoirs*, 166.
19 *C. J.*, iv, 114. BL, Harleian MSS 166, ff. 210, 214, 218.
20 Edmund Calamy, *An Indictment Against England*, 13–20, 26, 30–1, 33, 37.
21 *C. J.*, iv, 7, 11–12.
22 *C. J.*, iv, 27.
23 *C. J.*, iv, 11, 20, 21, 28.
24 *C. J.*, iv, 113–14. BL, Additional MSS 31, 116, f. 205.
25 *C. J.*, iv, 113. BL, Harleian MSS 166, ff. 202–3, 204, and Additional MSS 31, 116, ff. 204, 206.
26 *C. J.*, iv, 247, 276–7. *A. & O.*, i, 749–54.
27 BL, Additional MSS 37, 344, ff. 6–12.
28 *C. S. P. Dom.*, *1645–7*, 180.
29 BL, Harleian MSS 166, f. 265, and Additional MSS 31, 116, f. 233.

   C. J., iv, 280, 282.
30 BL, Harleian MSS 166, f. 266.
31 BL, Harleian MSS 166, ff. 267–8, and 646, ff. 80, 137, 158, 159.
32 *A. & O.*, i, 789–97.
33 BL, Additional MSS 31, 116, ff. 242–3.

CHAPTER 10   A LAME PRESBYTERIANISM

1 Thomas Hill, *An Olive Branch of Peace and Accommodation*, 16, 32–3, 35, 36, 38–9 (inaccurate pagination).
2 *A. & O.*, i, 796.
3 Sir James Harrington, *Noah's Dove*, 2–6, 9.
4 William Prynne, *A Fresh Discovery of Some Prodigious New Wandring-Blasing-Stars and Firebrands Stiling Themselves New-Lights* (Thomason Tracts, E.267(3)), 31.
5 Baillie, ii, 336.
6 *C. S. P. Dom., 1645–7*, 190. For the recruiter elections see D. Brunton and D. H. Pennington, *Members of the Long Parliament*, 21–37 and Robert Ashton, *The English Civil War*, 248–9. 279, 413.
7 BL, Additional MSS 10, 114, f. 4.
8 Clarendon, iv, 219–20, 223, 275.
9 BL, Additional MSS 24, 860, f. 149, 24, 861, f. 17; 37, 343, f. 280; and 37, 345, f. 47. *C. J.*, v, 604. George Yule, *The Independents in the English Civil War*, 126. Obadiah Sedgwick, *Christ the Life and Death the Gain*, epistle dedicatory by George Cokayne. For Boynton see above, 104–5.
10 *Hutchinson Memoirs*, 146, 166, 167, 169, 178.
11 Thomas Edwards, *Gangraena*, pt iii, 167.
12 Anthony Wood, *Athenae Oxonienses*, ii, col. 336. *Somersetshire Archaeological and Natural History Society*, xxxvii, 26.
13 *Staffordshire Record Society Historical Collections*, Fourth Series, ii, 29. BL, Additional MSS 11, 332, f. 45.
14 Richard Baxter, *Reliquiae Baxterianae* (ed. Matthew Sylvester), 59–60. BL, Portland MSS, BL Loan 29/177, ff. 76–7.
15 *C. J.*, iv, 443, 446. BL, Additional MSS 31, 116, ff. 255, 258. Baillie, ii, 359.
16 Baillie, ii, 357.
17 BL, Additional MSS 24, 860, f. 149.
18 BL, Additional MSS 31, 116, f. 259. Baillie, ii, 362.
19 *A. & O.*, i, 833–8.
20 BL, Portland MSS, BL Loan 29/175, ff. 13–14, and Additional MSS 31, 116, f. 262. *C. J.*, iv, 518.
21 Baillie, ii, 360.
22 BL, Additional MSS 10, 114, f. 11, and 31, 116, ff. 262–3.
23 BL, Portland MSS, BL Loan 29/175, ff. 13–14.

24 *C. J.*, iv, 506. BL, Additional MSS 31, 116, f. 264.
25 *C. J.*, iv, 511, 517–20. BL, Additional MSS 10, 114, ff. 12, 13, and 31, 116, f. 265.
26 A. F. Mitchell and J. Struthers (eds), *Minutes of the Sessions of the Westminster Assembly of Divines*, 448–56. Shaw, i, 308–10.
27 *C. J.*, iv, 552, 553. BL, Additional MSS 31, 116, f. 270.
28 BL, Additional MSS 31, 116, f. 272. *C. J.*, iv, 562–3. *A. & O.*, i, 852–5. Anthony Wood, *Athenae Oxonienses* (ed. Philip Bliss), iii, 1240.
29 William Prynne, *A Fresh Discovery of Some Prodigious New Wandring-Blasing-Stars and Firebrands Stiling Themselves New-Lights* Thomason Tracts, E.267(3)), 15, 17.
30 Thomas Edwards, *Gangraena*, pt i, 70–1.
31 BL, Additional MSS 31, 116, f. 271, and 37, 344, f. 52.
32 *C. J.*, iv, 556.
33 *C. J.*, iv, 653. BL, Additional MSS 10, 114, f. 17. *A. & O.,*, i, 865–74.
34 *C. J*, iv, 526. Bulstrode Whitelocke, *Memorials of the English Affairs*, ii, 88.
35 BL, Additional MSS 10, 114, f. 18, and 31, 116, f. 283. *Puritan Gentry*, 61.
36 BL, Additional MSS 31, 116, f. 283. *A. & O.*, i, 913–14.

CHAPTER 11   RELIGION IN THE PROVINCES

1 *Puritan Gentry*, 233–4. *Hutchinson Memoirs*, 54.
2 *C. J.*, iii, 57, 353, 389. *Oxford Royalist*, i, 254–5.
3 *C. J.*, iii, 220. *A. & O.*, i, 265–6.
4 BL, Portland MSS, BL Loan 29/389. *C. J.*, iii, 470, 486. BL, Harleian MSS 166, ff. 52, 57. *A. & O.*, i, 425–6.
5 *HMC, Fourteenth Report*, Appendix, pt ii, 132–4. BL, Harleian MSS 165, f. 221. *Oxford Royalist*, ii, 37, 44–5, 132. *HMC, MSS of Marquis of Bath*, i, 22, 40.
6 *Gentleman's Magazine*, New Series, xxxvi, 372.
7 *Oxford Royalist*, iii, 135–6, 205.
8 That is, stained glass windows.
9 C. H. Evelyn White (ed.), *The Journal of William Dowsing*, 6–7, 22, 32. *C. S. P. Dom., 1641–3*, 509–10.
10 BL, Additional MSS 15,669, and 15,670 (proceedings of the Committee for Plundered Ministers). John Walker, *Sufferings of the Clergy*, pt i, 73. For members of the committee see Additional MSS 15, 669, f. 1.
11 BL, Harleian MSS 165, f. 154. *C. J.*, iii, 214. See John White, *The First Century of Scandalous, Malignant Priests*.
12 *C. J.*, iii, 153, 231. Walker, *op. cit.*, pt i, 88, 90–1, 98. BL, Additional MSS 15, 669, f. 1.
13 Shaw, ii, 190–1.

14 *A. & O.*, i, 371–2. T. W. Davids, *Annals of Evangelical Nonconformity in the County of Essex*, 209–11. Clive Holmes (ed.), *The Suffolk Committees for Scandalous Ministers 1644–1646*, 14, 25. Alan Everitt, *Suffolk and the Great Rebellion 1640–1660*, 63–5. BL, Additional MSS 5829, ff. 6–8.

15 Holmes, *op. cit.*, 25. *Massachusetts Historical Society Collections*, Fourth Series, vi, 567.

16 Holmes, *op. cit.*, 98. John Walker, *Sufferings of the Clergy*, pt ii, 312.

17 Holmes, *op. cit.*, 53–6.

18 A. G. Matthews, *Walker Revised*, 343. BL, Harleian MSS 7043, 3. See also *C. J.*, iii, 129.

19 BL, Harleian MSS 387, f. 45. Matthews, *op. cit.*, 266.

20 BL, Additional MSS 5829, f. 8.

21 BL, Additional MSS 15, 669, f. 2. *C. J.*, iv, 123.

22 BL, Egerton MSS 787, ff. 10, 25, 87–8.

23 *C. J.*, iv, 212, 502. Shaw, ii, 263, 264.

24 *A. & O.*, i, 865–70.

25 A. G. Matthews, *Calamy Revised*, 170, 361, 517, 542. *L. J.*, ix, 374. PRO, Institution Books, Series A, iii, f. 125. Shaw, ii, 343. *Puritan Gentry*, 166, 184–5.

26 BL, Harleian MSS 376, ff. 90, 92, 94, 96, 98. *C. J.*, iii, 717, 725. PRO, Institution Books, Series A, iii, f. 252. Shaw, ii, 325. *DNB* (Gurnall).

27 *C. J.*, iv, 502, 628.

28 BL, Additional MSS 18, 979, f. 232.

29 Thomas Edwards, *Gangraena*, pt iii, 167.

30 Edwards, *op. cit.*, 32, 96.

31 *C. J.*, iv, 276.

32 *A. & O.*, i, 749–54.

33 BL, Additional MSS 24, 860, f. 145.

34 BL, Harleian MSS 165, f. 179. *C. J.*, iv, 463, 506, 552, and v, 108, 162, 179. For Norton see above, 127.

35 *C. J.*, iv, 7, 668–70, 673, and v, 7. Lancashire petition, 27 August 1646, Thomason Tracts, E.352(3). *L. J.*, viii, 509. Shaw, ii 394–8. Richard Parkinson (ed.), *The Life of Adam Martindale, Chetham Society*, iv, 61–4, 128. R. Halley, *Lancashire: Its Puritanism and Nonconformity*, 240–4.

36 Baillie, iii, 1.

37 Shaw, ii, 29, 31, 374–92, 423–31.

38 The classification of laymen as Presbyterians or Independents, whether in a religious or a political sense, is an extremely hazardous undertaking and much of the labelling in modern historical works is highly contentious. See J. H. Hexter, 'The Problem of the Presbyterian Independents', *Reappraisals in*

History, 163–84; George Yule, *The Independents in the English Civil War*; David Underdown, *Pride's Purge*; A. B. Worden, *The Rump Parliament 1648–1653*; Valerie Pearl, 'The 'Royal Independents' in the Civil War' , *Transactions of the Royal Historical Society*, xviii, 69–96; Stephen Foster, 'The Presbyterian Independents Exorcized', *Past and Present*, no. 44, 52–75; and 'Debate: Presbyterians, Independents and Puritans', *Past and Present*, no. 47, 116–46.

39 Shaw, ii, 375, 377, 380, 382, 388, 389, 423, 427, 428, 429.
40 BL, Additional MSS, 39, 218, ff.43–73.
41 *HMC, Seventh Report*, Appendix, 559. Shaw, ii, 375. A. G. Matthews, *Calamy Revised*, 554.
42 Thomas Edwards, *Gangraena*, pt i, 41.
43 Edwards, *op. cit.*, pt ii, 3.
44 *C. J.*, iv, 556. *L. J.*, viii, 338.
45 Shaw, ii, 29. T. W. Davids, *Annals of Evangelical Nonconformity in the County of Essex*, 305–6.
46 Shaw, ii, 430.
47 Shaw, ii, 431–2. *HMC, Thirteenth Report*, Appendix, pt i, 582, and *Fourteenth Report*, Appendix, pt ix, 477.
48 Shaw, ii, 413–21. David Underdown, *Pride's Purge*, 36. BL, Sloane MSS 1519, f. 188.
49 BL, Portland MSS, BL Loan 29/175, ff. 18, 26, 80, and 176, ff. 5, 12, 34. *A. & O..* i, 840–1.

CHAPTER 12   THE GROWTH OF FACTION

1 Rushworth, vi, 2.
2 Thomas Edwards, *Gangraena*, pt ii, 151–4.
3 Bulstrode Whitelocke, *Memorials of the English Affairs*, i, 464, 468, 479. BL, Additional MSS 37, 344, f. 4. Clarendon, iv, 218–19.
4 BL, Harleian MSS 165, f. 152. Sir Simonds D'Ewes, *The Primitive Practise for Preserving Truth*, 3, 40.
5 *Hutchinson Memoirs*, 153, 158, 166, 167, 172, 179, 186.
6 Edmund Ludlow, *Memoirs of Edmund Ludlow*, 80, 84, 102.
7 *Ibid.*, 74, 80. See David Underdown, *Pride's Purge*, 68–72, and A. B. Worden, *The Rump Parliament 1648–1653*, 4–11.
8 Clarendon, iv, 238, 295.
9 See, for example, *C. J.*, iv, 3, 136, 428, 463, 506, and v, 108, 162.
10 Clarendon, iii, 497. Patricia Crawford, *Denzil Holles, 1598–1680*, 10.
11 *Yorkshire Archaeological Journal*, viii, 459. Dr Williams's Library: Morrice MSS, J, no pagination.
12 Sir William Waller, *Vindication of the Character and Conduct of Sir William Waller*, 227–8.

13 Underdown, *op. cit.*, 64. *DNB* (Francis Rous).
14 BL, Egerton MSS 786, ff. 20, 25–7, 33, and 787, ff. 5, 15, 58, 70, 79, 84. See also above, 101–2.
15 Clarendon, iv, 302.
16 Clarendon, iv, 157.
17 Clarendon, iii, 497. *Puritan Gentry*, 229.
18 BL, Harleian MSS 165, ff. 156–7. *C. J.*, iv, 463, 506, 542, 552, 558, and v, 25, 108, 162, 179, 415. For Crewe and Evelyn see Valerie Pearl, 'The 'Royal Independents' in the Civil War', *Transactions of the Royal Historical Society*, xviii, 84–5, 87.
19 Thomas Edwards, *Gangraena*, pt i, 55.
20 Sir William Waller, *Vindication of the Character and Conduct of Sir William Waller*, 10.
21 J. T. Rutt (ed.), *Diary of Thomas Burton*, ii. 407.
22 Clement Walker, *The Compleat History of Independency*, pt i, 16.
23 Bulstrode Whitelocke, *Memorials of the English Affairs*, i, 327 and ii, 88, 118. BL, Additional MSS, 37, 344, ff. 1, 4, 6. Violet A. Rowe, *Sir Henry Vane the Younger*, 73.
24 BL, Harleian MSS 165, f. 179.
25 Waller, *op. cit.*, 15.
26 *A. & O.*, i, 604–5. Denzil Holles, *Memoirs of Denzil Lord Holles*, 29.
27 *C. J.*, iii, 748, and iv, 88, 100. Rushworth, vi, 4, 6.
28 *Oxford Royalist*, iii, 434–7.
29 *C. J.*, iv, 44. H. G. Tibbutt, (ed.), *The Letter Books 1644–45 of Sir Samuel Luke*, 140, 430, 435, 438–9.
30 *C. J.*, iv, 123. *A. & O.*, i, 677. *Oxford Royalist*, iv, 43.
31 Clarendon, iii, 506, 507.
32 Tibbutt, *op. cit.*, 144–5, 213, 430. BL, Egerton MSS 787, f. 81.
33 For references to the replacement of MPs as military commanders see, for example, *C. J.*, iv, 131, 136–7, 140 and BL, Harleian MSS 166, f. 208.
34 *C. J.*, iv, 169–70. Sir Henry Ellis, *Original Letters*, Third Series, iv, 248.
35 *C.S.P. Dom., 1660–1*, 8. *C. J.*, v, 239.
36 BL, Additional MSS 11, 331, ff. 4, 35, 44, 85, 97. *C. J.*, iv, 139, 284, 302, 412, 416. *C. S. P. Dom., 1645–7*, 158. *VCH, Cheshire*, ii, 108.
37 *HMC, Sixth Report*, Appendix, 178. *C. J.*, v, 182.
38 *C. J.*, iv, 80. BL, Harleian MSS 166, f. 184. Sir William Waller, *Vindication of the Character and Conduct of Sir William Waller*, 109.
39 BL, Harleian MSS 166, ff. 176, 201, and Egerton MSS 767, f. 55. *The Poetry of Anna Matilda*, 128, 131. Waller, *op. cit.*, 8–9, 11, 12.
40 See, for example, *C. J.*, iii, 236, and BL, Egerton MSS 787, f. 77.
41 This may have been Lord Robartes with whom Sir Samuel was

corresponding at this time. (BL, Egerton MSS 786, ff. 7, 12, 72).
42 BL, Egerton MSS 786, f. 21, and 787, ff. 30–2, 41, 46, 48, 58, 70, 79, 81. BL, Harleian MSS 166, ff. 207–8. *C. J.*, iv, 164, 166. *HMC, Eighth Report*, Appendix, pt i, 8.
43 BL, Egerton MSS 786, ff. 20, 25, 26–7, 44, 47, 48. William Prynne, *A Fresh Discovery of Some Prodigious New Wandring-Blasing-Stars and Firebrands Stiling Themselves New-Lights*, Thomason Tracts, E.267(3), epistle dedicatory. For Paul Hobson see also Thomas Edwards, *Gangraena*, pt i, 33–4.

CHAPTER 13 REVOLUTION

1 D. Brunton and D. H. Pennington, *Members of the Long Parliament*, 205, 208, 216, 223. *Hutchinson Memoirs*, 164. Edmund Ludlow, *Memoirs of Edmund Ludlow*, 73.
2 Ludlow, *op. cit.*, 74.
3 Denzil Holles, *Memoirs of Denzil Lord Holles*, 43.
4 BL, Additional MSS 37, 344, f. 53. *C. J.*, iv, 558.
5 *C. J.*, v, 20–1, 24–5, 34–5.
6 Sir William Waller, *Vindication of the Character and Conduct of Sir William Waller*, 24–5.
7 Bulstrode Whitelocke, *Memorials of the English Affairs*, ii, 146.
8 *C. J.*, v, 192. Waller, *op. cit.*, 128–30.
9 *C. J.*, v, 236. Whitelocke, *op. cit.*, ii, 162, 179. Waller, *op. cit.*, 163, 171–2. *Camden Society*, lviii, 231.
10 *C. J.*, v, 259, 260, 262, 263, 265, 266. Edmund Ludlow, *Memoirs of Edmund Ludlow*, 88–90. *Hutchinson Memoirs*, 171. Whitelocke, *op. cit.*, ii, 182. Waller, *op. cit.*, 191. *HMC, Earl of Egmont MSS*, i, 440. *L. J.*, ix, 385–6. Rushworth, vii, 754–5.
11 *C. J.*, v, 268. Rushworth, vii, 785, 789. Whitelocke, *op. cit.*, ii, 168, 179, 189–91. Waller, *op. cit.*, 200–2, 213.
12 *HMC, Tenth Report*, Appendix, 177. Ludlow, *op. cit.*, 84–5.
13 *C. J.*, v, 234, 235, 329–30. For Drake see above, 66.
14 *HMC, Earl of Egmont MSS*, i, 462.
15 *HMC, Sixth Report*, Appendix, 329–30.
16 BL, Portland MSS, BL Loan 29/176, f. 201.
17 *Camden Society*, lviii, 232. BL, Portland MSS, BL Loan 29/175, ff. 85–6, 89–90, 97–8.
18 *C. J.*, v, 584.
19 David Underdown, 'Parliamentary Diary of John Boys, 1647–8', *Bulletin of the Institute of Historical Research*, xxxix, 155.
20 BL, Harleian MSS 166, ff. 282–5.
21 *C. J.*, v, 415–16.
22 Bulstrode Whitelocke, *Memorials of the English Affairs*, ii, 331, 332, 336, 338–9, 341, 352, 365, 374. *HMC, Thirteenth Report*,

Appendix, pt i, 468. Samuel Fairclough, *The Prisoners' Praises for their Deliverance from their Long Imprisonment in Colchester*, a sermon preached at Romford on 28 September 1648 (Thomason Tracts, E.589/4).

23 *Hutchinson Memoirs*, 186.

24 *C. J.*, v, 584, 589. *A. & O.*, i, 1188–1215.

25 Clarendon, iv, 392–4, 426–52. *C. J.*, v, 697. Whitelocke, *op. cit.*, ii, 383, 396. *HMC, Thirteenth Report*, Appendix, pt i, 593.

26 *C. S. P. Dom.*, *1648–9*, 296–7, 300, 302–3, 306–7.

27 Henry Cary, *Memorials of the Great Civil War in England*, ii, 36.

28 BL, Portland MSS, BL Loan 29/176, f. 47.

29 *C. J.*, vi, 62–3. Whitelocke, *op. cit.*, ii, 423, 433.

30 *Puritan Gentry*, 227, 229.

31 *C. S. P. Dom.*, *1648–9*, 319–20.

32 *C. J.*, vi, 74.

33 *Parliamentary History*, xviii, 286–302. *C. J.*, vi, 93. Violet A. Rowe, *Sir Henry Vane the Younger*, 111–13.

34 *C. J.*, vi, 102. *Parliamentary History*, xviii, 482–4.

35 *Hutchinson Memoirs*, 187.

36 David Underdown, *Pride's Purge*, 212.

37 See Underdown, *op. cit.*, and A. B. Worden, *The Rump Parliament 1648–1653*.

38 *Hutchinson Memoirs*, 188. For Whitelocke's account of Pride's Purge see *Memorials of the English Affairs*, ii, 468–72.

39 BL, Sloane MSS 1519, f. 188. *HMC, Thirteenth Report*, Appendix, pt i, 447–8.

40 *Parliamentary History*, xviii, 467–8, 471. Rushworth, vii, 1353, 1356. Edmund Ludlow, *Memoirs of Edmund Ludlow*, 116.

41 *Parliamentary History*, xviii, 453, 465, 473. Whitelocke, *op. cit.*, ii, 219, 224. *C. S. P. Dom.*, *1650*, 255.

42 Rushworth, vii, 1369. Whitelocke, *op. cit.*, ii, 478. *Parliamentary History*, xviii, 467. BL, Portland MSS, BL Loan 29/176, ff. 64, 66, 67.

43 Frances P. Verney and Margaret M. Verney, *Memoirs of the Verney Family*, i, 444.

44 Sir William Waller, *Vindication of the Character and Conduct of Sir William Waller*, 272, 301, 302.

45 Whitelocke, *op. cit.*, ii, 480, 487. BL, Additional MSS 37, 344, ff. 239–41. *C. J.*, vi, 102, 113. *A. & O.*, i, 1253–5.

46 Rushworth, vii, 1395–1426. *Hutchinson Memoirs*, 190.

47 Rushworth, vii, 1426. *The Tryal of Sir Henry Vane, Knight*, 31, 45, 46. J. T. Rutt (ed.), *Diary of Thomas Burton*, iii, 174. Dr Williams's Library: Baxter Letters, i, 257.

48 Rushworth, vii, 1395, 1426. *C. S. P. Dom.*, *1660–1*, 8. Rutt, *op. cit*, iii, 27, 96–7, 102.

49 Rushworth, vii, 1395, 1426. Edmund Ludlow, *A Voyce from the Watch Tower* (ed. A. B. Worden), *Camden Fourth Series*, xxi, 166–7.
50 *Hutchinson Memoirs*, 190.
51 Sir Edward Peyton, *The High-Way to Peace*, 13 and *The Divine Catastrophe of the Kingly Family of the House of Stuarts*, preface and 6–7, 71–2, 86, 125.
52 *Puritan Gentry*, 206, 208–11.
53 Ludlow, *op. cit.*, 183.

CHAPTER 14   THE TWILIGHT OF GODLINESS

1 *C. S. P. Dom.*, *1650*, 69–71.
2 David Underdown, *Pride's Purge*, 299–300.
3 Sir Robert Somerville, *Office-Holders in the Duchy and County Palatine of Lancaster from 1603*, 2. *C. J.*, vi, 121, 436. G. E. Aylmer, *The State's Servants*, 357–8.
4 BL, Portland MSS, BL Loan 29/175, ff. 283–4, and 176, ff. 80, 102, 111, 143–4, 177–8, 179–80. *C. J.*, vi, 210. *C. S. P. Dom.*, *1649–50*, 75, 130, 137, 142.
5 Sir William Waller, *Vindication of the Character and Conduct of Sir William Waller*, 30.
6 *A. & O.*, ii, 564–5. Derbyshire Record Office: Chandos-Pole-Gell MSS, Boxes 56/28 and 58/18. PRO, Chancery Proceedings, Six Clerks' Series, C.5/404/110. Other Puritan gentry who were affected by the act included Sir Thomas Alston of Bedfordshire and Sir Thomas Norcliffe of Yorkshire.
7 John Nicholls (ed.), *Original Letters and Papers of State Addressed to Oliver Cromwell*, 102.
8 Sir John Reresby, *Memoirs of Sir John Reresby* (ed. Andrew Browning), 22.
9 J. T. Rutt (ed.), *Diary of Thomas Burton*, i, 155, 169.
10 Clement Walker, *The Compleat History of Independency*, pt iv, 70.
11 *C. S. P. Dom.*, *1651–2*, 566. HMC, *Seventh Report*, Appendix, 458.
12 HMC, *Leyborne-Popham MSS*, 51.
13 *Ibid.*, 58–9.
14 HMC, *Ninth Report*, Appendix, pt ii, 394–6. *C. S. P. Dom.*, *1650*, 61, 75. *C. J.*, vi, 618, and vii, 33, 78, 119, 274.
15 BL, Portland MSS, BL Loan 29/119, and 176, ff. 185–190, 192, 202.
16 HMC, *Thirteenth Report*, Appendix, pt i, 582, 588, 593, 602.
17 HMC, *Fourteenth Report*, Appendix, pt ix, 477–8. *C. S. P. Dom.*, *1651*, 531.
18 *C. S. P. Dom.*, *1651*, 151. BL, Portland MSS, BL Loan 29/84. *C. S. P. Dom.*, *1651–2*, 90, 91, 125.

19 *Somers Tracts*, v, 258–62. John Nicholls (ed.), *Original Letters and Papers of State Addressed to Oliver Cromwell*, 66. See also Clarendon, v, 221–2.
20 Baillie, iii, 306–7.
21 BL, Portland MSS, BL Loan 29/177, ff. 42–3.
22 *A. & O.*, ii, 855–8. Details of presentations during the Commonwealth period are to be found in Jane Houston, *Catalogue of Ecclesiastical Records of the Commonwealth 1643–1660 in the Lambeth Palace Library*.
23 *A. & O.*, ii, 968–90.
24 Dr Williams's Library: Baxter Letters, i, ff. 226–9.
25 William Bridge, *Twenty One Several Books of Mr William Bridge*, ii, epistle dedicatory. *Puritan Gentry*, 207. Owfield had been nominated as a Presbyterian elder for Surrey in 1648 (Shaw, ii, 434).
26 BL, Portland MSS, BL Loan 29/88; 175, ff. 77–8, 79–80; 176, f. 5; and 177, ff. 2-3, 44-5.
27 Dr Williams's Library: Baxter Letters, iv, f. 279.
28 A. G. Matthews, *Calamy Revised*, 110–11. Samuel Palmer (ed.), *The Nonconformist's Memorial*, i, 417.
29 *Ibid.*, 116–17, 388. Clare signed a Presbyterian manifesto in 1648 (*The Joint-Testimonie of the Ministers of Devon*, Thomason Tracts, E.450 (1), 34).
30 See note 22 above for the main source of evidence.
31 *Massachusetts Historical Society Collections*, Fourth Series, vi, 568. J. J. Muskett, *Suffolk Manorial Families*, i, 283–5.
32 BL, Harleian MSS 7658, f. 39. *Archaeologia Cantiana*, iv, 148, 168.
33 John Nicholls (ed.), *Original Letters and Papers of State Addressed to Oliver Cromwell*, 19.
34 *C. S. P. Dom., 1651*, 173, 176, 179. BL, Egerton MSS 3517, ff. 32–42. Seth Wood, *The Saint's Enterance into Peace and Rest by Death*, 16–18, 20–2.
35 PRO, Wills, PROB 11/232/376.
36 Samuel Clark, *The Lives of Sundry Eminent Persons*, pt ii, 114–15. Samuel Fairclough, *The Saint's Worthinesse and the World's Worthlesnesse*, 13–14, 17–19, 23, 24.
37 *Suffolk's Tears*, 13.
38 BL, Portland MSS, BL Loan 29/88 and 177, ff. 84–91. Thomas Froysell, *The Beloved Disciple*, 99–101, 105–6, 109.
39 Sir James Harrington, *A Holy Oyl*, 243–4, 259.
40 Bristol Record Office: Ashton Court MSS, AC/02/13 and AC/C74/19. H. A Helyar, 'The Arrest of Col. William Strode of Barrington, in 1661', *Somersetshire Archaeological and Natural History Society*, xxxvii, 16, 18, 19, 24, 26, 38. *C. S. P. Dom., 1661–2*, 145, 437–8. *DNB* (William Strode). *HMC, Ninth Report*, Appendix, pt ii, 494.

41 J. T. Rutt (ed.), *Diary of Thomas Burton*, ii, 24, 165–6.

42 John Pyne used this term in a letter written in November 1659 (*HMC, Ninth Report*, Appendix, pt ii, 494).

43 East Devon Record Office: Drake of Buckland Abbey MSS, F738.

44 *Hutchinson Memoirs*, 209.

45 Dr Williams's Library: Baxter Letters, i, f. 22.

46 William Bray (ed.), *Diary and Correspondence of John Evelyn*, 147, 154, 163, 164.

47 Richard Baxter, *Reliquiae Baxterianae* (ed. Matthew Sylvester), 58. Dr Williams's Library: Baxter Letters, iv, ff. 128–9.

48 Seth Wood, *The Saint's Enterance into Peace and Rest by Death*, 23. Norfolk Record Office: Kimberley MSS, Box 17, book on Armyne family, p. 1. Christopher Shute, *Ars piè Moriendi: or The True Accomptant*, 25, 26, 29.

49 *HMC, Fourteenth Report*, Appendix, pt ii, 240–1.

50 *DNB* (Morton). John Walker, *Sufferings of the Clergy*, pt ii, 18. Sir Gyles Isham, *Easton Mauduit and The Parish Church of SS. Peter and Paul*, 5–7.

51 Sir Coplestone Bampfield, for example, was an ardent royalist who appears to have had no Puritan leanings.

52 Sir William Waller, *Divine Meditations*, 91.

53 Dr Williams's Library: Morrice MSS, J, no pagination.

54 *HMC, Fourteenth Report*, pt ix, 483–4.

55 Derbyshire Record Office: Chandos-Pole-Gell MSS, Box 29/51. John Gell's wife was in correspondence with Richard Baxter during the 1650s (Dr Williams's Library: Baxter Letters, iv, ff. 142, 183–4).

56 A. G. Matthews, *Calamy Revised*, 113, 215, 466, 492, 515. *HMC, Fourteenth Report*, Appendix, pt ii, 284, 316. *Camden Society*, lviii, 248–9.

57 *C. J.*, viii, 247, 258. Edmund Ludlow, *A Voyce from the Watch Tower* (ed. A. B. Worden), *Camden Fourth Series*, xxi, 288.

58 Matthews, *op. cit.*, 82, 102, 120. T. W. Davids, *Annals of Evangelical Nonconformity in the County of Essex*, 588. Thomas Cawton the younger, *The Life and Death of that Holy and Reverend Man of God Mr Thomas Cawton*, epistle dedicatory. *Puritan Gentry*, 166.

59 *Devon and Cornwall Notes and Queries*, xxi, 226, 284. Lyon Turner, i, 49.

60 Sir Thomas Barnardiston, for example, experienced great difficulty in finding a suitable minister to succeed Samuel Fairclough as rector of Kedington (Suffolk) (Samuel Clark, *The Lives of Sundry Eminent Persons*, pt i, 175).

61 Matthews, *op. cit.*, 99, 149, 266, 368, 473, 475.

62 *Devon and Cornwall Notes and Queries*, xxi, 284. James Small, a

Presbyterian, was serving as Sir John Davie's chaplain at this time (Matthews, *op. cit.*, 475).

63 Lyon Turner, i, 275, 277, 286, 315, 344, 451, and iii, 769–70. Matthews, *op. cit.*, 4.

64 Lyon Turner, i, 214, 318, 353, 359 and iii, 766.

65 William Trevethick, *A Sermon Preached at the Funeral of the Honourable Colonel Robert Rolle of Heanton Sachville in the County of Devon Esquire*. Matthews, *op. cit.*, 388, 474, 492.

66 Matthews, *op. cit.*, 56. *HMC, Fourteenth Report*, Appendix, pt ii, 321.

67 Richard Parkinson (ed.), *The Life of Adam Martindale, Chetham Society*, iv, 177, 196.

68 BL, Portland MSS, BL Loan 29/48.

BIBLIOGRAPHY

PRIMARY SOURCES
I MANUSCRIPT

British Library

ADDITIONAL MSS, in particular

4274,4460	Thoresby MSS
5829, 33,498	MSS of William Cole
10,114	Memorandum book of John Harrington
11,331, 11,332, 11,333	Letter-books of Sir William Brereton
15,669, 15,670	Proceedings of the Committee for Plundered Ministers
18,777, 18,778, 18,780	Parliamentary journals of Walter Yonge
18,979	Fairfax correspondence
21,922	Letter-book of Sir Richard Norton
24,860, 24,861	Papers of Richard Major
31,116	Parliamentary journal of Lawrence Whitaker
33,084 (also Additional Charters 29,276 and 29,277)	Pelham MSS
35,331	Diary of Walter Yonge
37,343, 37,344, 37,345, 53,726	Autobiography of Bulstrode Whitelocke
39,218, 39,231	Wodehouse MSS (papers of Sir Edmund Bacon)
41,308	Townshend MSS
46,381	Harrington MSS
53,728	Sermons of Bulstrode Whitelocke

ALTHORP MSS
B3	Clifford correspondence

EGERTON MSS
786, 787	Letter-books of Sir Samuel Luke
2546	Nicholas papers
2646, 2647, 2648, 2650	Barrington correspondence

229

3517	Armyne MSS

HARLEIAN MSS

163, 164, 165, 166, 374, 378, 379, 382, 383, 384, 386, 387, 646, 7658	D'Ewes MSS
6395	Account of East Anglian gentry
7132	Speeches in the Short and Long Parliaments

LANSDOWNE MSS

459	Commonwealth surveys of church livings

PORTLAND MSS

BL Loan 29/48, 84, 88, 119, 173, 175, 176, 177, 389	MSS of the Harley family

SLOANE MSS

1519	Fairfax correspondence
5247	Civil War mottoes

STOWE MSS

188	Grenville MSS

Public Record Office

CHANCERY
Proceedings, Six Clerks' Series (C.5–10)
Commonwealth Church Surveys (C.94)

COURT OF WARDS
Feodaries' Surveys (Wards 5)
Miscellaneous Books (Wards 9)

EXCHEQUER
Depositions (E.134)

INSTITUTION BOOKS
Series A, 1556–1660

STATE PAPER OFFICE
State Papers Domestic Series, Charles I (S.P.16), Committee for Compounding (S.P.23), Commonwealth Exchequer Papers (S.P.28)
WILLS
Wills proved in the Prerogative Court of Canterbury (PROB11)

Dr Williams's Library, London

Baxter Letters
Morrice MSS

House of Lords Library
House of Lords MSS

Bedfordshire County Record Office
St John of Bletsoe MSS

Bodleian Library, Oxford
Carte MSS
Tanner MSS
MS Top. Beds., d. 4

Borthwick Institute of Historical Research (University of York)
Wills in the York Registry

Bristol Record Office
Ashton Court MSS

Buckinghamshire County Record Office
Grenville MSS

Derbyshire Record Office
Burdett of Foremark MSS
Chandos-Pole-Gell MSS
Gresley of Drakelow MSS

Dorset County Record Office
Browne of Frampton MSS
MSS deposited by Mrs E. Cockburn
MSS deposited by Mrs J. M. Lane
MSS deposited by Mr G. D. Roper

East Devon Record Office
Drake of Buckland Abbey MSS

Essex County Record Office
Hatfield Broad Oak MSS

Guildford Muniment Room
Loseley MSS
Onslow MSS

Hampshire Record Office
Daly MSS
Jervoise of Herriard Park MSS

Hull University Library

Wickham-Boynton MSS

Humberside County Record Office

Howard-Vyse MSS
Legard of Anlaby MSS
Macdonald of Sleat MSS
Wickham-Boynton MSS

Leicestershire Record Office

Papers of Lord Hazlerigg of Noseley

Norfolk Record Office

Ketton-Cremer MSS
Kimberley MSS

Northamptonshire Record Office

Dryden (Canons Ashby) MSS
Finch-Hatton MSS

North Yorkshire Record Office

Darley MSS
Marwood MSS

Sheffield Central Library

Crewe MSS
Wentworth Woodhouse Collection, Bright MSS

Somerset Record Office

Harrington of Kelston MSS (documents deposited by Messrs Corbould, Rigby & Co.)
Popham MSS

West Devon Record Office

Strode MSS

Yorkshire Archaeological Society Library

Lister-Kaye MSS

II PRINTED

A Narrative of the Late Parliament and *A Second Narrative of the Late Parliament, Harleian Miscellany*, iii (1809).
A Reall Protestation of Many and Very Eminent Persons in the County of Yorke (1642) (Thomason Tracts, E.116 (17)).

ASHLEY COOPER, Anthony, Earl of Shaftesbury, *Memoirs, Letters and Speeches of Anthony Ashley Cooper, First Earl of Shaftesbury*, ed. W. D. Christie (1859).

AUBREY, John, *Aubrey's Brief Lives*, ed. Oliver Lawson Dick (1972).

BAILLIE, Robert, *Letters and Journals of Robert Baillie*, ed. David Laing, 3 vols (1841–2).

BAXTER, Richard, *Penitent Confession* (1691).

BAXTER, Richard, *Reliquiae Baxterianae*, ed. Matthew Sylvester (1696).

BAXTER, Richard, *The Autobiography of Richard Baxter*, ed. J. M. L. Thomas (1931).

BELL, R. (ed.), *Memorials of the Civil War*, 2 vols (1849).

Bibliotheca Gloucestrensis, 2 vols (1823).

BRERETON, Sir William, *Travels in Holland, United Provinces, England, Scotland and Ireland*, ed. Edward Hawkins, *Chetham Society*, i, (1844).

BRIDGE, William, *Twenty One Several Books of Mr William Bridge*, 2 vols (1657).

BURNET, Gilbert, *History of his Own Time*, 6 vols (1833).

BURTON, Thomas, *Diary of Thomas Burton*, ed. J. T. Rutt, 4 vols (1828).

CALAMY, Edmund (1600–1666), *An Indictment Against England Because of Her Selfe-Murdering Divisions* (1645).

CALAMY, Edmund (1600–1666), *England's Looking-Glasse, The English Revolution. I. Fast Sermons to Parliament*, ii (1970), 11–80.

CALAMY, Edmund (1600–1666), *The Noble-Man's Patterne of True and Reall Thankfulnesse* (1643).

CALAMY, Edmund (1671–1732), *An Account of the Ministers, Lecturers, Masters and Fellows of Colleges and Schoolmasters who were Ejected or Silenced after the Restoration in 1660*, vol.ii of a 2-vol work (1713).

CALAMY, Edmund (1671–1732), *The Nonconformist's Memorial*, ed. Samuel Palmer, 2 vols (1775).

Calendar of State Papers, Domestic.

Calendar of the Proceedings of the Committee for Compounding.

Calendar of the Proceedings of the Committee for the Advance of Money.

CARY, Henry, *Memorials of the Great Civil War in England*, 2 vols (1842).

CAWTON, Thomas, the younger, *The Life and Death of that Holy and Reverend Man of God Mr Thomas Cawton* (1662).

CHAMBERLAIN, John, *The Letters of John Chamberlain*, ed. N. E. McClure, 2 vols (1939).

CLARK, Samuel, *The Lives of Sundry Eminent Persons* (1683).

COLLINGES, JOHN, *Par Nobile. Two Treatises* (1669).

Commons Journals.

233

D'EWES, Sir Simonds, *The Journal of Sir Simonds D'Ewes. From the Beginning of the Long Parliament to the Trial of the Earl of Strafford*, ed. W. Notestein (1923).

D'EWES, Sir Simonds, *The Journal of Sir Simonds D'Ewes. From the First Recess of the Long Parliament to the Withdrawal of King Charles from London*, ed. W. H. Coates (1942).

D'EWES, Sir Simonds, *The Primitive Practise for Preserving Truth* (1645).

EDWARDS, Thomas, *Gangraena*, 3 parts (1646).

ELLIS, Sir Henry, *Original Letters*, Third Series, iv (1846).

FAIRCLOUGH, Samuel, *The Prisoners' Praises for their Deliverance from their Long Imprisonment in Colchester* (1650), Thomason Tracts, E.598/4.

FAIRCLOUGH, Samuel, *The Saint's Worthinesse and the World's Worthlesnesse* (1653).

FAIRCLOUGH, Samuel, *The Troublers Troubled* (1641).

FIRTH, Sir Charles and RAIT, R. S. (ed.), *The Acts and Ordinances of the Interregnum, 1642–1660*, 3 vols (1911).

FROYSELL, Thomas, *The Beloved Disciple* (1658).

FULLER, Thomas, *The Church-History of Britain* (1655).

GARDINER, Dorothy (ed.), *The Oxinden Letters, 1607–1642* (1933).

GELL, Sir John, *The Severall Accompts of Sir John Gell, Baronet and Colonell, and of his Brother Thomas Gell, Esquire, Lieutenant Colonell* (1645) (Thomason Tracts, E.273.1/15).

GILLESPIE, George, *Notes of Debates and Proceedings of the Assembly of Divines* in vol ii of *The Presbyterian's Armoury*, 3 vols (1846–53).

HAMPER, W. (ed.), *The Life, Diary and Correspondence of Sir William Dugdale* (1827).

HARLEY, Lady Brilliana, *Letters of the Lady Brilliana Harley*, ed. T. T. Lewis, *Camden Society*, lviii (1854).

HARRINGTON, Sir James, *A Holy Oyl, and a Sweet Perfume* (1669).

HARRINGTON, Sir James, *Noah's Dove* (1645).

HILL, Thomas, *An Olive Branch of Peace and Accommodation* (1648).

HILL, Thomas, *The Right Separation Incouraged* (1645).

HILL, Thomas, *The Trade of Truth Advanced* (1642), *The English Revolution. I. Fast Sermons to Parliament*, iii (1970), 286–351.

HISTORICAL MANUSCRIPTS COMMISSION:
Fourth, Fifth, Sixth, Seventh, Eighth, Ninth, Tenth and *Eleventh Reports*
Twelfth Report (Coke MSS)
Thirteenth and *Fourteenth Reports (Duke of Portland MSS)*
Duke of Buccleuch MSS
Duke of Portland MSS

Earl of Egmont MSS
Earl of Verulam MSS
Leyborne-Popham MSS
MSS of Marquis of Bath
HOLLES, Denzil, *Memoirs of Denzil Lord Holles* (1699).
HOLMES, Clive (ed.), *The Suffolk Committees for Scandalous Ministers 1644–1646, Suffolk Records Society*, xiii (1970).
HOUSTON, Jane, *Catalogue of Ecclesiastical Records of the Commonwealth 1643–1660 in the Lambeth Palace Library* (1968).
HUTCHINSON, Lucy, *Memoirs of the Life of Colonel Hutchinson*, ed. James Sutherland (1973).
HYDE, Edward, Earl of Clarendon, *State Papers Collected by Edward Earl of Clarendon*, ed. R. Scrope and T. Monkhouse, 3 vols (1767–86).
HYDE, Edward, Earl of Clarendon, *The History of the Rebellion and Civil Wars in England . . . by Edward, Earl of Clarendon*, ed. W. D. Macray, 6 vols (1888).
JOHNSON, G.W. (ed.), *The Fairfax Correspondence. Memoirs of the Reign of Charles the First*, 2 vols (1848).
JOSSELIN, Ralph, *The Diary of the Rev. Ralph Josselin 1616–1683, Camden Third Series*, xv (1908).
KNOWLER, W. (ed.), *The Earl of Strafforde's Letters and Despatches*, 2 vols (1739).
LEY, John, *A Patterne of Pietie* (1640).
Life and Death of Mr Henry Jessey (1671).
Lords Journals.
LUDLOW, Edmund, *Memoirs of Edmund Ludlow* (1671).
LUDLOW, Edmund, *A Voyce from the Watch Tower*, ed, A. B. Worden, *Camden Fourth Series*, xxi (1978).
LUKE, Sir Samuel, *Journal of Sir Samuel Luke*, ed. I. G. Philip, *Oxford Record Society* (1947).
LUKE, Sir Samuel, *The Letter Books 1644–45 of Sir Samuel Luke*, ed. H. G. Tibbutt (1963).
MARTINDALE, Adam, *The Life of Adam Martindale*, ed. R. Parkinson, *Chetham Society*, iv (1845).
MAY, Thomas, *The History of the Parliament of England* (1812).
MILTON, John, *Complete Prose Works of John Milton*, 6 vols (1653–73).
MITCHELL, A. F. and STRUTHERS, J. (ed.), *Minutes of the Sessions of the Westminster Assembly of Divines* (1874).
MORTON, Thomas, *The Episcopacy of the Church of England Justified to be Apostolical* (1670).
NALSON, John, *An Impartial Collection of the Great Affairs of State*, 2 vols (1682–3).
NICHOLLS, John (ed.), *Original Letters and Papers of State*

Addressed to Oliver Cromwell (1743).

NORTON, Luke, *Elegies on the Death of that Worthy and Accomplish't Gentleman Colonel John Hampden Esquire* (1643).

PEYTON, Sir Edward, *The High-way to Peace* (1647).

PEYTON, Sir Edward, *The Divine Catastrophe of the Kingly Family of the House of Stuarts* (1652).

PRINCE, John, *The Worthies of Devon* (1701).

PRYNNE, William, *A Fresh Discovery of Some Prodigious New Wandring-Blasing-Stars and Firebrands Stiling Themselves New-Lights* (1645) (Thomason Tracts, E.267(3)).

PRYNNE, William, *Hidden Workes of Darkenes Brought to Publike Light* (1645).

RERESBY, Sir John, *Memoirs of Sir John Reresby*, ed. A. Browning (1936).

RICRAFT, Josiah, *A Survey of England's Champions* (1647).

ROUS, John, *Diary of John Rous*, ed. Mary Anne Everett Green, *Camden Society*, lxvi (1856).

RUSHWORTH, John, *Historical Collections of Private Passages of State, Weighty Matters in Law, Remarkable Proceedings in Five Parliaments*, 8 vols (1721).

SCHOFIELD, B.(ed.), *The Knyvett Letters (1620–1644)* (1949).

SEDGWICK, Obadiah, *Christ the Life, and Death the Gain* (1650).

SHUTE, Christopher, *Ars piè Moriendi: or the True Accomptant* (1658).

SIKES, George, *The Life and Death of Sir Henry Vane, Knight* (1662).

SLINGSBY, Sir Henry, *The Diary of Sir Henry Slingsby, Bart.*, ed. D. Parsons (1836).

SPRINGETT, Lady Mary, memoirs and account of Springett family, *Gentleman's Magazine*, New Series, xxxvi (1851).

Suffolk's Tears (1653).

The Dissenting Ministers' Vindication of Themselves from the Horrid and Detestable Murder of Charles I (1649), *Somers Tracts*, (1811).

The English Revolution. I. Fast Sermons to Parliament, 34 vols (1970–1).

The English Revolution. III. Newsbooks I. Oxford Royalist, 4 vols (1971).

The Parliamentary or Constitutional History of England, 24 vols (1762–3)

Thomason Tracts (British Library) (The more important works are listed individually.)

TREVELYAN, Sir Walter Calverley and Sir Charles Edward (ed.), *Trevelyan Papers*, pt iii, *Camden Society*, cv (1872).

TREVETHICK, William, *A Sermon Preached at the Funeral of the Honourable Colonel Robert Rolle of Heanton Sachville in the County of Devon Esquire* (1661).

TURNER, G. Lyon (ed.), *Original Records of Early Nonconformity under Persecution and Indulgence*, 3 vols (1911–14).

TWYSDEN, Sir Roger, 'Sir Roger Twysden's Journal', *Archaeologia Cantiana*, iv (1861).

VANE, Sir Henry the younger, *The Tryal of Sir Henry Vane, Knight* (1662).

VANE, Sir Henry the younger, *A Healing Question, Somers Tracts*, vi (1811).

Vindiciae Veritatis (1654).

WALKER, Clement, *The Compleat History of Independency* (1661).

WALKER, John, *Sufferings of the Clergy* (1714).

WALLER, Sir William, *Divine Meditations upon Several Occasions, with a Dayly Directory* (1680).

WALLER, Sir William, *Recollections* (in *The Poetry of Anna Matilda*, 1788).

WALLER, Sir William, *Vindication of the Character and Conduct of Sir William Waller* (1793).

WHITE, C. H. Evelyn (ed.), *The Journal of William Dowsing* (1885).

WHITE, John, *The First Century of Scandalous, Malignant Priests* (1643).

WHITELOCKE, Bulstrode, *Memorials of the English Affairs*, 4 vols (1853).

WILDRIDGE, T. Tindall, *The Hull Letters* (1886).

WOOD, Anthony, *Athenae Oxonienses* (1691).

WOOD, Anthony, *Athenae Oxonienses*, ed. Philip Bliss, 4 vols (1815).

WOOD, Seth, *The Saint's Enterance into Peace and Rest by Death* (1651).

WOODROFFE, Timothy, *A Religious Treatise upon Simeon's Song* (1659).

WORTH, R. N. (ed.), *The Buller Papers* (1895).

SECONDARY SOURCES

I BOOKS

ANDRIETE, Eugene A., *Devon and Exeter in the Civil War* (1971).

ASHTON, Robert, *The English Civil War* (1978).

ATKYNS, Sir Robert, *The Ancient and Present State of Glostershire* (1712).

AYLMER, G. E., *The State's Servants: The Civil Service of the English Republic 1649–1660* (1973).

BALL, Bryan W., *A Great Expectation. Eschatological Thought in English Protestantism to 1660* (1975).

BARNARD, E. A. B., *The Rouses of Rous Lench, Worcestershire* (1921).

BLACKWOOD, B. G., *The Lancashire Gentry and Great Rebellion 1640–60*, Chetham Society, Third Series, xxv (1978).

BOLAM, C. G., GORING, Jeremy, SHORT, H. L. and THOMAS, Roger, *The English Presbyterians* (1968).

BRADY, W. M., *Annals of the Catholic Hierarchy in England and Scotland, 1585–1876* (1877).

BROOK, Benjamin, *The Lives of the Puritans*, 3 vols (1813).

BRUNTON, D. and PENNINGTON, D. H., *Members of the Long Parliament* (1954).

CAPP, B. S., *The Fifth Monarchy Men* (1972).

CLIFFE, J. T., *The Yorkshire Gentry from the Reformation to the Civil War* (1969).

CLIFFE, J. T., *The Puritan Gentry* (1984).

COATE, Mary, *Cornwall in the Great Civil War* (1963).

COBBETT, William, *Cobbett's Parliamentary History of England*, 36 vols (1806–20).

CRAWFORD, Patricia, *Denzil Holles, 1598–1680* (1979).

DAVIDS, T. W., *Annals of Evangelical Nonconformity in the County of Essex* (1863).

Dictionary of National Biography.

DORE, R. N., *The Civil Wars in Cheshire* (1966).

DURRANT, C. S., *A Link between Flemish Mystics and English Martyrs* (1925).

ELIOTT-DRAKE, Lady, *The Family and Heirs of Sir Francis Drake*, 2 vols (1911).

EVERITT, Alan M., *Suffolk and the Great Rebellion, 1640–1660*, Suffolk Records Society, iii (1960).

EVERITT, Alan M., *The Community of Kent and the Great Rebellion, 1640–1660* (1966).

FIRTH, Katharine R., *The Apocalyptic Tradition in Reformation Britain 1530–1645* (1979).

FLETCHER, Anthony S., *A County Community in Peace and War: Sussex 1600–1660* (1975).

FLETCHER, Anthony S., *The Outbreak of the English Civil War* (1981).

GRENVILLE, George, Lord Nugent, *Some Memorials of John Hampden*, 2 vols (1832).

HALLER, William, *Liberty and Reformation in the Puritan Revolution* (1955).

HALLEY, Robert, *Lancashire: its Puritanism and Nonconformity* (1872).

HEXTER, J. H., *Reappraisals in History* (1961).

HEXTER, J. H., *The Reign of King Pym* (1968).

HILL, Christopher, *Intellectual Origins of the English Revolution* (1965).

HILL, Christopher, *Puritanism and Revolution* (1958).

HILL, Christopher, *Society and Puritanism in Pre-Revolutionary England* (1965).

HIRST, Derek, *Authority and Conflict. England 1603–1658* (1986).

HOLMES, Clive, *The Eastern Association in the Civil War* (1974).

HOLMES, Clive, *Seventeenth-Century Lincolnshire* (1980).

HUNTER, Joseph, *South Yorkshire: the History and Topography of the Deanery of Doncaster*, 2 vols (1828).

HUTTON, Ronald, *The Restoration* (1985).

IRBY, P. A., *The Irbys of Lincolnshire and the Irebys of Cumberland*, 2 vols (1938).

ISHAM, Sir Gyles, *Easton Mauduit and the Parish Church of SS. Peter and Paul, Northamptonshire Record Society* (1974).

KEELER, M. E., *The Long Parliament, 1640–1641. A Biographical Study of its Members. American Philosophical Society* (1954).

KETTON-CREMER, R. W., *Norfolk in the Civil War* (1969).

LAMONT, William M., *Godly Rule, Politics and Religion, 1603–1660* (1969).

MACDONALD of the ISLES, Lady Alice, *The Fortunes of a Family. Bosville of New Hall, Gunthwaite and Thorpe* (1928).

MANNING, Brian (ed.), *Politics, Religion and the English Civil War* (1973).

MATTHEWS, A. G., *Calamy Revised* (1934).

MATTHEWS, A. G., *Walker Revised* (1948).

MORRILL, J. S., *Cheshire 1630–1660* (1974).

MORRILL, J. S., *The Revolt of the Provinces* (1976).

MUSKETT, J. J., *Suffolk Manorial Families*, 3 vols (1900–10).

NASH, Thomas, *History and Antiquities of Worcestershire*, 2 vols (1781–99).

PRESTWICH, John, *Prestwich's Respublica* (1787).

ROWE, Violet A., *Sir Henry Vane the Younger* (1970).

RUSSELL, Conrad (ed.), *The Origins of the English Civil War* (1973).

SEAVER, Paul S., *The Puritan Lectureships. The Politics of Religious Dissent 1560–1662* (1970).

SHAW, W. A., *A History of the English Church, 1640–1660*, 2 vols (1900).

SMITH, Harold, *The Ecclesiastical History of Essex under the Long Parliament and Commonwealth* (n.d.).

SOMERVILLE, Sir Robert, *Office-Holders in the Duchy and County Palatine of Lancaster from 1603* (1972).

SPALDING, Ruth, *The Improbable Puritan. A Life of Bulstrode Whitelocke, 1603–1675* (1975).

STONE, Lawrence, *The Causes of the English Revolution 1529–1642* (1972).

TOLMIE, Murray, *The Triumph of the Saints. The Separate Churches*

of London 1616–1649 (1977).
UNDERDOWN, David, *Pride's Purge* (1971).
UNDERDOWN, David, *Somerset in the Civil War and Interregnum* (1973).
VERNEY, Frances P. and Margaret M., *Memoirs of the Verney Family During the Seventeenth Century*, 2 vols (1907).
Victoria County History: various counties.
VULLIAMY, C. E., *The Onslow Family 1528–1874* (1953).
WATSON, A. G., *The Library of Sir Simonds D'Ewes* (1966).
WILSON, John F., *The Pulpit in Parliament: Puritanism during the English Civil Wars, 1640–1648* (1969).
WOOD, Alfred C., *Nottinghamshire in the Civil War* (1937).
WOOLRYCH, Austin, *Commonwealth and Protectorate* (1982).
WORDEN, A. B., *The Rump Parliament 1648–1653* (1974).
YULE, George, *The Independents in the English Civil War* (1958).
YULE, George, *Puritans in Politics. The Religious Legislation of the Long Parliament 1640–1647* (1981).

ARTICLES

BLACKWOOD, B. G., 'The Cavalier and Roundhead Gentry of Suffolk', *The Suffolk Review*, New Series, no. 7 (1986).
CHETWYND-STAPYLTON, H.E., 'The Stapletons of Yorkshire', *Yorkshire Archaeological Journal*, viii (1884).
CLAY, J. W., 'The Gentry of Yorkshire at the Time of the Civil War', *Yorkshire Archaeological Journal*, xxiii (1915).
DUCKETT, Sir George, 'Civil Proceedings in Yorkshire', *Yorkshire Archaeological Journal*, vii (1881–2).
FOSTER, Stephen, 'The Presbyterian Independents Exorcized', *Past and Present*, no.44 (1969).
HELYAR, H. A., 'The Arrest of Col. William Strode of Barrington, in 1661', *Somersetshire Archaeological and Natural History Society*, xxxvii (1891).
KIDSON, Ruth M., 'The Gentry of Staffordshire, 1662–3', *Collections for a History of Staffordshire, Staffordshire Record Society*, Fourth Series, ii (1958).
MORRILL, J. S., 'The Religious Context of the English Civil War', *Transactions of the Royal Historical Society*, Fifth Series, xxxiv (1984).
NEWMAN, P. R., 'Catholic Royalists of Northern England, 1642–1645', *Northern History*, xv (1979).
PEARL, Valerie, 'The "Royal Independents" in the Civil War', *Transactions of the Royal Historical Society*, Fifth Series, xviii (1968).
UNDERDOWN, David, 'Parliamentary Diary of John Boys, 1647–8', *Bulletin of the Institute of Historical Research*, xxxix (1966).

240

WARD, Seth, Bishop, letters 1663–7, *Devon and Cornwall Notes and Queries*, xxi (1940–1).

WORDEN, A. B., 'Providence and Politics in Cromwellian England', *Past and Present*, no.109 (1985).

WORDEN, A. B., PEARL, Valerie, UNDERDOWN, David, YULE, George, HEXTER, J. H. and POSTER, Stephen, 'Presbyterians, Independents and Puritans', *Past and Present*, no.47 (1970).

Index

245

Index

Brian Merriman's
THE MIDNIGHT COURT

for Cast and Crew
past and future

Brian Merriman's

THE MIDNIGHT COURT

a one act play

Celia de Fréine

translated and dramatised
by
Celia de Fréine

ARLEN
HOUSE

The Midnight Court

is published in 2012 by
ARLEN HOUSE
42 Grange Abbey Road
Baldoyle
Dublin 13
Ireland
Phone: 00 353 86 8207617
Email: arlenhouse@gmail.com
arlenhouse.blogspot.com

International distribution
SYRACUSE UNIVERSITY PRESS
621 Skytop Road, Suite 110
Syracuse, NY 13244–5290
Phone: 315–443–5534/Facs: 315–443–5545
Email: supress@syr.edu
www.syracuseuniversitypress.syr.edu

ISBN 978–1–85132–055–4, hardback
978–1–85132–056–1, paperback, 2013

Design ¦ Arlen House
Printing ¦ Brunswick Press
Fale & Flowers, 1991 ¦ Poppy Melia
Gouache on Handmade Paper, 790mm x 560mm,
www.poppymelia.com

CONTENTS

Cúirt an Mheán Oíche : The Midnight Court, a poem of approximately 1,000 lines written by Brian Merriman in or around 1780, is unique in Irish literature. Drawing its inspiration from the *Aisling,* the Irish vision-poem, and from the European Courts of Love which date from the Middle Ages, it gives a bawdy account of society in late eighteenth century Ireland. Little is known of its author other than that he was the master of a hedge-school, a tutor to the gentry, a farmer, a violinist, and that *The Midnight Court* is his only work of note. It is almost certain also that he was the illegitimate son of a member of the gentry, raised by the stonemason his mother married.

When I set about translating *Cúirt an Mheán Oíche* in 1982, I decided to explore its dramatic potential rather than reproduce it as a poem in English. To this end, I re-sequenced lines, and allocated some to newly-created characters: the wenches, the codgers and the fairy maidens.

In 2009 I revised the script, allocating lines to the defendant's wife so that she could speak on her own behalf. I also felt that the bailiff would not have remained silent during some of the more raucous exchanges. The few lines I gave her and others spoken by the codgers, the wenches, and the defendant's wife, are the only additions to my translation into English of Merriman's text.

I decided to explore other aspects of the text, i.e., its genesis, the attitude of the clergy to the sexual mores of the day, and the dilemma of the single expectant mother, by writing the play *Meanmarc.*

This translation and dramatisation of *Cúirt an Mheán Oíche* forms Part II of the *Lorg Merriman* project.

CHARACTERS

BRIAN MERRIMAN	a poet in his thirties
BAILIFF TO THE COURT	a hag
AOIBHEALL	a Fairy Queen
PLAINTIFF	a buxom well-dressed woman in her twenties
DEFENDANT	an elderly man
FIRST WENCH	a young woman
SECOND WENCH	a young woman
FIRST CODGER	an elderly man
SECOND CODGER	an elderly man
FIRST FAIRY MAIDEN	a young maiden
SECOND FAIRY MAIDEN	a young maiden
THE PRIEST	a young man
DEFENDANT'S WIFE	a young woman

MUSICIANS

THE SET
This play can be performed in any venue. All that is required are stools and a throne.

Lights are brought up on a summer's day at a crossroads where the PLAINTIFF, the FIRST WENCH, the SECOND WENCH, the DEFENDANT, the DEFENDANT'S WIFE, the FIRST CODGER and the SECOND CODGER are gathered.

The MUSICIANS are playing, the WOMEN are dancing, the MEN are watching and gossiping.

MERRIMAN enters, engrossed in thought. The FIRST WENCH flaunts herself at him; the PLAINTIFF invites him to dance. Ignoring them both, he sits, takes from his pocket a piece of vellum on which he has jotted a poem and casts his eye over it.

The dancing finishes and the crowd disperses and exits, bar the MUSICIANS who remain onstage, one of whom accompanies MERRIMAN as he stands and reads, from the vellum, the opening of Cúirt an Mheán Oíche. *(These lines have been left in Irish to suggest a newly-penned poem; their translation into English is on page 63).*

MERRIMAN
Ba ghnáth mé ag siúl le ciumhais na habhann
ar bháinseach úr 's an drúcht go trom,
in aice na gcoillte, i gcoim an tsléibh',
gan mhairg, gan mhoill, ar shoilse an lae.
Do ghealadh mo chroí nuair chínn Loch Gréine,

13

an talamh, 's an tír, is íor na spéire;
taitneamhach aoibhinn suíomh na sléibhte
ag bagairt a gcinn thar dhroim a chéile.
Do ghealfadh an croí bheadh críon le cianta,
caite gan bhrí, nó líonta de phianta,
an séithleach searbh gan sealbh gan saibhreas
d'fhéachfadh tamall thar bharra na gcoillte
ar lachain 'na scuainte ar chuan gan cheo
's an eala ar a bhfuaid 's í ag gluaiseacht leo,
na héisc le meidhir ag éirí in airde,
péirse im' radharc go taibhseach tarrbhreac,
dath an locha agus gorm na dtonn
ag teacht go tolgach torannach trom.
Bhíodh éanlaith i gcrainn go meidhreach mómhar
is léimneach eilte i gcoillte im' chóngar,
géimreach adhairce is radharc ar shlóite,
tréanrith gadhar is *Reynard* rómpu.

MERRIMAN puts away his poem and addresses the audience.

MERRIMAN
Yesterday morning the sky was clear,
the sun arose a blazing sphere
and having put paid to the black of night
set to work with force and might.

Above me the boughs sagged and creaked;
beside me swathes of grass and reeds
flourished alongside flowers and wort
that would banish the darkest doleful thought.

MERRIMAN settles himself on the grass.

MERRIMAN
Heavy and languid I lay on a bank,
deep in a swaying blanket of grass;

beneath the trees, beside a trench,
I supported my head and stretched myself.

Making sure to shelter from flies,
I closed my eyes, clammed them together,
sealed them shut in slumber's fetter.

I drifted off to a place of dreams,
round and round on a circular course;
stripped to the bone and cut to the deep,
I lay there senseless, chained in sleep.

*MERRIMAN sleeps. The sky becomes overcast; the earth shakes;
the wind howls. The FIRST and SECOND FAIRY MAIDENS enter
and are lit as though by flashes of lightning.*

FIRST FAIRY MAIDEN
He drifted off to a place of dreams,
round and round on a circular course.

SECOND FAIRY MAIDEN
Stripped to the bone and cut to the deep,
he lay there senseless, chained in sleep.

FIRST FAIRY MAIDEN
Round and round on a circular course,
stripped to the bone and cut to the deep.

SECOND FAIRY MAIDEN
He drifted off to a place of dreams,
as he lay there senseless, chained in sleep.

BOTH FAIRY MAIDENS
Stripped to the bone and cut to the deep.

The FAIRY MAIDENS move into shadow until their next lines.
Enter BAILIFF who should fit Merriman's description below. (It's
worth bearing in mind also that she's an officer of the court and
an otherworld creature). MERRIMAN awakes and recoils. The
storm abates. Night falls.

MERRIMAN
In my sleep I thought that I felt and heard
the ground beneath me tremble and rumble,
and a storm from the North, vicious and wild,
hammer sparks from the nearby jetty.

Glancing around me, what did I see
advancing inland from the harbour's edge,
but a huge, full-bummed, fat-bellied female,
big-boned, bristling, brash and broad.

Her correct height I reckoned to be
about eighteen or twenty feet, or more;
forty four feet of her grime-spattered cloak
trailed behind in the mud and the mire.

She was big, she was bold, and a sight to behold
was her wrinkled brow all ploughed and furrowed;
a stalking terror, a fright to be seen
were her gawping gums and her grotesque grin.

Oh, Heavens above! Strong and firm
was her beam of a hand that held in its grasp
a staff – a brazen sign above on its spike
with the power of bailiff inscribed upon it.
These rasping words she boldly uttered
from the gravelly depths of her gaping gorge.

Bodhrán is played during the following passage.

BAILIFF
The Irish race has no land, no freedom,
no control of law, no income, or leaders.
Your country's been ravished and all that remains,
in place of the lush, the noxious and rank.

The clans of the nobles are scattered abroad
and wanton upstarts usurp their places,
quick to pillage, to rob, and to plunder,
flaying the feeble, destroying the frail.

The hapless survivors have been led astray,
without right, or title, or recourse to law,
bewildered by wrangles and legal banter
that inflict upon them hardship and ruin.

For the judges are false and the counsels are crooked –
callous connivers, corrupt and cunning.
Justice is clouded, her radiance defiled,
blinded by fees, by falsehood and bribes.

*FAIRY MAIDENS take up position behind the BAILIFF, one on
either side.*

FIRST FAIRY MAIDEN
It has heavily grieved his highness the king
and the tribes and the clans of our Sovereign Shee.

SECOND FAIRY MAIDEN
And its countless companies, far and wide,
that Ireland has suffered such a tragedy.

BAILIFF
But worst of all, for this demoralized nation,
the choice of your youth are without copulation,
and few of them marry or settle at all.

'Tis clear that your lands have been desolated:
incessant battle and bloodshed have drained them;
a regal race has quitted these shores –
high time you were making more to replace them.

(to MERRIMAN)
Look at ye all without chick or child
when there's passionate women on land and on sea:
buxom beauties and well-built wenches,
handsome hussies and hot-blooded straps,
languid lassies and shy little slips,
the haughty and high, waiting to be harnessed.

'Tis a shame that these damsels are not reproducing;
'tis a shame that their bellies and breasts aren't bloated
Fair dues to their endurance – I praise their patience –
while they wait to be wooed and rendered with child.

FIRST FAIRY MAIDEN
We're proud to announce to the Irish people
that the scribes of the Shee have all agreed
to take action regarding your country's plight.
After two days and nights on top of the mountain,
in a court convened by the Moy Graney Shee,
our scribes and sages have reached a decision:
one of our number has been chosen by lot
and sent to this land to set matters right.

SECOND FAIRY MAIDEN
Aoibheall the just, her heart without falsehood,
Craglea's Fair Queen, beloved of Thomond,
has agreed to be exiled from the hosts of the Shee,
and abide here awhile on the judgement bench.

FIRST FAIRY MAIDEN
This fair-minded maiden has already sworn
to stand for the poor, the frail and infirm,
to crush underfoot the fraudulent lawyer,
and speak against the might of the powers that be.

SECOND FAIRY MAIDEN
The stance of usurpers will be soon set aside
and right once more returned to its place.

BAILIFF
Arise and stir, you dozing degenerate!
You're a sorry sight stretched out on your arse,
while the court is in session and hordes headed there.

For 'tisn't a court without statute or rule,
or a booty court, the kind that you're used to,
but a court convened by the gentlest of hosts,
a court of compassion, of triumph, of muses.

And I can tell you now that tricks and treason,
collusion, conspiracy, and underhand deeds,
will not feature here as they are wont to do.

This court is convened in Feakle today.
Answer the call – without further delay.
'Tis there you are summoned, begin the trek
or I'll drag you there by the scruff of your neck.

MERRIMAN tries to rise but stumbles. The BAILIFF grabs hold of him with her staff. As he is marched towards the court the rest of the cast re-enter and promenade across the stage, bringing with them stools and a throne.

FIRST FAIRY MAIDEN
She cocked her crook in the back of his cape.

SECOND FAIRY MAIDEN
And started to strut in determined strides.

FIRST FAIRY MAIDEN
Through woodland and glen she marched him down.

SECOND FAIRY MAIDEN
She cocked her crook in the back of his cape.

FIRST FAIRY MAIDEN
And started to strut in determined strides.

SECOND FAIRY MAIDEN
Through woodland and glen she marched him down.

BOTH FAIRY MAIDENS
Till at last they arrived at the Midnight Court
convened by the gable of the church at Moinmoy.

*AOIBHEALL appears and the FAIRY MAIDENS fall into step
behind her, attending to her needs and helping her to be seated.*

MERRIMAN
And there, before me, flooded in torchlight,
shimmered a household that was richly adorned:
firm, well-built, refined and handsome,
solid of frame with its doors fortified.

*The BAILIFF bangs her staff and everybody sits, apart from
MERRIMAN, the BAILIFF, and the PLAINTIFF who takes up
position downstage. The FIRST WENCH and SECOND WENCH
and the DEFENDANT'S WIFE are seated on one side; the
DEFENDANT and the FIRST CODGER and SECOND CODGER are
on the opposite side. The directions for the actors' movements
during the court proceedings are guidelines only. As this is not a
regular court it is envisaged that there should be much horse-*

play and pushing and shoving. Music, in particular the bodhrán,
may be played at the discretion of the director.

MERRIMAN

I entered and saw the well-mannered Shee Woman
seated above at the head of the court,
while a band of maidens, forceful and strong,
formed by her side a cohort of beauty.

I saw at once a house filled full
from top to middle with women and people.

Standing alone was a comely maiden
sweet, wet-mouthed, pleasing, yet wan,
lively, beguiling, with a long fair mane,
she was placed before the dock of the court.

Her hair cascaded about her in tresses,
there was a troubled, tormented look in her eye.
Her speech was repressed in her heaving bosom,
she was soundlessly silent, completely o'ercome –
'twas clear to all that she'd prefer to be dead.

A flood of tears flowed down her cheeks,
as she stood beyond, straight as an arrow,
wringing her hands and clenching her fists.
The tears rolled on, without sign of abating.

Then sighs released her power of speech,
her sobbing ceased, and a change occurred.
She dried her eyes and gave vent to these words.

MERRIMAN *sits alongside the men.*

PLAINTIFF
A thousand welcomes, I rejoice in your coming,
Aoibheall, Queen and Prophet of Craglea.

Oh Light of Day and Moon without limit,
the fullness of life here is in fetters chained.
Majestic Monarch of the Hosts of Shee,
you've been sadly missed in Thomond and Ireland.

The source of my sorrow, the cause of my woe,
the cause that distressed me and left me defeated,
the cause that distracted and left me insane,
enveloped and engulfed me in burning pain,
is the women deprived of marriage fulfillment:
throughout this land myriads of maidens
become black hags without husbands' aegis,
never to know the zeal of the conjugal bed.

In the course of my travels I've seen much of this,
a hundred and one who wouldn't refuse
and me among them, for it's my loss too.

Morose I've become, without husband or child.
My hurt, my sorrow, my pain that we're left
without comfort or chattels, peace or repose,
gloomy, forlorn, distressed and in need,
without sleep or slumber or succour at night,
but confronted with grief, stretched with no rest
on a cold drab bed, tormented with thoughts.

Oh Venerable Queen, take a good hard look
at the women of Ireland – we're so deprived –
if the men of the country remain as they are,
I swear upon oath, we'll resort to abduction.

By the time they wish to espouse a wife
no one wants them, they're old and exhausted.
By then there's no value in lying beneath them –
ancient antiques, shriveled and useless.

On those rare occasions in youthful heat
when one in seven with a growth of down
takes up with a woman, you can be certainly sure
she's no fine specimen, genteel, well-got,
well-bred and comely, with delicate graces
who'd know when to sit or rise in your presence,
but an old brown hag, a remorseful cow
who has amassed riches by meanness and drudging.

The PLAINTIFF falls to her knees. FIRST WENCH and SECOND WENCH rush forward and support her, one on either side.

FIRST WENCH
It's broken her heart and rent it in twain –
left her mind and her body drained.

SECOND WENCH
Ill, indisposed, unfit and feeble,
depleted, defeated, lamenting and weeping.

FIRST WENCH
By the time we spot a stalwart lad
manly, magnetic, alert and active,
level-headed, learned, steady and sure,
smooth-cheeked, humorous, handsome and blest ...

SECOND WENCH
or a light-hearted lad, lively, well-heeled,
self-righteous and strong, sturdily shaped ...

FIRST WENCH
they're won and trapped in the bonds of wedlock
by wretches, witches, fools and buffoons ...

SECOND WENCH
or dirty sluts or slatterns or slobs
or arrogant know-alls who gossip and yap.

PLAINTIFF
My shame, my ruin, there's a bad-mannered heifer,
a wench whose feet and hair are right squalid,
getting married tonight and it sears me through.
What fault have I that he chose her over me?

*FIRST WENCH and SECOND WENCH help the PLAINTIFF to her
seat. MERRIMAN addresses the audience as the incensed
DEFENDANT rises.*

MERRIMAN
Up there leapt, ferocious and fast,
a mean old codger, seething with venom.
His limbs a-tremble, his breath in gasps,
rage and rancour flowed through his veins.
An awesome sight to the assembled court,
he approached the bench and I heard him speak

BAILIFF bangs her staff. MERRIMAN sits.

DEFENDANT
Damnation and damage! And unending heart scald!
You streel of a hussy are the progeny of a whore!

'Tis no wonder the sun has faded to wanness
and that, without statute, our laws have declined;
'tisn't enough the tribulations befallen the land:
our cows left dry, without milk or calves.

What of the widespread ruin that's been caused
by the fashions worn by yourself and your ilk?

You notorious trollop, isn't it well we remember
the wicked breed from which you issued:
not a word of praise is due to your elders –
slovenly louts and churlish beggars.

We know full well which dawdler's your father,
without friend or fame, backbone or cash,
a drooling fool, without sense or learning,
plate or pleasure, food or relish,
with no coat for his back, his crotch exposed,
a shoot of willow tied about his waist.

Believe you me, if sold at a fair
himself and his tribe, by the saints above,
having paid all the bills, he'd barely be able
to purchase a tankard of ale with the leavings.

PLAINTIFF rises and pushes DEFENDANT into his seat.

PLAINTIFF
I'm bright and smart, well-drawn and buxom:
my throat, my bosom, my hands, my limbs
are ever vying to surpass each other.

Look at my waist, and my slender frame.
I'm not lean or lank, crooked or gangly.
Here's bum and thigh and figure to be proud of,
while under cover lies my finest property.

FIRST WENCH rises.

FIRST WENCH
And my mouth is neat, my teeth, my laugh;
my form is lithe, my forehead tender.
My eye is green, my locks are in whorls
that fall in abundant tresses and curls.
My cheek, my face are without smudge or blemish.

SECOND WENCH rises.

SECOND WENCH
And I'm not a hag or a witch of a woman,
but a bonnie lass, milk-white and pleasing.
Not a slut or a slattern, or a slovenly slob,
or an awkward idiot without joy or pleasure.
Or a rotten drone, or a useless wench,
but a choice young lady – one of the best.

PLAINTIFF
If I was a drip like some of my neighbours,
tattered and torpid, with no sense or learning,
without vision or cunning in seeking fair play,
what would it matter if I turned to despair?

What is the reason that no one will love me?
I was never yet seen in the company of men,
fawning on, watching the young or the old
on the level ground of a match or a dance,
or racing with rabble on full grassy plains.

Calm is my demeanour – I'm dressed without flaw
in well-made clothes from top to toe:
the poll of my head is powdered with care,
starched, well-shaped is the back of my bonnet,
my hood is bright, with lashings of ribbons,
my dress is patterned and boasts many ruffles.

I always make sure there's an outstanding border,
attractive and bright on my crimson cloak.
Branches and plants adorn in profusion
my apron of cambric with its bold bird-ed stripes.

My heels are well-shaped, slender and narrow;
tall and sleek screwed under my shoes.
Hoops, bracelets, embroidered laces,
and gloves of silk adorn my hands and my wrists.

Applause and cheers. The DEFENDANT *leaps up and pushes the*
women aside. BAILIFF *bangs her staff.*

DEFENDANT
Almighty prophet, how boldly she blathers –
this strutting strap, so mighty and high
in her proper colours and crimson mantle!

Wait a while, love, tell where you got it.
Tell where you got this beauty you boast of.
Tell how you came by these useless garments.
Were they honestly got? That's surely the question.

A short while ago you had nowt of your own.
Tell where you got the price of the hood.
Tell where you got the price of the dress.
Forget for a minute the price of the apron,
tell where you got the price of the shoes.

'Tis a widespread scandal and topic for gossip
that a slut of your sort, without cow or sheep,
with buckles on your shoes and a silken mantle,
your placket agape for all the world to see,
should blind so many with your wile and deceit.

I remember you well when you'd only a cap.
'Tis been a long time since your back knew a shift.
Beneath your silk skirts your backside is bare,
but only the wicked would know what you lack.

With the best of ruffles on your cambric sleeves,
a band of cheap canvas adorns your small waist –
who knows it's not stays that are holding it in place?
The country sees all your frills and your flounces,
but your gloves conceal the blotches and cracks.

Up jumps FIRST CODGER.

FIRST CODGER
Confess to the court, or I'll tell it myself,
how long since you had a drink with your meal?
You poor wretched woman, your feet are filthy
and you're ruining your body with sauceless spuds.

SECOND CODGER
And I've seen myself the hovel you live in.
The stuff laid beneath you is not soft or fine,
tow or flax on a wheel purely-crafted,
but a dirty mat without sheet or quilt,
bare with no stitch, not even a blanket,
in a shell of a cabin, with nowhere to sit,
its air fetid, its floor a squalid mess –
where the tracks of hens are as plain to be seen
as the weeds that run wild in the soggy screed –
its roof sagging, its gables cracked and bending
beneath the downpour that's forever descending.

PLAINTIFF *pushes her way forward.*

PLAINTIFF
Watch it, don't think I'm frightened or shy,
a fool with no mind or a shameful child
afraid or alone, skittish or wild,
a mindless maniac who's lost control.

Why should I hide from the gaze of admirers
when my face and my brow are uncommonly bright?
Why shouldn't I be proud to show myself off
at each field where a game's being played,
at bonefires and dances, races and revels,
at fairs and markets and Sunday mass,
to see and be seen and pick out a man?

But I've spent my days in a useless hunt:
they've codded me all and broken my heart,
after my friendship, my giving, my loving,
after I've suffered a thousand afflictions,
after I've listened to the reading of cups
by hard-faced hags and card-cutting sluts.

PLAINTIFF sinks to the floor. FIRST WENCH rushes forward.

FIRST WENCH
There isn't a trick that I haven't resorted to
when the moon was new, or when it was full,
at Shrovetide, Hallowe'en, and other occasions,
but how foolish I was, expecting results.
I never yet slept on one of these vigils
without a sock-full of fruit by my ear.

Fasting and praying to me were no bother,
for three days I'd swallow no bite or no sup.
Against the current I have washed my shift
hoping for a husband's whisper in sleep.

Often indeed I have swept out the stack;
my nails and my hair I have left in the ashes;
the flail I have placed beneath the gable
and under my pillow concealed the spade;
I've put my distaff in the eye of the oven
and my ball of yarn in MacReynold's limekiln;
I've put the flaxseed out in the street
and under my bedding a head of cabbage.

During each of these tricks that I'm after recounting
I invoked the Devil and all of his minions.

The outcome of my story is plain to be seen,
after all my hard-trying, I still have no man.

The cause of my worry, alack and alas,
is my fierce fending off of advancing years.
The long grey days are fast approaching,
I'm afraid I'll expire with n'ere a proposal.

*FIRST WENCH sits beside PLAINTIFF. SECOND WENCH rushes
forward.*

SECOND WENCH
Oh Pearl of Paradise, I beg and implore you,
take my soul, I pray and beseech you.

Dismiss me not as a worthless old crone,
an incomplete streel who'd no chance to blossom,
without kith or kin or credit or cash,
a fireside scold without use or welcome.

By the Holy Book, by fire and by thunder,
the world has deceived me and called me a fool,
while the lowest of the dregs have all that I yearn for.

I can see them now, the scum of the earth:
Sive has a suckling, she's rich and cosy,
Muireann rejoices in getting a man,
Maura and Orla are bloated with babies,
great is their derision and mockery of me.
Marcella and Maeve are all airy fairy,
Celia and Anna are surrounded by litter,
and more of the unlikeliest women the same,
and me barren, like this, without issue or offspring.

SECOND WENCH sits with FIRST WENCH. PLAINTIFF rises.

PLAINTIFF
Too long I'm abused, my patience is leaving.
I'm longing with lust and the one cure in sight
is devilish herbs that are dried-out and seasoned
with magic potions that will tame yet for me
a handsome lad, or a gallant garsoon,
and win with effect his affection and love.

Dozens of these tricks I've seen done before,
and I will resort to the very same means.
A good strong help in the coupling of people
are the cores of apples and powdered herbs,
the purple orchid and flax-of-toad,
the knotted knapweed and Lady's Slipper,
beard-of-the-goat with Solomon's seal,
the yellow wort with its magic for lust,
leaves that are singed and shrivelled in secret,
and more of this sort that I don't care to mention.

Indeed, 'twas a wonder all over Ireland
that heifer above, when she captured a man –
at Shrovetide she told me, aside, in secret,
you see she's been married since last Hallowe'en –

'twas only the clear milky aid that she drank
with moorland midges pickled in ale.

I've been patient for long, please give me release,
watch me set to with the speed of an arrow.
If a cure for my trial isn't found in your court,
I'll give vent to my rage – you're my last hope.

PLAINTIFF sits.

FIRST CODGER
Almighty Aoibheall, benevolent, benign,
I pray you, beseech you to save and protect me.
I know, 'tis true, that the brave men of Ireland
are baited and trapped by rogues of this kind.

SECOND CODGER
By the hand of my friend, I know a young lad,
a neighbour of mine, living close by,
an innocent soul, a poor simple slob,
till one of these ones he took unto wife.

It breaks my heart whenever I see her,
her bearing, her holding, her pomp and her pride.
She has a few cows and a field of fine barley,
money in her pocket and gold on her hand.

FIRST CODGER
I saw her today on the side of the road –
she's fine and strong, a hefty young trollop,
but always fault-finding, jeering, cajoling,
with her great fat thighs and a leer on her puss.

Only I'm not one who's given to gossip,
to seek out scandal or to search for yarns,
'twould be easy repeat what I've heard –

how by day she was dragged and sorely tired out,
torn in the middle with shouts all about her,
stretched on the street, or laid in a stable,
by a rabble of bogmen near the mill at Gaurus.

SECOND CODGER
Listen, she was warped and after what he's said,
I'd freely forgive her all her digressions,
but a plague on her: by night I'd oft see her
thrown on the road that skirts Derryduff,
her legs spread and no stitch beneath her.

Reports will thrive, and there'll forever be talk,
discourse on her name and her coarse rough deeds,
in Ibrickane, famed for its wine and its bread,
and in Tirmaclane of the lush green fields,
by high and by low in Bansha and Inch,
Kilbreckan, Clarecastle, not to mention Quin;
among the bully-boys of bean-pod Tradree
and the bulky bouncers of Corduroy Cratloe.

FIRST CODGER
My shock at this had me out of my mind,
for I'm fain to tremble with fright when I think
of how she used to be slim, in spite of the squeezing,
but pregnant she got the moment she wished.

'Tis a relief to me to put this in words –
for there didn't go by a moment in time
from oaths on the altar in front of the candles,
the 'I join ye together' ordained by the Lord
till milk erupted in streams from her breasts
nine months and a week to the day.

DEFENDANT *rises.*

DEFENDANT
Beware of the danger to him that's unwed.
Beware of the tie under yoke until death
where envy and sufferance thrive and abound.
In vain, alas, no lesson I learned.

This part of the country knows how I was –
my early career in the days before:
proud and strong with fine rich possessions,
a welcome awaited guests to my house.

I'd friends in Court and the legal profession,
status, renown, on a par with the learned,
poise in my speech, assurance and strength;
land and riches were proof of my standing.

I was a settled man, content in my ways
till a woman seized my strength and my health.

FIRST CODGER
A pleasing woman, a strapping young lass.

SECOND CODGER
Stout was her trunk, limber her limbs.

FIRST CODGER
Her hair held up in ringlets and rolls.

*FIRST CODGER drags the DEFENDANT'S WIFE out of her seat
and up before the court.*

SECOND CODGER
The blush on her cheek was rosy and bright.

FIRST CODGER
Her girlish appearance rippled with laughter.

SECOND CODGER
She'd a shape that seduced and demanded a kiss.

DEFENDANT
Oh, stupid and daft, I shook with desire
from top to bottom to take her in love.
My only reward was a savage penance,
harshly doled out for going astray.

Because of my deeds it rained down in teems
from the heavens above to cleanse my soul.

The church's knot was tied by the priest
and we were joined in a yoke to each other.

Without being mean, I cleared every bill
and paid for the day's disaster and folly.
Well ye all know I couldn't be faulted:
torches I lit and gathered in neighbours.
Music was played and the drink it flowed free;
plenty of victuals were stacked on the table.

The mouths of the riff-raff I stuffed with provisions,
not to mention the clerk – even the priest
was content with the feast – well he had reason:
a fine hearty banquet was eaten by all.

My utter loss that I didn't smother
the night I was christened, or ere I lusted
to lie on a bed with the woman who greyed me,
and drove me insane without wits or sense.

FIRST CODGER
Reports that he got from the young and old:
she was a gamey one, bringing her custom

to country pubs where they bang on the tables;
for married and single she parted her legs.

Her name and her fame were much talked about,
but it took a long time for him to comprehend.

*DEFENDANT'S WIFE escapes back to her seat where she is
comforted by the WENCHES.*

SECOND CODGER
When we ourselves heard we were afraid
he'd run wild in his pelt and be heard of no more.

DEFENDANT
Blind fool that I was, I wouldn't give in
and the warning voice I banished and silenced.

Oh daft derision, oh wicked jest –
her womb confirmed the obvious fact
that it wasn't gossip or tittle-tattle –
a woman told me that a woman told her:
what she delivered spoke loud and clear –
a premature son was presented to me.

My rugged, rampant, roaring rage!
Oh, God, not a drop of my blood in his veins,
and so, overnight, I'd a readymade clan.

The child was swaddled and she convalesced.
They heated a posset on burning hot embers.
A churn of milk was brought to the boil.
A mountainous feed on a fine full plate
was given to Camley, the midwife from Crucka.

A committee had formed of the rest of the neighbours
who sat by the fire, hissing and spitting.

There were three or four of these baldy old hags
huffing and puffing on their pipes of tobacco,
profoundly swearing a rake of black lies
and loudly whispering close to my ear:

FIRST CODGER *(imitating hag)*
Glory be to God in the heavens above.
Although the wee creature isn't mature
you can clearly see he's the spit of his da.

SECOND CODGER *(imitating hag)*
Oh Sive, take a look at the set of his limbs!
His shape is so lithe, his form and his fingers,
the power in his hand and his fighting fists,
the build of his bones, well-covered in flesh,
an exact replica of one of their kin.

FIRST CODGER *(imitating hag)*
His form and his face and the cut of his features,
the line of his nose and his prominent brow,
his nimble mouth, his member, his guise,
the glint in his eye, and even his smile,
from top to bottom, his father complete.

DEFENDANT
I didn't catch sight or styme of the brat
through the crowd assembled that were set on deceit.

FIRST CODGER *(imitating hag)*
A gust of wind would extinguish the creature.
The merest draught would surely destroy him.

DEFENDANT
I harshly spoke and called the Lord Jesus.
I threatened destruction with rough incantation.
With violent tongue I gave vent to my

37

The hags of the house trembled before me,
not wanting a fight they handed him over.

FIRST CODGER *(imitating hag)*
Take him gently, watch you don't bruise him.
He's easy upset, handle him with care.

SECOND CODGER *(imitating hag)*
A fall that she took must have brought him on early.
Watch you don't squeeze him, please leave him be.
He's close to death, the poor little mite;
may he live till day when the priest arrives.
He'd be better off dead than the state that he's in.

DEFENDANT
I undid the knot on his swaddling clothes,
and stretched him out flat and had a good look.
And lo and behold, he was solid and sturdy,
a lusty lump, supple and strong.

His square-cut shoulders were broad and wide,
he'd limber feet and a full head of hair.
His ears were cocked, and his nails full-grown;
hard were his elbows, his hands, his bones.
His eyes were alert and even his nostrils.

I felt his knees, they were active and strong.
A powerful, pulsating, overgrown pup,
wholesome and hardy, healthy and long.

PLAINTIFF *rises and grapples with the* DEFENDANT. *FIRST
WENCH, SECOND WENCH and the* DEFENDANT'S *WIFE rise.
Uproar in the court.*

DEFENDANT'S WIFE
Lies! All lies! Let me claw out his eyes!

FIRST WENCH
Fabrication! Falsification!

SECOND WENCH
Fallacious falsehoods!

The BAILIFF bangs her staff.

BAILIFF
Let both sides be heard! The truth in words!

The crowd becomes calmer. MERRIMAN rises.

MERRIMAN
Having listened awhile, the plaintiff arose:
her patience was gone, she was losing control.
With rage in her bones and tears in her eyes,
she turned and addressed the court once more.

The crowd cheers. The BAILIFF bangs her staff.

BAILIFF
Respect our queen as is right and fitting.
Back to your seat, you, and remain sitting!

MERRIMAN sits.

PLAINTIFF
By Craglea's Crown, if I didn't allow
for your shortage of wits, you snivelling snot,
and the wish to revere this awesome assembly,
I'd claw with my nails your snout from your neck.

I'd knock you flat with a mighty thump
that'd be marvelled at for many a day.

With delight I'd rip out your scrawny life-strings
and dispatch your soul down to Acheron's flood.

I wouldn't be bothered with a measured reply,
you grovelling dotard, with your cankerous tongue.

You don't deserve this woman you've impugned:
she was weak, poor thing, without cash or cows,
a long time roaming without warmth or shelter,
tired of living and wandering astray
from pillar to post, without kith or kin,
without comfort or ease in the day or the night,
but begging her bread from women she scorned.

FIRST WENCH
This man promised her a spell of ease.
This thing promised her warmth and cover,
clean fair play and plenty of milch cows.

SECOND WENCH
And a good long rest in a bed of down.
A warm hearth in the house and plenty of peat.
Sodded walls without gust or breeze.

FIRST WENCH
Shelter above and a roof from the weather,
with wool and flax to weave into cloth.

PLAINTIFF
'Tis known to the world and to this maggot here
that lust, or liking, or the least bit of love,
didn't lure to his arms this pearl of a woman,
but desperate need and comfort from want.

DEFENDANT'S WIFE
No sooner married than I saw his shortcomings.
I'm ashamed to relate how I'd pass the night:
squeezing the sluggard, and shaking, and shuddering,
twisting and turning with the sheet beneath me,
dashing my elbows, my heels and my knees,
my limbs and teeth chattering with shivers,
not sleeping a wink till the dawning of day.

PLAINTIFF
Is there a woman alive who wouldn't turn grey
had she been wed to a maggot like this,
who didn't find out even twice in the year
whether she was a girl or a lad, flesh or fish?

And this cold wizened thing lying beside her
half-dead and decayed, without budge or bounce –
oh, how she longed for a lively thrust
twice in the night as was only her right.

DEFENDANT'S WIFE
The joy of the night was indeed a cold comfort –
his legs were of lead and his shoulders stooped in.
His bony knees were hard as the ice;
his feet were withered and burnt by the embers,
and his poor sick body was shrivelled and sapped.

PLAINTIFF
It won't, I hope, be thought she was guilty,
or that she would flinch or falter or fall,
this handsome, gentle, sweet woman –
'tis clear she's received the opposite rearing.

SECOND WENCH
Nor would she baulk or pout like a prude,
or lunge like a cat, or scrape or scratch,

but stretch herself out on the marriage bed
side by side, with her arm about him,
tale after tale his thoughts provoking,
her mouth on his, mauling him down.

DEFENDANT'S WIFE
'Twas often indeed that I threw my leg over
and brushed him slow from his waist to his knee,
or tore the blanket and quilt from his groin
and fumbled and groped with the leaden lump.
Not to mention the nights that I grasped his organ,
held it in my hand and fondled it dearly,
with n'ere a result, for 'twas dead to the world.

FIRST WENCH
Her misery's been long, deprived of her dues,
dulled and defeated by an ossified corpse.

SECOND WENCH
And well may this leper talk about women ,
without force in his groin or power in his bones.
If this woman has sinned, then her need has been strong.
And if she's had fun, then it should be condoned.

PLAINTIFF
Is there a fox on the hill or a fish in the sea,
an eagle that hunts or a deer that runs wild
so deprived of reason for a year or a day
that they'd go without food when prey is at hand?

Where in the world do you think that you'd find
the warped little beast or the queer little bird
who'd pick at the earth, the heather, the hedge,
when there's hay in bales and grass to be had?

Tell straight out, you crafty old codger,
answer me, show me the sense in your talk.
Where is your loss, sitting down for a meal,
if it happens the plate has already been used?

FIRST WENCH
Is the corner smaller, the place more minute,
if it happens a million have walked there before?

SECOND WENCH
Woe to your head, you stiff old dotard,
do you think there'll be famine 'cause the want is on you?

FIRST WENCH
Do you think there is danger, you hectoring prattler,
of the bountiful Shannon being emptied of water?
The sea being drained or the tide sucked dry?

PLAINTIFF
Examine in time your foolish thoughts,
and tie your head about with a band.

Again beware, don't lose your senses,
because a woman was open and kind.
If she spent the day looking after them all,
by night there'd be more than your fill left behind.

Can't you see, you old fool, jealousy'd be fine
in a stalwart slasher who's willing and brave,
who's greedy and gushing, gentle yet strong,
dashing and daring, with the gift of the gab.

A welcome visitor who crosses the threshold,
a powerful piercer who long abides,
besides an old man, withered and weak,
a blubbering idiot whose sceptre is dead.

Applause and cheers. The BAILIFF bangs her staff.

BAILIFF
You've made your point, now please be seated.
The rest of you stay quiet or be evicted.

*The WOMEN sit. The DEFENDANT rises, followed by FIRST
CODGER and SECOND CODGER.*

DEFENDANT *(to Aoibheall)*
I humbly beseech you, on behalf of the people.
I lay the country's case in your lap.
Consider it with care and grant us compassion.

If it's true that the human race is dwindling
in Ireland of the green and pleasant hue,
it'd be easy to fill the country with heroes
by rescinding an inept and inadequate rule:
revoke the Law, the Bonds of Marriage.

Where is the need to be having these weddings
with quarts of drink and fees for musicians,
this sitting at table and gross over-feeding,
this prattling and noise and guzzling of drink?

Before ever a priest had joined us together,
by the grace of God, I'd been given a son.

FIRST CODGER
Throughout the land one finds natural children.
They're healthy and hearty, strong and robust.

'Tis often I've seen these brawny young boys,
respectful, obedient, and brim-full of life.

I don't see defects, or blindness, or dimness
in love-children reared by the women I know.
They're bigger, livelier, hardier, more tough
in form and mind than many legitimates.

DEFENDANT *(pointing at Merriman who squirms)*
What has been said can be proved without doubt –
in this very Court there is one of these kind.

Do you see him beyond, so meek and so mild?
Cast your eye over to the right of the bench!

Take a good look, even though he's young,
you can see he's a well-set lump of a lad,
a bouncer in bulk, in body and limb.

Find me a fault in his leg or his arm,
he's no wizened stray or a bagful of bones,
or an old bent slob or an over-fed gander,
a shapeless mass or a miniscule minor,
but a man, I'll bet, with a forceful lance.

SECOND CODGER
'Tis clear as well that 'twas no useless sprig –
without potence or power, form or figure,
without loving or courting, desire or vigour –
harnessed in dutiful yoke to a harridan,
who produced in passion this stalwart champion,

but one who entered a handsome woman
with the venom and lust of a stalwart stallion
in the flush of youth and fullness of health
proving his prowess beyond a doubt
by the power of his organ and the set of his frame.

DEFENDANT
Therefore, oh Queen, abolish all marriage:
the rule that brings misfortune to millions.

The problem, as I see it, can be easily resolved:
let the issue of tramps and the highest gentry
lie down together without cover or binding;
let the noble race and the race of slaves
copulate and beget as nature intended.

Make this announcement throughout the land –
give freedom in love-making to young and to old.

This law will make the Irish wise:
the heroes' vigour will arise once more,
beget strength of limb and back and fist
in earthy men like Goll Mac Morna;
the sky will brighten, there'll be fish in teems;
on land and hill fresh herbs will grow.

If this Act is enforced once and for all,
men and women will praise you in song.

The MEN *applaud. The* PLAINTIFF *rises. During the following disturbance the* PRIEST, *drawn to the proceedings, sneaks in and sits at the back of the court.*

FIRST CODGER *(dancing)*
Abolish all marriage! Marriage is for fools!

SECOND CODGER *(dancing)*
Abolish this ancient stupid rule!

FIRST CODGER *(dancing)*
Enact this law, once and for all!

SECOND CODGER *(dancing)*
Who needs to be married – no one, no one at all!

The BAILIFF bangs her staff.

BAILIFF
I've said it before and I'll say it again –
let the plaintiff be heard, without stress or strain!

The MEN sit.

PLAINTIFF
God didn't chose an unmarried mother!
And women are favoured by the Laws of the Prophets!

'Ancient stupid rule' – who are you to interfere,
to upbraid Church Law, to count the cost
of giving a girl and her folks a day out?

Applause. BAILIFF bangs her staff.

PLAINTIFF
And now that I mention the Laws of the Church,
there's one that gives me cause for concern,
my heart must needs be filled with sorrow –
for I know this is no foolish thought:
what keeps apart from wedlock tie
the complete clergy of the Catholic Church?

My incurable anguish and unending woe,
my patience is strong though I'm raging inside:
for all the time that we lack for a man
our heart's desire is in clerical black.

'Tis a sorry sight for a loving maiden
to see their beauty and strength of limb,

their happy faces and joyous laughter,
their bodies and waists and rods that are pining.

*FIRST WENCH and SECOND WENCH drag the PRIEST before the
court and encircle him. The PRIEST opens his mouth but words
fail him. Bodhrán plays.*

FIRST WENCH
Freshness of beauty and flower of youth.
Stoutness of bone and fullness of flesh.
Staunchness of trunk and un-stooped back.
Doubtless strength and desire uncooling.

They're always powerful, exceedingly young,
and they're flesh and blood – we know full well.

SECOND WENCH
At the clergyman's table they have every sport,
gold and silver, and drink and devilment.

Downy beds to lie on and bacon to eat,
flour, sweetbreads, the choicest of wines.

FIRST WENCH
I've no desire for a whimpering eunuch,
or a diseased decrepit or a weak little foal.

These lusty louts and potent piercers
are fast asleep while there's work to be done.

PLAINTIFF
Although 'tis well known that some are rakes,
I'm certainly sure they're not all the same –
I wouldn't be one to condemn any man –
or to sink the ship because of one rogue.

I honestly believe that some of them wish
to requite my love, and it wouldn't cost much.

FIRST WENCH
And some are uncurbed by law or restraint,
some are skinflints and lacking in virtue,
fierce and frigid with a hatred for women.

SECOND WENCH
I know not all are the likes of these –
some have plenty of love and grace.
Many's the household that acquired its riches,
cattle and churns after a clergyman's visit.

PLAINTIFF
Indeed, I well remember their qualities praised,
their many deeds that were clever and lusty.
I have often heard throughout the land
a lively whisper dispersed widespread:

the results of their pranks are plain to be seen
on some of their issue with false surnames;
it racks me through from the core of my heart,
them wasting their health on middle-aged women.

And 'tis known in the country that the maidens' loss
is the wanton waste of the sacred seed.

Harsh and distressing is the law of celibacy,
Ireland has lost by this useless rule.

I submit to you, oh, Paragon of Sense,
the terms of my case regarding the clergy.

Till now my hopes are deceived and destroyed.
I'm blind without vision, please give me knowledge.

Recall and recite the Saying of the Prophet,
and the moving words of the Lord's Apostle.

Where are the powers that nature ordained?
The single life causes the flesh to be hardened.

Paul I don't think ever told anyone
to refuse marriage, but to shun fornication.
Leave your kin, if that is your wish,
and tie your heart to a woman for life.

The PLAINTIFF pushes the PRIEST towards the back of the court.
Relieved, he beats a hasty retreat. End of bodhrán.

PLAINTIFF
But it's needless work for women like us
to quote from this law in your divine presence.

Oh Pearl of Riches, 'tis well you remember:
the merits of each case are known to your Grace.

I loudly beseech you, High Prophetess,
oh Celestial Issue of Royal Kings,
oh Light of Glory, oh Crown of People,
listen to my plea, help and relieve us.

Weigh in your mind the maidens' loss
and the needs of the many would-be brides:
those gawky girls, those gaggles of geese
who are bursting the seams of their clothes.

The smallest urchins that walk the streets:
black little waifs who are dirty and scant,
if they get their fill of spuds and whey,
they'll surely shoot up in the shortest of time;

but their breasts will swell in futile growth
and they'll proceed to a crusty old age.

My heart-scald, oh, I'm a foolish wench
to be talking of a husband in fiery rages.
'Tis hard for me to hope for bliss
when there's three women to every one man.

And since this barren place is so needy,
giants are scarce and time is so precious.
Ireland is empty, weeds freely abound.
Our youth will soon become grey and withered,
lost and depressed because of their status.

Give me some man, anyone on earth.
Let him, in time, slip into my harness
and leave him to me forever hereafter.

*Applause. The WOMEN are seated. MERRIMAN rises. The
FAIRY MAIDENS accompany AOIBHEALL as she moves to the
head of the court. Music/Bodhrán.*

MERRIMAN
The stately queen moved to the head of the court.
Her radiant presence illumined the place.
Gentle and young were her face and her form;
strong was her voice – the voice of truth.

She clenched her fist, and ordered
direct that the bailiff silence the court.
She parted her lips and began to proclaim
to the enrapt court who'd waited so long.

The BAILIFF bangs her staff.

BAILIFF
Aoibheall, the just, her heart without falsehood!
Craglea's fair queen, beloved of Thomond!

AOIBHEALL
Having listened at length to both sides presented,
I find in your favour, dear gentle maiden.

Cheers and applause. BAILIFF bangs her staff.

BAILIFF
Silence in the court! Silence, I said!

AOIBHEALL
I've heard in your speech sorrow and pining;
undeniable hardship has led to your triumph.

I've also noticed and it sears me through,
the seed of Orla, Maura, Maeveen,
of lowly litter and mediocre issue
who aspire to be joined to the noblest seers;
sly schemers and cowardly creatures
with crooked queries and scurrilous scrounging –
their needs I'll ignore when answering your petition,
nor will I condone their yearning for grandeur,
or interfere with the church's teaching on marriage.

I hereby enact this law for maidens:
all men of age who are as yet unwed
shall be stopped and seized and spared no pity,
Bind them to the tree beside the tomb;
there strip them bare of their shirts and their vests,
and flay their backs and their rumps with a rope.

Take all, like him, well on in years *(indicating MERRIMAN)*
who have the cheek to conceal their manhood,

who wantonly waste, without giving pleasure,
the scrotum's urge and the member's vigour,
whose tools are limp, with women to be had,
already ripe and waiting to be plucked.

Lascivious ladies, aching with lust,
I give you leave to get on with these deeds,
and any others you may decide upon – no matter
how painful – you have my permission.

Torture them at will, with fire and force:
a painless death isn't what they deserve.

I wouldn't be bothered, if I were you,
with the wizened old man, weak and worn out,
the bee with no sting, the fork with no prong,
the barren crotch, or the impotent male;
let the youth get on with the breeding
and let this sort become their cloak.

'Tis often I've seen dull-witted men
tied to the house and I'm grateful to them;
bossed by women by day and by night,
they pretend to act, but once their names
are placed on the children, I'll be content.

Regarding that other matter that gives you concern:
'tis clear I'm not given to false promise;

I'll share with you what has been predicted to me,
though I'm aware it will cause some surprise,
not least in that its date is uncertain as yet,
but some day soon, the priests will wed.

Heed my advice; what is needed is patience:
a time will come with the Vatican's leave,

when a seal will go on a Papal Bull;
the Cardinals will consider the country's woes
and having debated the issue, agree
to release forthwith these spancelled lads.

Full of desire, with a longing thrust,
an answer to prayer are these hot-blooded men.

But beware, anyone else of woman born,
listen to me well, let me see you respond.

By my authority, abolish all around,
any pansy boy or mollycoddled man;
chase out all the withered grey codgers
and clear the country once and for all.

I must away and leave ye now,
I'm already late, with a journey ahead:
the trip I'm committed to, brooks no delay,
too much business has yet to be done,
several more courts await my judgment.

I'll return again soon and woe betide
those whose ways aren't mended by then.
Those men who are base in mind,
the sort who need their fame announced,
who loudly boast of deeds with women.

I see through their jest and derision:
'tis pleasing to them, and they think it's heroic,
to seduce and taunt both married and single;
the urge of their will doesn't provoke their desire,
a rush of blood or a lusty swelling;

not passion or pleasure found in the act,
or greed or fury that drives them,

but talk and waffle and windy bragging,
too much boasting and unruly rushing,
their efforts are weak, without yield or purpose;
small and feeble their faulty sceptres,
with women furious with want in their wake –
I can see this court understands what I mean.

In yoke and shackles I'll put this gang
when I return before the harvest moon;
meanwhile more urgent needs await me.

Storm effects as at beginning of play. AOIBHEALL and the FAIRY
MAIDENS move towards the exit.

FIRST FAIRY MAIDEN
In yoke and shackles she'll put this gang
when she returns before the harvest moon.

SECOND FAIRY MAIDEN
Those whose ways aren't mended by then,
those of them who are base in mind.

Exit AOIBHEALL. The FAIRY MAIDENS wait by the exit.

MERRIMAN
I looked around at the stately Queen;
my heart grew weak when she had finished.

I felt in the air a vicious frenzy,
fear in tremors swept through my bones.

I felt the land and the household swaying;
the echo of her speech danced in my ears.

The tall and terrible bailiff came;
my complexion greyed as she stretched out her hand.

My ear she grabbed, rough and harsh,
and dragged me up to the top of the court.

Up leapt the maid who had won her case;
she clapped her hands and at me yelled.

The BAILIFF drags MERRIMAN to the head of the court.

PLAINTIFF
You cute old crust, it's been a long time
that I've been wanting to thrash your back.

You hard old heart that I've often tempted,
submit you must to the Law of Maidens.

Who'll stand up and defend you now –
not a word you deserve, you whey-faced coward.

The WOMEN attack MERRIMAN and tear at his shirt and waistcoat.

FIRST WENCH
Where are the maidens who would be thankful
for all the deeds you've never done?

SECOND WENCH
Look at his limbs, come here till ye see,
there's no blemish here that's kept him from women.

PLAINTIFF
Indeed he's handsome, and fairly-well-built
from the top of his head to the soles of his feet.

FIRST WENCH
Though I don't like them pale, I have to say,
I would never revile a torso like this.

SECOND WENCH
Even if he was humped or bent in two,
shoulders are stooped on the best of men.

FIRST WENCH
Often a runt has an active lance,
or them with bow legs, a lively thrust.

PLAINTIFF
Indeed some other unknown cause
has left Brianeen single all these years.

FIRST WENCH
And him well-liked by the country gentry,
and a great friend of the high and mighty.

SECOND WENCH
Making music, and sport and fun
in the presence of people, and playing and drinking,
with vigour and pleasure at the table's top.

PLAINTIFF
I'd find it easy to proffer respect to the wretch –
studious, though useful, pleasing, accomplished,
merry, high-spirited, famous, though fickle.

Still a celibate and starting to grey –
an animal of your sort wasn't made by God.

Your poetic speech is of no use to you now.
You've heard the queen: 'tis an offence
to be thirty years of age and to have no wife.

You paragon of patience, listen to me,
can't you see you're the cause of my outburst?

Anguish, and desire have left me lifeless.
Oh, dear women, I must make him pay.

The WOMEN hand the PLAINTIFF a whip. MERRIMAN tries to escape. The PLAINTIFF, FIRST WENCH, SECOND WENCH, and the DEFENDANT'S WIFE capture MERRIMAN and spread-eagle him on the ground where the PLAINTIFF raises the whip.

BAILIFF
Help I tell ye, catch him, grab him,
Una, come here and get me a rope.
Where are you Annie? Don't be left out.
Maureen, tie down his hands and his feet.
Muireann, Maeve, Sive and Sheila,
put into effect with flaming zeal
the height of torture ordained by the Queen:

raise your arms and lift the scourge;
the woven cords sink into his flesh;
measure out, showing no mercy,
the cruellest of pain on Brian's arseen.

Ladies dear, he's a very fine specimen.
Cut into him deep, he deserves no favour.
Flay his hide from top to bottom.

Let his cries be heard throughout the land,
striking terror in bachelors' hearts.

I think this is a good sensible act.
'Tis best to record the date it was passed:
let me see, subtract in a hurry
exactly a hundred and ten from a thousand,
then correctly double what there is left,
the week before God's Son arrived.

Music/Bodhrán. The BAILIFF *writes on Merriman's piece of vellum.*

MERRIMAN
She grabbed the pen; my head was spinning,
in fear of flaying and terror of flogging.

Then all the while she was writing the date,
the women of the house stood by as guards.

BAILIFF *moves towards exit. She and* FAIRY MAIDENS *exeunt.* MUSICIANS, *the* PLAINTIFF, *the* FIRST WENCH, *the* SECOND WENCH, *the* DEFENDANT, *the* DEFENDANT'S WIFE, *the* FIRST CODGER *and the* SECOND CODGER *regroup as at the beginning of the play. Lights suggest daylight.* MERRIMAN *lies where he was positioned at the beginning of the play.*

MERRIMAN
Then I ended my dream, and opened my eyes,
and leapt from my pains – wide – wide – awake.

The musicians play, the WOMEN *dance, the* MEN *watch and gossip. The* PLAINTIFF *approaches* MERRIMAN *and invites him to dance. Freeze. Lights are extinguished as he deliberates whether or not to accept.*

Acknowledgements

This script was first performed by the Dublin Shakespeare Society, as part of their centenary celebration, at Club 36, Dublin, in May, 2007, with the following cast and crew:

Brian Merriman	Ben Mulhern
Bailiff to the Court	Marie Gallagher
Aoibheall, a Fairy Queen	Mary Dowling
Fairy Maidens	Sarah Byrne
	Orla O'Donoghue
Plaintiff	Rachel Carey
Wenches	Cliona Cleary
	Marguerite McCarthy
Defendant	Val O'Donnell
Codgers	Peter Prior
	Jim Corcoran
Priest	John Murphy
Defendant's Wife	Mary O'Connor
Musicians	Peter McDunphy
	Darragh McManamon
	Aisling Ní Cheallaigh
Assistant to Directors	John Murphy
Set Design	John Flood
Lighting Design	Patrick R Burke
	Gerry O'Connor
Stage Manager	John Murphy
Set Construction	John Flood
	Jim Butler
Programme	Dan O'Mahony
Co Director	Debbie O'Sullivan
Director	Helen Byrne

An earlier version of this script was performed at the Dublin Shakespeare Society Studio, 50 North Great George's Street, Dublin, in May, 1982, with the following cast and crew:

Brian Merriman	Martin Maguire
Bailiff to the Court	Helen Byrne
Aoibheall, a Fairy Queen	Brenda McSweeney
Fairy Maidens	Orla Golden
	Fiona Skehan
Plaintiff	Michaele Traynor
Wenches	Bríd Ní Chumhaill
	Noëlle O'Reilly
	Anne Byrne
Defendant	Paul Fox
Codgers	John Flood
	Michael Clarke
Priest	Rory McCloskey
Defendant's Wife	Annick Rolle
Musicians	Liam Ó Maonlaí
	Nuala O'Sullivan
Set Design	John Flood
Costume Design	Reg Deane
Poster/Programme Design	Orla Golden
Lighting Design	Willie Byrne
Backstage	Jack Brereton
	Fred Roche
	Rosemary Warner
Front of House	Grania Gilroy
Publicity	Kevin Madden
Assistant Director	Willie Byrne
Director	Celia de Fréine

OPENING LINES

I was wont to stroll by the river bank
where the softest dew covered the grass,
beside the woods in a mountain dale,
without bother or care at break of day.
My heart would soar when I'd see Lough Graney
and the lush pasture stretching before me;
pleasant and bright the set of the mountains
raising their heads to rival each other –
a sight that would cheer the wizened heart,
one without vigour, spent and in pain.
A bitter wretch, without wealth or land,
could look for a while beyond the woods
at a flock of ducks in the clear-lit bay,
a single swan sailing among them,
at the joyous fish leap through the air –
perch and trout their bellies aglisten –
at the hue of the lough and the blue of the waves
as they rumbled landward in tumultuous din.
Birds would chirp as they flew through the trees,
and the doe flit past below in the clearing,
a blare of horns would herald a pack
of fast-running hounds in pursuit of Reynard.

Celia de Fréine is a poet, playwright, screenwriter and librettist who writes in Irish and English. She has published five collections of poetry: *Faoi Chabáistí is Ríonacha* (2001) and *Fiacha Fola* (2004) from Cló Iar-Chonnachta; *Scarecrows at Newtownards* (Scotus Press, 2005); *imram ⦙ odyssey* (2010) and *Aibitír Aoise ⦙ Alphabet of An Age* (2011) from Arlen House. Her poetry has won many awards including the Patrick Kavanagh Award (1994) and Gradam Litríochta Chló Iar-Chonnachta (2004). She has four times won Duais an Oireachtais for best full-length play. Arlen House published three of these plays in *Mná Dána* (2009). In the same year the Abbey Theatre presented a rehearsed reading of her play *Casadh* which it had commissioned. The short films *Lorg*, *Seal* and *Cluiche*, inspired by her poems, have been shown in festivals in Ireland and the US. In association with Biju Viswanath, she wrote the film *Marathon* which won best screenplay award at the New York International Film Festival in 2009. Also in 2009 *Living Opera*, in association with *Opera Ireland*, presented a showcase performance of the opera *The Earl of Kildare*, composed by Fergus Johnston, for which she wrote the *libretto*.

Further information: www.celiadefreine.com